OECD Reviews ~~~~~ ral Policies

South Africa

OECD

ORGANISATION FOR ECONOMIC CO-OPERATION AND DEVELOPMENT

ORGANISATION FOR ECONOMIC CO-OPERATION AND DEVELOPMENT

The OECD is a unique forum where the governments of 30 democracies work together to address the economic, social and environmental challenges of globalisation. The OECD is also at the forefront of efforts to understand and to help governments respond to new developments and concerns, such as corporate governance, the information economy and the challenges of an ageing population. The Organisation provides a setting where governments can compare policy experiences, seek answers to common problems, identify good practice and work to co-ordinate domestic and international policies.

The OECD member countries are: Australia, Austria, Belgium, Canada, the Czech Republic, Denmark, Finland, France, Germany, Greece, Hungary, Iceland, Ireland, Italy, Japan, Korea, Luxembourg, Mexico, the Netherlands, New Zealand, Norway, Poland, Portugal, the Slovak Republic, Spain, Sweden, Switzerland, Turkey, the United Kingdom and the United States. The Commission of the European Communities takes part in the work of the OECD.

OECD Publishing disseminates widely the results of the Organisation's statistics gathering and research on economic, social and environmental issues, as well as the conventions, guidelines and standards agreed by its members.

This work is published on the responsibility of the Secretary-General of the OECD. The opinions expressed and arguments employed herein do not necessarily reflect the official views of the Organisation or of the governments of its member countries.

This document has been produced with the financial assistance of the European Union. The views expressed herein can in no way be taken to reflect the official opinion of the European Union.

Foreword

This Review of Agricultural Policies in South Africa was undertaken as part of an initiative to provide analyses of agricultural policies for four major agricultural economies outside the OECD area, the others being Brazil, China and India. It takes a thorough look at the situation of agriculture in South Africa and issues for the future. The study also measures the extent of support provided to agriculture using the same method that OECD employs to monitor agricultural policies in OECD countries. In addition, it focuses on key interactions between South Africa and OECD countries, including the impacts of trade and agricultural policy reforms. The country study aims at strengthening the policy dialogue with OECD members on the basis of consistent measurement and analysis, and to provide an objective assessment of the opportunities, constraints and trade-offs that confronts South Africa's policy makers.

The study was carried out by the OECD Directorate for Food, Agriculture and Fisheries. The principal author was Václav Vojtech who received valuable contributions from Hsin Huang, Olga Melyukhina and Pete Liapis. Research and statistical support were provided by Laetitia Reille, technical and secretarial assistance by Stefanie Milowski and Anita Lari.

The study benefited from the substantive input of a range of South African experts. The following contributions were provided: contextual information to Chapter 1 by Jan Groenewald (retired Professor from Free State University); information on domestic policies by Mohamad Makhura, Ted Stilwell and Nico Meyer from the South African Development Bank (SADB), Johan von Schalkwyk from the Free State University (FSU), and Simphiwe Ngqangweni from the Pretoria University (PU); information on trade policies by André Jooste from the FSU; the data and information for the estimation of support to agriculture by André Jooste and David Spies (FSU) and Johan Kirsten (PU). The analysis of changes in incomes, poverty and inequality was prepared by Scott McDonald (University of Sheffield, UK) based on the Social Accounting Matrix data collected under the project PROVIDE and made available by the South African National and Provincial Departments of Agriculture. The study also benefited from inputs from the FAO and the World Bank.

The study benefited greatly from the support from the South African Ministry of Agriculture and Land Affairs, coordinated by Ben van Wyk, whose experts provided essential information on the functioning of agricultural programmes in South Africa as well as comments on the draft report.

The study was made possible through voluntary contributions from Germany, the Netherlands, New Zealand, Spain, Switzerland, United Kingdom, the Unites States, as well as funding from the European Union.

The study was reviewed in a roundtable with South African officials and experts in Pretoria in October 2005. Subsequently, South African agricultural policies were examined by the OECD's Committee for Agriculture at its 143rd session in December 2005, bringing together policy makers from South Africa, OECD member countries and some non-OECD countries. The report is published under the authority of the Secretary-General of the OECD.

Stefan Tangermann
Director
Directorate for Food, Agriculture and Fisheries

Table of Contents

Highlights and Policy Recommendations 11

   1.   Reforms and their impacts 13

   2.   Current agricultural policies 18

   3.   Effects of policy reforms 23

   4.   Policy challenges and recommendations 25

Chapter 1. **The Policy Context** 31

   1.1. A historical perspective 32

   1.2. The agriculture and food sector in South Africa 39

   1.3. Deregulation of agricultural marketing and impacts on the agricultural
       markets 55

   1.4. South Africa's trade in agricultural products 58

   Notes 64

Chapter 2. **Policy Evaluation**... 65

   2.1. Agricultural policy framework 66

   2.2. Domestic policies 69

   2.3. Agro-food trade policies.. 90

   2.4. Government expenditures on agro-food policies....................... 94

   2.5. Evaluation of policy instruments and institutional arrangements 98

   2.6. Evaluation of support to South African agriculture..................... 105

       Aggregate results 107

       Commodity profile of producer support 113

       Conclusions 115

   Notes 115

Annex 2.A1. Supporting Tables and Figures.................................. 117

Chapter 3. **Policy Effects** 131

   3.1. Market access barriers to South African agricultural exports 132

   3.2. Welfare impacts of trade and agricultural policy reforms 137

   3.3. Household impact of trade and agricultural policy reforms 141

   3.4. The impact of liberalisation on South African agricultural commodity
       markets... 145

   3.5. The effects of policy reform on food security.......................... 153

   Notes 158

Annex 3.A1. Supporting Tables for Chapter 3, Section 3.1...................... 160

Annex 3.A2. Supporting Analysis for Chapter 3, Section 3.3 163

Acronyms 177

List of boxes

1.1. Remuneration of hired farm labour 53
2.1. Principal National Land Reform Acts 71
2.2. OECD indicators of support to agriculture: Definitions 106
2.3. Fluctuations in exchange rates and world prices: Implications
for interpretation of producer support 109
3.1. Implementation of assumed South Africa policy changes 146

List of tables

1.1. Selected macroeconomic indicators for South Africa, 1994-2003 35
1.2. Changes in the South African tariff structure 37
1.3. Composition of South African labour force, 2002-04 39
1.4. Principal statistics on farm structure in South African commercial agriculture
by group of farms according to economic size 40
1.5. Land production potential in South Africa................................. 42
1.6. Livestock numbers and slaughterings, 1990 to 2004....................... 47
1.7. Extent of wind and water erosion of agricultural land in South Africa, 1998 49
1.8. Total application of nitrate, phosphorus, and potassium in South African
agriculture, 1987-2003 49
1.9. Agricultural water needs in South Africa, 10-year averages and projections
for 2000 and 2010 50
1.10. Farm employment in South Africa, 1985-2002 52
1.11. Employment and employees' remuneration on commercial farms,
1993 and 2002 52
1.12. Input use structure in South African agriculture, 1947-96................. 53
1.13. Intermediate input purchases in South African agriculture, 1980-2003 54
1.14. Capital assets and debt of commercial farmers, 1980-2003................. 54
1.15. Total incomes of small-scale farmers based on survey in Limpopo Province 55
1.16. South Africa's agro-food trade, 2000-2004 59
2.1. Differences in Marketing Acts of 1968 and 1996 70
2.2. Cumulative statistics on settled restitution claims, as of 31 March 2004 73
2.3. Provincial spending on structured training 81
2.4. Provincial and national agriculture expenditure, 2000/01 to 2006/07 95
2.5. Provincial agriculture expenditure by programme, 2000/01 to 2006/07....... 95
2.6. Provincial agriculture expenditure by programme, 2004/05 96
2.7. National agriculture expenditure by programme, 2000/01 to 2006/07........ 97
2.8. Budgetary expenditure on Land reform 98
2.9. South Africa: Percentage PSEs and CSEs, 1994-2003...................... 107
2.10. Total support to South African agriculture, 1994-2003.................... 111
2.A1.1. The roles of Departments serving agriculture.......................... 118
2.A1.2. Import duties applied on maize and wheat, 1998-2005 118
2.A1.3. Import duties applied for sugar, 1994-2005 119
2.A1.4. Settled restitution claims: cumulative statistics, 1995 to 30 June 2005 119
2.A1.5. Total Estimate of Support to South African Agriculture 120
2.A1.6. Producer Support Estimate by commodity............................. 121
2.A1.7. Estimates of support to agriculture in selected non-OECD and OECD countries.. 123
2.A1.8. Consumer Support Estimate by commodity 125

3.1. Tariffs levied and faced.. 138
3.2. Welfare effects of multilateral policy reform........................ 139
3.3. Principal assumptions of the liberalisation scenarios 146
3.4. Profile of the South African social security public policy framework, 2002....... 157
3.A1.1. Protection of the wine sector in South African export markets 160
3.A1.2. Protection of the fresh fruit sector in South African export markets 161
3.A1.3. Protection of the sugar sector in South African export markets............. 162
3.A2.1. Imposed percentage changes in world prices of exports and imports..... 165
3.A2.2. Commodity price results 166
3.A2.3. Commodity quantity results – Base volume (for imports and exports)
and percentage changes 167
3.A2.4. Activity prices... 169
3.A2.5. Components of household incomes – Base levels and changes............ 171
3.A2.6. Household incomes and consumption expenditures – by province 174
3.A2.7. Household incomes and consumption expenditures – by race 174

List of figures

0.1. South Africa: Total exports, imports and trade of goods as % of GDP, 1990-2004 . 14
0.2. South African agricultural exports and imports, in 1992-2004 15
0.3. South African agro-food exports by destination and imports by origin 16
0.4. PSE by country, EU and OECD averages, 2000-03 average 20
0.5. Composition of Producer Support Estimate, 1994-2003 21
0.6. South African PSEs by commodity, 2000-03 average 22
0.7. Composition of the Total Support Estimate in South Africa 22
0.8. Total Support Estimate in South Africa and selected countries, 2001-03 average. 23
0.9. Welfare gains in South Africa by source of liberalisation 24

Map of South Africa...................................... 33
1.1. Annual GDP growth rates in South Africa, 1961-2003 35
1.2. Inflation and interest rates in South Africa, 1980-2004 36
1.3. Exchange rates of the South African Rand against selected currencies, 1990-2004 37
1.4. South Africa: Total exports, imports and trade of goods as % of GDP, 1990-2004 . 38
1.5. Agriculture's share of GDP, 2000-02 average 41
1.6. Agriculture's share of total employment, 2000-02 average 41
1.7. Share of agriculture in GDP, agricultural exports and imports, 1990-2004 42
1.8. Agricultural output indices, 1990-2004............................... 43
1.9. Structure of the gross value of agricultural production, 1990-92 and 2001-03 . 44
1.10. Field crop plantings, 1990-2004 45
1.11. Field crop production, 1990-2004.................................. 45
1.12. Field crop yield, 1990-2004 45
1.13. Domestic consumption and exports of apples, table grapes and oranges
in South Africa, 1990 and 2004................................... 46
1.14. Domestic consumption and exports of other main fruit in South Africa,
1990 and 2004 46
1.15. Production of main livestock products in South Africa, 1990-2004 48
1.16. Number of farm employees and domestic servants on commercial farms,
1971-1996. 51
1.17. South African agricultural exports and imports, 1992-2004 59

1.18. South African agricultural exports by destination, 2002-04 average......... 60

1.19. Changes in export shares to South Africa's main export destinations
between 2000 and 2004... 60

1.20. South Africa's agricultural exports by products, 2002-04 average 61

1.21. Changes in export volume of South Africa's main exportables between 2002
and 2004... 61

1.22. South African agricultural imports by source, 2002-04 average 62

1.23. Changes in import shares from South Africa's main countries of origin
between 2000 and 2004.. 62

1.24. South Africa's agricultural imports by products, 2002-04 average........... 63

1.25. Changes in import volume of South Africa's main importables between 2000
and 2004... 63

2.1. Restitution of agricultural land, by 31 March 2004 72

2.2. Settled rural claims by type of compensation, as of 31 March 2004......... 73

2.3. Progress with land restitution since 1994............................. 74

2.4. Progress with land redistribution since 1994.......................... 74

2.5. Composition of total provincial agriculture expenditure by programme,
2000/01 to 2006/07 96

2.6. Shares of provinces in aggregate provincial-level expenditures on agricultural
programmes, 2004/05 97

2.7. Composition of total national agriculture expenditure by programme,
2000/01 to 2006/07 98

2.8. PSE by country, EU and OECD, 2000-03 average 108

2.9. Composition of Producer Support Estimate, 1994-2003 108

2.10. Total Support Estimate in South Africa and selected countries, 2000-03 average. 112

2.11. Composition of the Total Support Estimate in South Africa, 1994-2003 112

2.12. South African PSEs by commodity, 2000-03 average 113

2.13. Distribution of total producer support by commodity, 2000-03 average...... 114

2.14. Percentage CSE by commodity, 2000-03 average........................ 114

2.A1.1. WHEAT: Percentage PSEs, producer and reference prices.................. 126

2.A1.2a. WHITE MAIZE: Percentage PSEs, producer and reference prices 126

2.A1.2b. YELLOW MAIZE: Percentage PSEs, producer and reference prices........... 127

2.A1.3. SUNFLOWER: Percentage PSEs, producer and reference prices 127

2.A1.4. GROUNDNUTS: Percentage PSEs, producer and reference prices............ 127

2.A1.5. SUGAR CANE: Percentage PSEs, producer and reference prices 128

2.A1.6. MILK: Percentage PSEs, producer and reference prices 128

2.A1.7. BEEF: Percentage PSEs, producer and reference prices.................... 128

2.A1.8. PIGMEAT: Percentage PSEs, producer and reference prices................ 129

2.A1.9. SHEEP MEAT: Percentage PSEs, producer and reference prices 129

2.A1.10. POULTRY MEAT: Percentage PSEs, producer and reference prices.......... 129

2.A1.11. EGGS: Percentage PSEs, producer and reference prices 130

3.1. Tariff protection of the wine sector in South African export markets, 2005.... 133

3.2. Tariff protection of the fresh grapes sector in South African export
markets, 2005.. 134

3.3. Tariff protection of the fresh oranges sector in South African export
markets, 2005.. 135

3.4. Tariff protection of the fresh apples sector in South African export
markets, 2005 135

3.5. Tariff protection of the raw sugar sector in South African export markets, 2005 . 136

3.6. Tariff protection of the refined sugar sector in South African export
markets, 2005 137

3.7. Welfare gains (losses) in South Africa by source of liberalisation 140

3.8. Real factor per unit returns to agriculture and non-agriculture 140

3.9. Household incomes and consumption expenditures by region 142

3.10. Household incomes and consumption expenditures by race 143

3.11. Equivalent variation in household welfare by province – Based on consumption 144

3.12. Equivalent variation in household welfare by race – Based on consumption 144

3.13. Summary changes in factor incomes – 50% cut in South Africa's trade
barriers with full employment and fiscal neutrality 145

3.14. Impact of 50% liberalisation on world crop markets, 2005-13 average 148

3.15. Impact of 50% liberalisation on South African crop markets,
2005-13 average 149

3.16. Impacts of 50% liberalisation on world livestock markets, 2005-13 average . . 150

3.17. Impact of 50% liberalisation on South African livestock markets,
2005-13 average 151

3.A2.1. Major real macroeconomic variables 164

3.A2.2. Activity output 168

3.A2.3. Household income by province 172

3.A2.4. Equivalent variation in household welfare by province – Based on consumption 173

3.A2.5. Household income by race 173

3.A2.6. Equivalent variation in household welfare by race – Based on consumption 174

ISBN 92-64-03679-2
OECD Review of Agricultural Policies
South Africa
© OECD 2006

Highlights and Policy Recommendations

South Africa has undergone enormous economic, social and political change since the beginning of the democratisation process in 1994. The overall results have been positive with a stronger and stable macro economy, better integration into the global trading system, and progress in redressing past injustices and reducing poverty. There are still many challenges facing the government and South African society as a whole, including widespread unemployment and poverty, a large unskilled workforce excluded from the formal economy, weak social and educational systems, a significant level of crime and a high prevalence of HIV/Aids.

Agriculture contributes less than 4% to GDP but accounts for 10% of total reported employment. The sector is increasingly export oriented with about one-third of total production exported. The conditions for agricultural production are not favourable in most regions (with the notable exception of the winter rain area in Western Cape) due to poor land quality, highly variable climatic conditions and a scarcity of water.

South African agriculture is of a highly dualistic nature, where a developed commercial sector co-exists with large numbers of subsistence (communal) farms. Agriculture is well diversified with field crops, livestock and horticulture the main sectors. However, there can be large annual fluctuations in output due to weather conditions. Fruit production has seen the most dynamic development in the past ten years with a large share of total output exported, mainly to Europe.

Important and wide ranging reforms liberalising domestic and foreign trade and lowering support to agriculture were implemented in the 1990s. The current level of support (PSE of 5%) is low relative to the OECD average and is comparable to that in Australia, Brazil, Russia and China. Border protection has been significantly relaxed, which is consistent with an emphasis on new regional trade agreements. Market price support remains the largest component of producer support. The level of support is uneven across commodities and sugar is by far the most supported commodity. Budgetary payments have been reduced and there has been a shift in payments away from established commercial farms to development of the small farm sector that is emerging from the land reform. Almost one half of the budgetary expenditures are for the provision of general services, such as research, training, inspection and infrastructure development.

The commercial agricultural sector adapted well to the policy reforms and liberalisation efforts. However, economic and financial pressure on commercial agriculture is substantial, and as with other sectors, farmers must adapt their production and investment decisions to the market situation and overall economic developments. These market pressures need to be considered in the context of land reform and Black Economic Empowerment (BEE). The new entrants into commercial agriculture (and into agricultural based services) are at a considerable disadvantage relative to the more experienced operators in responding to these challenges.

Continued land reform is one of the most important agricultural policy challenges, in particular how to a) improve the land acquisition and resettlement process; and b) create stakeholder consensus around the implementation strategy. Greater flexibility in land acquisition options and more decentralised community-driven decision-making would be positive steps. Moreover, adjustment assistance is required to ensure that land reform results in the emergence of viable farms. Development of the necessary technical and social infrastructure, as well as an effective service sector, are critical measures.

Facilitating economic integration between small and large-scale commercial units is another policy challenge. The ability of the commercial sector to respond to increased market opportunities will ultimately determine any gains from global trade liberalisation. Farming policies need to be conducive to the adoption of quality and productivity improvements for this sector to become more internationally competitive and exploit its export potential.

1. Reforms and their impacts

*South Africa is undergoing radical reforms towards market orientation and more
equitable distribution of resources with all racial groups participating in the economy*

The Republic of South Africa occupies the southern-most part of the African continent. With a surface area of 1.22 million km^2 and a population of 46.9 million, South Africa is one of the largest countries on the African continent. It is also the largest African economy, with a per capita GDP of USD 3 530 (USD 10 492 in PPP terms) more than four times the African average. However, the distribution of income is among the most unequal in the world, and high levels of unemployment, poverty and HIV/Aids are major concerns. Also, the potential of South African agriculture is limited by the relative scarcity of arable land and water resources.

South Africa has undergone immense social and economic change over the last 20 years, following the abolition of apartheid and fundamental reforms aimed at creating a more open and market-oriented economy. An underlying principle for virtually all government policy is to bring the previously excluded black community into the mainstream economy through job creation and entrepreneurship. Macroeconomic reforms have stabilised the economy, but serious problems of high unemployment and poverty remain.

*Tight monetary and fiscal policies have kept inflation down and stabilised
the economy, and more growth-oriented policies have prevailed since 2001*

Over the past ten years, the South African government introduced important reforms throughout the whole economy. Since the start of the democratisation process in 1994, South Africa has made tremendous progress in stabilising macroeconomic fundamentals. From 2000, the South African Reserve Bank (SARB) has conducted monetary policy based on inflation targeting. It has allowed the exchange rate to float and there are no exchange rate targets. Inflation has been reduced to less than 5% and interest rates were reduced as well. However, real interest rates are higher than in the past periods with high inflation. Also, in the most recent years fluctuations in the South African Rand (ZAR) exchange rate influenced the economy which is more open to world markets than in the 1990s.

A gradual transition from fiscal austerity to a growth-oriented policy has taken place since 2001/02. However, despite a growing emphasis on poverty reduction and increased social spending, the impact on employment and poverty has been limited. Many social needs remain unmet with a large segment of the population excluded from the formal economy and having limited access to services. A high and rising rate of unemployment is a major concern. One crucial factor is the low skills level for a large part of the South African workforce. Moreover, the country faces major social challenges including the need to improve management of social and educational systems, a high prevalence of HIV/Aids infection, and a high level of crime.

Market liberalisation accelerated after 1994 and lead to increasing integration of the South African economy into global markets

The Marketing Act, in force since 1937, gave the government control over domestic markets and trade. Partial reforms, mainly concerning domestic markets, were implemented during the 1980s and early 1990s. However, it was in 1994-97 that the government introduced radical reforms, liberalising domestic markets, foreign trade, and prices in the whole economy.

Overall, the South African economy is increasingly oriented towards world markets both in terms of exports and imports. The share of exports of goods and services in total GDP increased from 22% in 1994 to 34% in 2002, while that of imports increased from 20% to 31% (Figure 0.1).

Figure 0.1. **South Africa: Total exports, imports and trade of goods as % of GDP, 1990-2004**

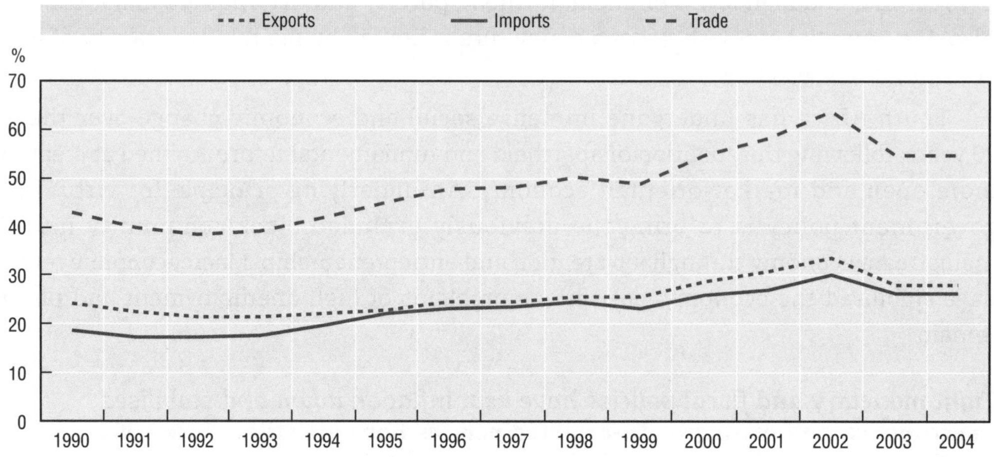

Source: World Development Indicators CD-ROM, World Bank, 2004.

South African agriculture is of a dualistic nature, with a well-developed commercial sector and large numbers of subsistence farms...

South African agriculture is highly dualistic with a small number of commercial operations run predominantly by the white farmers and large numbers of subsistence farms run by the black farmers. The problems and opportunities are quite different for each group. Agricultural reform continues with a series of measures to address past injustices including land redistribution, agricultural support programmes to disadvantaged farming communities, and a broad based programme of economic empowerment of the black population in the agricultural and food sector.

... and its potential for growth is constrained by availability of arable land and water

The importance of agriculture in the overall economy has been declining over the long term. Agriculture's share of GDP fell from around 6% in the 1980s to less than 4% in 2001-02. However, agriculture remains an important sector in terms of employment, accounting for around 10% of formal (officially reported) employment. Overall, the conditions for agricultural production are not favourable in most of the country. Only 16% of agricultural area is potentially arable and water resources are scarce in most regions. Natural pastures in desert and semi-desert areas represent 83% of total agricultural area, and the remaining area is used mostly for field crops and horticulture. The winter rain area in Western Cape is the only region with very favourable production conditions.

The three main sectors of agricultural production in South Africa are field crop production (33% of total agricultural output in 2001-03), livestock production (40%) and horticulture (27%). Overall, agricultural production is well diversified. However, due to adverse regional conditions, farmers in some regions have little scope to diversify. The southern and western interior (semi-arid area) is only suitable for extensive livestock production (sheep, cattle). Intensive livestock farming (dairy, poultry and pork production) is practised in the arable areas of the country, generally closer to the major metropolitan markets or on the coast where access to imported feed is easier. The country is a net importer of meat, most imports being from the neighbouring Botswana and Namibia.

The South African agro-food sector is increasingly integrated with world markets...

The South African economy, including agriculture, is increasingly integrated in world markets. Three major political and economic developments of the 1990s contributed to this process. The most important was the lifting of economic sanctions against South Africa following the accession in 1994 of a democratic government. The next radical change was the repeal of the Marketing Act of 1937, which led to establishment of a much freer economic and entrepreneurial environment with major reductions in government interventions in domestic production, marketing and trade. Finally, on the international front, the Uruguay Round Agreement of Agriculture (URAA) introduced new disciplines governing agricultural trade.

Figure 0.2. **South African agricultural exports and imports, 1992-2004**
Million USD

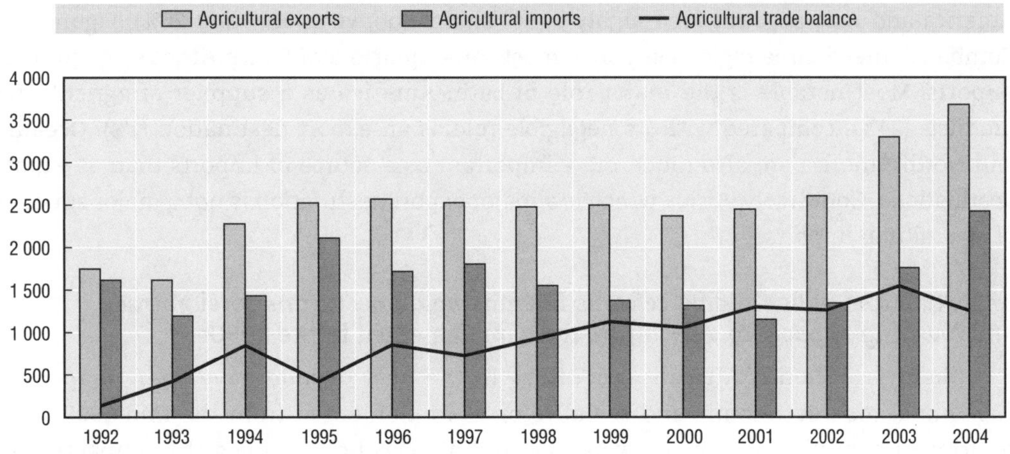

Source: Calculated from data of the Department of Trade and Industry.

... with a sharp growth in agricultural exports...

The opening of the agricultural sector placed South Africa among the world's leading exporters of such agro-food products as wine, fresh fruits and sugar. The country is also an important trader in the African region. The beginning of the current decade witnessed particularly strong agricultural export growth. South Africa's agricultural export revenues reached almost 9% of the total value of national exports. Europe is by far the largest importer, absorbing almost one-half of the country's agricultural exports. The African market is the second most important destination, accounting for around 26% of exports, with the Asian market slightly less important with an 18% share. North America (the United States and Canada) plays a relatively modest role as an export destination, absorbing only around 7%, while exports to Latin America and Oceania are marginal (Figure 0.3).

Figure 0.3. **South African agro-food exports by destination and imports by origin**
% of total

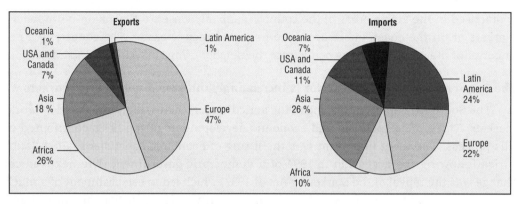

Source: Comtrade Database, 2005.

... and agricultural imports are also increasing somewhat

Agricultural imports are also growing but less rapidly than exports. Agricultural imports have accounted for 5% to 6% of total imports on an annual basis since 2000. They are distributed more evenly than exports with less emphasis on Europe. Europe, Latin America and Asia account for roughly equal shares (between 22% and 26%) (Figure 0.3). Combined, these three regions supply almost three-quarters of South Africa's agricultural imports. Most notable is the major role of Latin America as a supplier of agricultural products (24%), compared with its negligible role as an export destination (1%). Oceania and North America are also much more important as a source of imports than as export destinations. Conversely, Africa which is a major export destination is not a major supplier of agricultural imports.

Important and wide ranging reforms liberalising domestic and foreign trade and lowering support to agriculture were implemented in the 1990s...

Changes in South African agriculture in the past decade have been shaped by substantial macroeconomic and social reforms implemented from the mid-1900s, but reforms of agricultural policies were also initiated. Policy changes that impacted on agriculture included deregulation of the marketing of agricultural products; abolition of certain tax concessions favouring the sector; reductions in budgetary expenditure on the sector; land reform (restitution, redistribution and tenure reform); trade reform, including the tariffication of farm commodities; and the broadening/introduction of new labour legislation.

At the end of the 1980s and early 1990s there was increasing evidence that the continuation of highly interventionist policies was not economically sustainable due to their distorting effects. In addition to economic factors, globalisation and domestic social reforms contributed towards a relaxation of stringent interventionist measures. Market reforms implemented in 1996 (Marketing of Agricultural Products Act) liberalised prices and trade in large parts of the agro-food sector, including foreign trade (one notable exception is the sugar industry).

The main development in trade policies was the replacement of direct controls over imports by tariffs, which were set below the bound rates of the URAA, and elimination of state controls over exports. South Africa has also established a number of preferential trade arrangements with countries inside and outside the Southern African Development Community (SADC) region. These reforms resulted in the lowering of the average level of tariffs and simplification of the tariff structure while maintaining a tariff escalation profile. The new trade arrangements improved access to foreign markets for farmers but also exposed them more to external competition.

... and lead to a more market-oriented sector

Price liberalisation and market deregulation were accompanied by the development of trade and market institutions and an increase in the number of traders. Marketing reform has resulted in significant private sector response across the agro-food chain.

The withdrawal of most forms of support to commercial farmers created adjustment pressures for the sector, while deregulation of the input and services markets provided benefits. Effects on the sector were far reaching and included: i) shift of production out of grain to livestock in marginal production areas, and an increase in intensive farming in high potential areas, particularly horticultural production; ii) more farmer involvement in risk management by means of storage (especially in the case of maize, forcing the co-operatives which own the vast majority of grain silos to become more commercially oriented), forward contracts and diversification; iii) a strengthening of the role of organised markets (SAFEX, Auction markets) and producer responsiveness to price signals; and iv) an acceleration in the establishment of new enterprises in agriculture and downstream food processing sectors and foreign trade.

Less dependence on state support...

Although the deregulation of markets created some uncertainty, at the same time it opened opportunities for entrepreneurial farmers and led to a more efficient allocation of resources in agriculture. The net effect of these changes is that the South African agricultural industry has become less dependent on state support and internationally more competitive, although many sectors within the industry experienced a difficult period of adjustment.

... contributed to rationalisation of commercial farms

The structure of commercial farms in South Africa has been influenced by both deregulation and by the land reform programme. In response to deregulation, commercial farmers (especially in the field crop sector) adopted a wide variety of risk management strategies to cope with the declining and fluctuating producer prices that resulted from deregulation. These strategies included income diversification, e.g. on-farm agro-tourism, off-farm employment; farm diversification, e.g. different products, different regions; and farm consolidation and expansion. This latter trend has resulted in a smaller number of larger commercial farms, contrasting with a large number of very small subsistence farms.

Land reform is a fundamental element of agricultural reforms, aimed at redressing past injustices

After democratisation, the government introduced land reforms to redress past injustices, foster reconciliation and stability, support economic growth, improve household welfare and alleviate poverty in rural areas. The Land Reform Programme consists of three main programmes: restitution of land unjustly taken from people and communities; land redistribution; and land tenure reform.

Some of the components of land reform are well advanced...

The land restitution is well advanced (61% of claims settled). The beneficiaries had an option to be compensated in kind, with agricultural land and assets, or in cash. Some 65% of beneficiaries opted for the compensation in kind while the remaining 35% were compensated in cash. Cash restitution contributed directly to poverty alleviation. During the past ten years, about ZAR 1.6 billion (USD 200 million) have been spent by the government for financial compensation. Restitution beneficiaries tended to invest in home improvements, education and other livelihood projects. Concerning the restitutions in kind, around 916 500 hectares of agricultural land were restored to their former owners.

... while others are lagging behind expectations

Land redistribution is aimed at providing people with access to land for either settlement or agricultural purposes. The aim is, *inter alia,* to settle small and emerging farmers on viable farming operations in the commercial farming areas. The land redistribution programme aims to transfer 30% of all white-owned agricultural land to previously disadvantaged individuals within 15 years. In contrast with land restitution, the land redistribution programme in South Africa has performed below its expectations due to inadequate institutional capacity, financial resources, lack of appropriate agricultural support services, and co-ordination.

2. Current agricultural policies

Border protection has been significantly relaxed...

The trade liberalisation in South Africa after 1994 involved lowering the average tariff level by one-third by 1999. Licenses and quotas are restricted to tariff quota administration in respect of trade agreements, and non-tariff import controls consist of sanitary and phytosanitary measures in accordance with the WTO SPS Agreement. For a range of products, safeguard clauses exist but they have not been applied, mainly because of the substantial margin between bound and applied tariffs.

For most agro-food products, *ad valorem* tariffs or specific tariffs (or a combination of both) are applied. Formula tariffs exist for maize, wheat (replaced with and *ad valorem* tariff in July 2005) and sugar. Domestic market intervention has not been applied since the deregulation of markets in the mid-1990s. The exception is the sugar cane/sugar market where a price pooling system is maintained, and the South Africa Sugar Association is the only sugar exporter.

... and there is an emphasis on negotiating new regional trade agreements

Trade agreements have increasingly become an important tool for opening up markets for South African agricultural products. A general principle is that no agreement should exclude the negotiation of other agreements. South Africa is the most important member of the Southern African Customs Union (SACU), the others being Botswana, Lesotho, Namibia and Swaziland (BLNS countries). The customs union has been in existence since 1910 and was renegotiated in 2002. Within the African trade the most important development was the Southern African Development Community (SADC) Free Trade Agreement signed in 2000. Within this agreement the SACU tariffs were phased down in five years (by 2005). Other countries will do so in 12 years (by 2012).

South Africa is a beneficiary of several preferential trade agreements such as the US initiative African Growth and Opportunity Act (AGOA), and a Generalised System of Preferences (GSP) status with Canada, Norway, United States, Japan, Switzerland and the European Union. A Trade, Development and Co-operation Agreement (TDCA), between South Africa and the European Union was implemented from January 2000. On the other side, the European Union rejected South Africa's application to join the African Caribbean and Pacific (ACP) group. South Africa was accepted as a qualified member of the ACP which means that it can participate in/qualify for only tendering and procurement but not market access concessions to the European Union.

South Africa with other SACU partners is currently negotiating FTAs with the United States, the European Free Trade Association (EFTA) and Mercosur. Further negotiations with Africa's most populated country and second largest economy, Nigeria and the giant Asian markets of India and China have been planned but not yet started.

The budgetary support is increasingly targeted to the beneficiaries of the land reform aiming to develop their agricultural businesses and integrate with markets

An important share of public financial resources is devoted to the implementation of the land reform and especially land redistribution. To support this programme, Land Redistribution and Agricultural Development (LRAD) grants are given to the black disadvantaged population to acquire land or for other forms of on-farm participation. It allows farmers who can provide personal contributions (financial and/or own labour) to acquire more land. The implementation is demand led, and decentralised (applied by Provinces). Beneficiaries can access a range of grants depending on the amount of their own contribution in labour and/or cash. The programme is financially costly and budgets have become a constraint. Approval of the grant is based on the viability of the proposed project which takes into account project costs and expected profitability.

From 2005, new programmes are implemented to support the development of market oriented family farms emerging from the land reform process. The *Comprehensive Agricultural Support Programme* (CASP) is targeted to the beneficiaries of land reform willing to establish commercial farms. The support is to be provided mainly through investment grants allocated to viable projects. The CASP is complementary to the Micro-Agricultural Finance Schemes of South Africa (MAFISA), which is a newly established state-owned scheme to provide micro and retail financial services in rural areas.

The sector is also implicitly supported by tax relief schemes

The Diesel Refund System, introduced in 2000, provides a refund on the fuel and road accident fund levies paid on diesel. The concession applies to farming, mining and forestry. This is one of the few types of support which benefits the commercial farming sector.

Research and development, education and training, inspection and control, infrastructure are other major areas of public support

The publicly financed research and dissemination activities have been increasingly oriented towards the needs of the emerging small farming sector. The Agricultural Research Council in co-operation with the National Department of Agriculture and Departments of Agriculture in the Provinces are the main institutions involved. The inspection and control (regulatory) services of South Africa are relatively well developed. The Department of Agriculture programme, *National Regulatory System* (NRS), focuses on managing risks associated with animal and plant diseases; food safety, including the use of genetic resources and the importing and exporting of food; and bio-safety legislation pertaining to agricultural products entering South Africa and genetically modified products.

There are relatively low and declining levels of support to producers...

As part of the present review the OECD has for the first time calculated the Producer Support Estimate (PSE) for South Africa for the period 1994 to 2003. As measured by the aggregate percentage PSE, producer support in South Africa equalled on average 5% of gross farm receipts in 2000-03. A comparison of producer support in South Africa and the principal world agricultural players shows that the percentage PSE in South Africa is roughly at the level of such non-OECD economies as Brazil, China and Russia, and such OECD country as Australia and somewhat above that in New Zealand – the OECD country with the least policy interventions measured (Figure 0.4). The support level in South Africa is well below that in the United States and far below that in the European Union.

The measured average level of support in South Africa indicates a relatively moderate degree of policy interventions at the agricultural producer level and the overall trend shows some reduction of support since 1994. As is seen from Figure 0.5, the overwhelming share of producer support in South Africa is delivered in the form of Market Price Support (MPS). Budgetary transfers, although showing a tendency to increase in the current decade (mainly due to the introduction of the fuel tax rebate and spending on land reform), have less importance as a source of producer support.

Figure 0.4. **PSE by country, EU[1] and OECD averages, 2000-03 average**

% of gross farm receipts

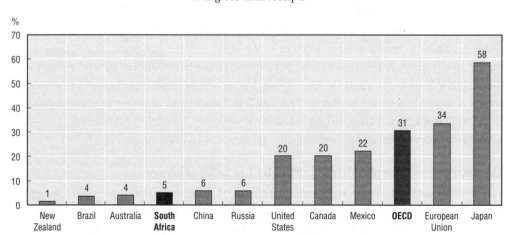

1. 2000-03: EU15.

Source: OECD PSE/CSE Database, 2005.

Figure 0.5. **Composition of Producer Support Estimate, 1994-2003**

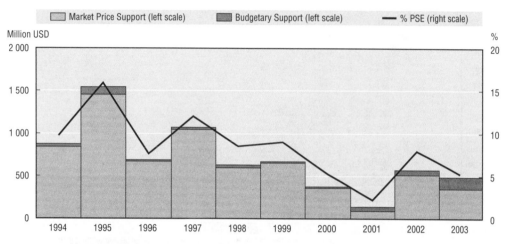

Source: OECD PSE/CSE databases, 2005.

... but strong variations between the years...

The moderate average level of support in South Africa, however, goes along with marked year to year variations – especially in the initial and the most recent years over the analysed period – with the percentage PSE fluctuating between 2% and 16% (Figure 0.5). The strong variations in the support level are the result of diverse – and sometimes opposing – policy impacts. One major force was the progressive overall trade deregulation, with the reduction in border protection and elimination of export subsidies. This overall pressure towards lesser protection, and therefore, lesser producer support, was partly counter-balanced by the system of variable import tariffs, which was maintained for such principal commodities as maize, wheat and sugar. Over and above these specific policies, strong exchange rate fluctuations, without an immediate equivalent transmission to domestic agricultural prices, produced shifts in relative levels of domestic and external prices, thus strongly contributing to annual changes in the measured support.

... and uneven distribution of support among commodities

There are marked differences in the levels of support across individual commodities – with the average percentage PSE ranging from 23% for sugar to nearly zero for a range of other commodities (Figure 0.6). Sugar is the most supported commodity receiving support far above the average level. This is notable given that sugar is one of South Africa's key exports (around one-half of sugar production is exported). The high level of sugar support is maintained through high import tariffs and the pricing system under which South African sugar producers are effectively compensated for export losses by higher prices for domestic sales compared to that destined for exports.

Sheep meat, milk and maize are the other commodities receiving above-average support, though far below that for sugar and closer to the average level. Support for these commodities is based predominantly on border protection. It should be also noted that a relatively high average PSE for maize in 2000-03 largely reflects an abnormal price spike for white maize in 2002.

Figure 0.7 illustrates the relative importance of each component – the PSE and the General Services Support Estimate (GSSE) – in South Africa's Total Support Estimate (TSE).

Figure 0.6. **South African PSEs by commodity, 2000-03 average**

% of gross farm receipts

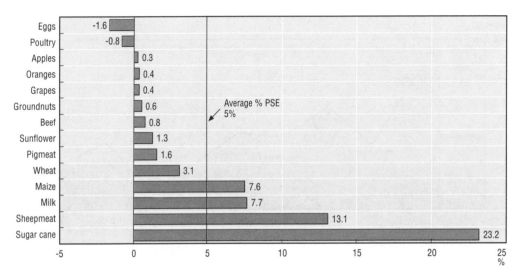

Source: OECD PSE/CSE databases 2005.

Figure 0.7. **Composition of the Total Support Estimate in South Africa**

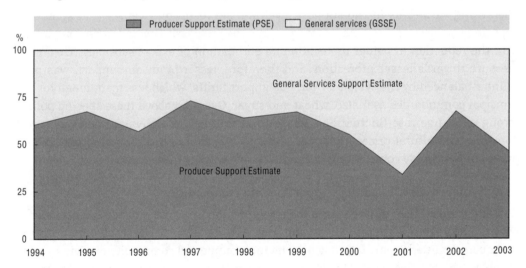

Source: OECD PSE/CSE databases, 2005.

Around 55% of total support to agriculture in 1994-2003 was delivered in the form of the transfers to producers (the PSE). The remaining assistance was provided through general services to the sector. The budgetary spending on general services finances mainly the research, development and training, the investments in infrastructure, inspection and control services, and administration of land reform. Most of the general services (training, infrastructure, *etc.*) are increasingly targeted to the emerging small farmers benefiting from the land reform.

The South African percentage TSE fluctuated over the analysed period, averaging 0.6% of GDP in 2000-03, which is slightly above one-half of the OECD level, and approximately between the percentage TSE in Russia and Brazil. The relative cost of total support in South

OECD REVIEW OF AGRICULTURAL POLICIES – ISBN 92-64-03679-2 – © OECD 2006

Figure 0.8. **Total Support Estimate in South Africa and selected countries, 2001-03 average**

% of GDP

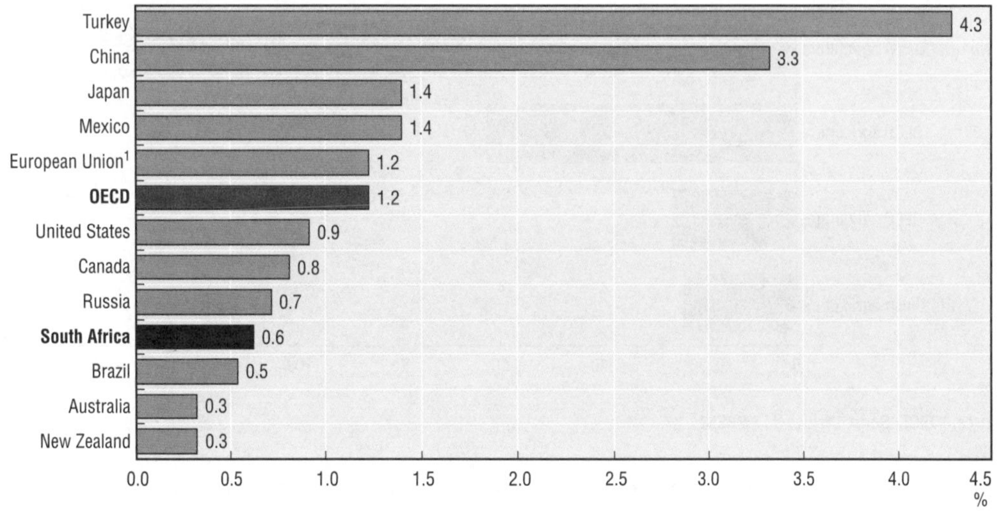

1. 2001-03: EU15.

Source: OECD PSE/CSE databases, 2005.

Africa is however, far less than in China or Turkey – countries with significant weights of the agricultural sectors in their economies (Figure 0.8).

3. Effects of policy reforms

Improving market access is one of the priorities of South African policies

A major share of South African key exports is directed to just a few destinations, among which the OECD markets – in particular, the European Union – are the most important. In general, wine and fresh fruit exports face relatively low levels of border protection, in part due to bilateral and general tariff concessions to South Africa. However, these preferences do not exclude South Africa from the seasonal elevation of tariff barriers and from implicit constraints of the entry prices, built into the EU regime for fresh fruits. This is an important issue for South Africa as the seasonal elevation affects the possibility of exporting fruit production from provinces which have similar harvesting seasons to those in Europe, as these provinces have a potential to increase their production.

OECD sugar markets are effectively restricted to raw sugar exports from South Africa. Although reduction in protection of the sugar sector in the large OECD economies could provide important gains for the low-cost sugar producers, South Africa, with domestic prices higher than world levels, is unlikely to have the comparative advantage to reap those gains.

South Africa benefits from global trade liberalisation, mostly from reforms in non-agricultural sectors...

Quantitative scenario analysis shows that South Africa would benefit from global liberalisation and the expected effect is dominated by the reform in the manufacturing industry (Figure 0.9). Nevertheless, the gains from reform in agriculture are also important, accounting for one-third of total welfare gains. The most significant contribution to gains from the reform in agriculture is from liberalisation of OECD agricultural policies. Under

Figure 0.9. **Welfare gains in South Africa by source of liberalisation**
Million USD

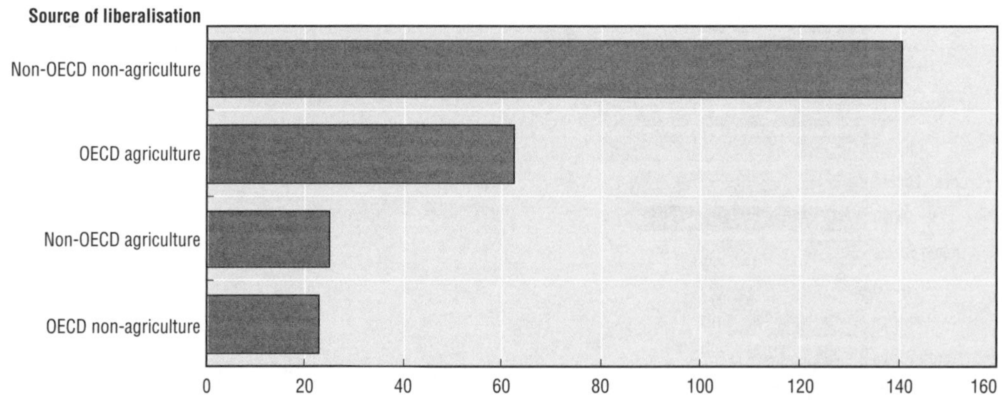

Source: OECD Secretariat, GTAPPEM.

the standard assumption of full employment, scenario analysis suggests that agriculture factor returns would increase slightly more than non-agricultural returns. However, an alternative assumption of no constraints on the unskilled labour supply shows that factor income inequality would be increased, though the creation of new jobs for unskilled workers helps to reduce poverty.

... but liberalisation by South Africa itself is an important component of these gains

An analysis of the distributional implications of multilateral liberalisation suggests that there would be redistribution in welfare both between racial groups and provinces, with the coastal provinces and white households being subjected to some small declines in welfare while the inland provinces and non-white households experience some increase in welfare.

The overriding conclusion is that while global liberalisation may open up market opportunities to South Africa, the primary determinants of the welfare changes in South Africa are under the control of the South African government, namely South Africa's own tax rates. As such, these results are consistent with the trade theory argument of "no gain without pain"; in this case the "pain" being imposed through the need to replace lost tariff revenue through higher domestic taxes.

Effects of agricultural policy liberalisation on South African agro-food markets are offsetting and relatively small

Liberalising OECD and South African agricultural policies would, to some degree, have opposite and therefore partly offsetting effects on South African domestic markets for crops and livestock. For a number of commodities, the resulting effects of a partial multilateral liberalisation would therefore be rather small. The effects of OECD and South African policies individually are generally more pronounced in dairy markets.

A partial liberalisation in OECD countries would generally result in higher world and domestic prices for most agricultural products and would therefore not only benefit South African producers, but also negatively affect food consumers. However, given the rather marginal size of price changes, the impacts remain small overall. Unilateral South African liberalisation, on the other hand, will have minor effects on world and domestic prices. The relatively little impact of unilateral liberalisation on South Africa's agricultural markets is not surprising given that the binding overhang in South Africa's tariffs leads to relatively little change.

4. Policy challenges and recommendations

Achieving higher and sustained economic growth is crucial for improvements in rural areas...

Although the recent performance of South Africa's economy has been generally positive, both investment and output growth are still below the levels necessary to reduce unemployment and to achieve a more equitable income distribution. Despite growing emphasis on reducing poverty and increasing social spending, enormous social needs remain unmet and a large segment of the population is excluded from the formal economy – as indicated by very high unemployment rates – and has limited access to social services.

Agricultural and rural development in South Africa is not possible without broad economic growth and macroeconomic stability. This in turn calls for well gauged fiscal and monetary policies designed to achieve economic growth above the rates prevailing currently. However, in a country like South Africa, broad economic growth is inconceivable without resolving profound humanitarian problems, such as social divisions, illiteracy and low education levels, and HIV/Aids. These problems are largely rooted in rural South Africa, and agricultural development has an important role to play in their resolution. There is therefore a circular dependence between agricultural and economic growth and human development, which ultimately represents the most difficult challenge facing South Africa's policy makers.

Policies to increase participation in the rural economy and diversify incomes are key to addressing rural poverty...

Rural poverty in South Africa appears to differ from other countries in three ways: among the rural poor, income generated directly from agricultural activities and food consumed from own farm production are minor components of household resources (estimated at 10% to 20% of the total); many households continuously rotate between rural and urban base; and rural society is closely linked to the social and health problems of urban areas. The reorientation of safety net and social programmes in the late 1990s which addressed poverty issues in rural areas through general social security schemes was a move in the right direction.

However, the long-term solution requires involving a greater part of the rural poor in economic activities generating sufficient income. While recognising the important role of agricultural development in addressing poverty and inequalities, it should also be clear that the potential of agriculture and agricultural (land) reform itself to reduce poverty is limited. The current and prospective role of agriculture in the economy and South Africa's relatively scarce natural resources (arable land, water) suggest that only a limited number of people may secure fair living standards from agriculture only. The main potential to reduce rural poverty and inequity lies in the development of overall frameworks providing social security, education and training as well as health care, and in developing adequate infrastructures in rural areas. There is a need to examine how recent and ongoing sectoral and economy-wide policies contribute to poverty reduction by integrating poor population in broader economic activities.

... including development of rural and social infrastructure

Rural economic infrastructure, such as rural transport, telecommunication and information technologies, is crucial for the development of economic activities in rural areas, including commercially sustainable farming. Not all farmers in South Africa have access to the telecommunication and/or electricity networks. Equally important are the provision of social services and investments in infrastructure that will provide a knowledgeable, skilled, healthy, economically active society in rural areas. Just as transport and communication are the priority drivers for economic activity, education, skills development and health are the priority drivers for human capital development and welfare.

Land reform has a long way to go and is facing implementation challenges

Land reform is driven by the need to redress inequitable land allocation which emerged from the apartheid past. There is a broad consensus in South Africa that the land issue needs to be resolved as a matter of urgency, although there is much controversy about the ways this should be done. The key issues are how to *a)* create stakeholder consensus around the implementation strategy; and *b)* improve the procedures of land acquisition and resettlement. If agreement can be reached on a policy framework which allows a menu of options to be pursued, the results can then be monitored, evaluated and modified as the programme proceeds. Clarity is needed about the role and functions of institutions involved and better co-ordination between them. Land reform is a massive, complicated process and not everything can be done simultaneously. The identification of realistic objectives and careful sequencing of activities are conditions for success.

Budgets have become a constraint on the land reform programme. Provincial budget allocations have been overcommitted with the result that in some provinces, new projects cannot be approved and existing projects are jeopardised. Some provinces have put a moratorium on new projects. The costs to government of all the actions required, time scales involved, and fiscal responsibilities of specified government agencies need to be estimated well in advance. Land programme budgets should also be subject to macroeconomic constraints and government prioritising on public spending.

Some of the beneficiaries of land reform suffered defaults, as they were inadequately prepared for running commercial farming in a high risk environment, or were unable to raise sufficient capital for commercial production. The experience thus shows that the proper selection and follow-up of beneficiaries is crucial for land reform to develop sustainable commercial farming. At the same time, training is essential, not only in farm technologies, but also in marketing and financial management. Some retraining of extension personnel could provide this service but the largest potential rests with the current commercial farming sector, and its mentor approach appears a useful route to be supported and developed. Attention is needed to ensure the availability of appropriate support services at the right place, time and cost (*e.g.* financial services, market information and access, purchased inputs, research, and transportation infrastructure).

The overall policy objective would be to have a ready set of complementary land acquisition methods that have been tested and made operational. Governments should add variants, adapted to local circumstances. Legal mechanisms which transfer the ownership directly, or almost directly, from the former owner to the beneficiaries may be considered to avoid a lengthy transfer of ownership during which the State has to ensure the security of the asset "in transit". Land acquisition options need to include the acquisition of subdivisions, rather than whole farms.

... and a more decentralised approach offers promise

South Africa's experience with land redistribution since 1994 confirms the international lessons that underline the need to decentralise and make programmes more community-driven. South Africa's flagship redistribution programme, LRAD, made the important step of decentralising decision-making down to the provincial level, and reaped immediate benefits in terms of speed and the quantity of projects implemented. By bringing them closer to the local level redistribution decisions would become more adjusted with local conditions and the capacities and needs of the beneficiaries. As vertical accountability is relaxed, horizontal and downward accountability, and integration between programmes should be strengthened. The land reform programmes could then become an integral part of the local development plans which in South Africa are the basis for local development budgeting and implementation.

The government needs to keep stakeholders engaged in dialogue around policy implementation. Local government structures, farmers' associations, NGOs, and churches, can assist in a number of ways. They can identify programme priorities, support applicants in accessing the various land reform programmes, and provide follow-up technical assistance to successful beneficiaries. NGOs and research institutions can provide valuable monitoring and evaluation services, and assist in policy development.

Developing a viable small-scale commercial agriculture requires well targeted support services

The dismantling of apartheid implied a strong commitment to develop a new class of black farmers and to integrate them into a market economy. This objective requires considerable investment in human capital and progress in this area has been slow. Smallholder farming, still located mostly in the former homelands, is an impoverished sector, dominated by low-input, labour-intensive production. Low productivity is a major handicap, coupled with tenure insecurity, very small size of land holdings and lack of support services (*e.g.* extension, finance and marketing). The black population in rural areas is the target of the land reform policies, but it is clear that adequate supporting infrastructure must also be in place if these new entrepreneurs are to survive.

The new entrants into commercial agriculture (and into agricultural based services) are at a considerable disadvantage relative to the more experienced operators in facing the challenges of the liberalised market. The government may address these issues by implementing well targeted support programmes and services, including research and development programmes tailored to the needs of the emerging commercial farms. The emerging commercial farmers may also benefit from the experience of commercial farmers, and the government (at different administration level) has a role to play in facilitating the exchange of information and promoting tutorial partnerships.

It is essential for the development of small-scale farms and for the less developed regions of South Africa, to have a financial system able to mobilise savings, allocate capital and monitor farmers, business firms and micro-enterprises. The Micro-Agricultural Finance Schemes of South Africa (MAFISA) was established to provide micro credit and related services to the rural poor. In principle, MAFISA is targeting those who, with the help of the loan, are able to establish a viable business and escape poverty. In this respect, careful client targeting and development/application of transparent selection criteria are of utmost importance to secure longer term financial viability of the programme.

Liberalisation of market and trade policies provide both challenges and opportunities, mainly to commercial farms

During the 1990s, South Africa liberalised its economy including the wide liberalisation of agricultural markets and agro-food trade. Although many sectors experienced a difficult period of adjustment, the deregulation of markets opened opportunities for entrepreneurial farmers and led to a more efficient allocation of resources in agriculture. The net effect of these changes is that the South African agricultural industry has become less dependent on state support and more competitive internationally.

The South African agro-food trade is increasingly integrated with world markets and South Africa is exporting around a third of its agricultural production. In general, the tariffs regime has been simplified and the level of tariffs reduced during the 1900s. In most cases the applied tariffs are well below the bound rates. However, for some products (maize, wheat, sugar) the tariff schedule remains complex (formula tariffs), and applied tariffs are changing frequently. This may create uncertainty for businesses that frequently import goods and isolate the domestic markets from price changes on world markets. A simplification of the tariff structure (as was done for wheat in July 2005) may be considered also for the other products.

Although there is no direct state intervention on the markets, the sugar market is still regulated by the South African Sugar Association (SASA). The sugar producers are subject to quotas when selling on domestic markets and a price pooling system is in place. SASA is also the only exporter of sugar. As a result sugar is the most highly supported commodity in South Africa and the system applied is implicitly taxing domestic consumers. The deregulation of the sugar market may bring benefit to consumers but also may lead to a better allocation of scarce resource in agriculture (arable land and water).

Conclusion

Within the past ten years, wide-ranging reforms created a good base for continuation of efforts to address further, often profound, economic and social challenges facing South Africa. While important progress has been made, there is much more to be done in South Africa to redress social inequalities, reduce poverty, and increase equitable access to economic opportunities for all segments of the population. Balancing more inclusive social policy with a stable and open macroeconomic environment, in which both the role of further agricultural development and the limits of agriculture's contribution are clearly recognised, is the fundamental challenge.

Review of Agricultural Policies in South Africa

ISBN 92-64-03679-2
OECD Review of Agricultural Policies
South Africa
© OECD 2006

Chapter 1

The Policy Context

Chapter 1 of this study sets out the policy context. Section 1.1 provides a brief historical perspective of the main macroeconomic developments, earlier policy reforms and resulting current economic situation. Section 1.2 looks at the role of agriculture in the South African economy and how the structure of the sector is evolving. Section 1.3 examines agricultural trade in more detail in terms of both exports and imports. Section 1.4 then highlights some of the main impacts of policy reform on the sector.

South Africa has undergone immense social and economic change over the last 20 years led by the abolition of apartheid and extensive domestic policy reforms aimed at creating a more open and market-oriented economy, as well as by the general global changes like the international trade regimes. An underlying principle for virtually all government policy is to bring the previously excluded black community into the mainstream economy through job creation and entrepreneurship. Macroeconomic reforms have strengthened and stabilised the economy but serious problems of high unemployment and poverty remain.

South African agriculture is highly dualistic with a small number of predominately commercial operations run by the white community and large numbers of small-scale and subsistence farms run by the black community. The problems and opportunities are quite different for each group. Agriculture has had to adjust to greater reforms than any other sector with the deregulation of domestic markets, liberalisation of foreign trade, lowering of support, and the land reform. Agricultural reform continues with a series of measures to address past injustices including land redistribution, agricultural support programmes to disadvantaged farming communities and a broad based programme of economic empowerment in the agricultural and food sector.

1.1. A historical perspective

The Republic of South Africa occupies the southernmost part of the African continent. With a surface area of 1.22 million km^2 and the population of 46.9 million,[1] South Africa is one of the largest countries on the African continent. It is also the largest African economy, whose per capita GDP of USD 3 530 (USD 10 492 in PPP terms)[2] is more than four times the African average. However, the distribution of income is among the most unequal in the world, and high levels of unemployment, poverty and HIV/Aids are major concerns.

Based on the 2001 Census, 79% of South African citizens identified themselves as African; 9.6% as white; 8.9% as coloured; and 2.5% as Indian/Asian. To cater for South Africa's diverse peoples, the Constitution recognises 11 official languages.[3] The country is very unevenly populated. An average population density is 36.7 inhabitants per km^2, but it reaches 519.5 inhabitants per km^2 in Gauteng (a small region with two large cities, Johannesburg and Pretoria) and is only 2.3 persons per km^2 in the Northern Cape. The latter is the largest province with 30% of total land area and just 1.8% of total population. Some 21% of the population is located in KwaZulu-Natal on 7% of the total land area.

South Africa is becoming progressively more urbanised. The share of urban population currently reaches 58%, which is well above the Sub-Saharan Africa average of 34%. Six cities, Johannesburg, Tshwane (Pretoria), Cape Town, Ethekwini (Durban), Ekurhuleni (Greater East Rand) and Nelson Mandela (Port Elizabeth), each count for over 1 million inhabitants. The rapid urbanisation is consistent with the trends in the developing world and is an increasingly important factor to consider in policy making.

Map of South Africa

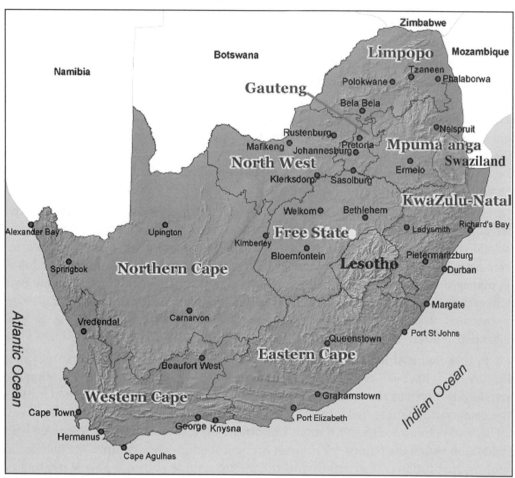

Regional and local governments play an important role in the delivery of agricultural and rural policy and programmes. For administrative purposes, South Africa is divided into nine provinces: Western Cape, Eastern Cape, Northern Cape, Free State, KwaZulu-Natal, North-West, Gauteng, Mpumalanga, Limpopo Province). Sub-provincial level is represented by District Councils, the Metropolitan Areas and the municipalities, which in 1999 were given higher authority and responsibilities, in particular in the area of local development. District municipalities also cover the rural and agricultural areas surrounding the towns and villages and are therefore responsible for infrastructure and other developmental aspects in rural areas. At the local level, formal governance co-exists with the traditional leadership. The institution, status and the role of traditional leadership, according to customary law, are recognised within the limits set by the Constitution.

Agriculture adjusts to a democratic society

By 1910, when the Union of South Africa was founded, the whole country was under white rule, and most farmland was occupied by white farmers. Land ownership by indigenous people had largely been constrained to designated *reserves*, later renamed *homelands*. Over the next seven decades, discrimination against Blacks continued, and particularly intensified after 1948, when the new government adopted the policy of segregation (known as "apartheid"). A series of legislative acts that emerged during the decades of racial discrimination, substantially limited access of Blacks to agricultural land, financial and other services, and state assistance.

Such discriminatory policies widened the gap between commercial farming as practiced predominantly by white farmers and subsistence farming represented mainly by black farmers. Drought and flood aid, interest rate subsidies, tax concessions on purchased farm machinery, as well as government expenditure on agricultural education, research and advisory services, including extension, were targeted mainly to commercial farming. The labour force in commercial agriculture mostly consisted of Blacks with low skills. Since the 1960s, increasing mechanisation has resulted in shedding much of this unskilled farm labour from agriculture.

A slow movement away from the discriminatory legislation and towards the deregulation of the economy began in the 1980s. However, with increasing international isolation of the country in social, cultural, political and intellectual spheres, the reforms were partial and aimed at the domestic market only. Foreign trade continued to be based on managed imports and exports or monopoly export schemes, in order to manipulate domestic prices. Overall, the policy changes implemented during the 1980s/early 1990s, represented changes within the existing institutional structure, despite the general relaxation of intervention.

In 1994, South Africa held its first democratic elections. Since then, all statutory race discrimination has been abolished and policies introduced to reduce the inequalities of the past, largely driven by the principles contained in the "Freedom Charter" adopted in 1955. The democratic changes had a major impact on agriculture as with all other aspects of social and economic life. The most important agricultural policy initiatives – all undertaken within the framework of wider macroeconomic policy reforms – included land reforms, institutional restructuring of the public service sector, a new Marketing of Agricultural Products Act and Water Act, trade liberalisation and labour market policy reform. (The impacts of these reforms on South African agriculture are highlighted in Section 4. These reforms are discussed in detail in Chapter 2.)

Economic growth rebounds

The South African economy grew at relatively high rates after the Second World War. The real GDP growth was 4% to 5% a year during the 1950s and 1960s. The rate of growth started to decline in the 1970s and slowed significantly during the 1980s and the first half of the 1990s, but increased to around 2% to 3% per annum in the second half of the 1990s (Figure 1.1). This restricted growth is commonly described as the real cost of apartheid, and the result of social and political instability that preceded the first democratic elections. However, the mining recession, especially after the gold price boom of the late 1970s, was also a major contributing factor. GDP per capita reached a peak in 1981, then declined before increasing again after 1994, partly explained by a decline in the population growth rate.

While GDP growth resumed in 1994, the momentum was lost in 2003 owing to the strong appreciation of the rand and a serious drought that led the growth to fall to 1.9% (Table 1.1). Despite this generally positive recent economic performance, both investment and output growth are still below the levels necessary to reduce unemployment and to achieve more equitable income distribution. Moreover, the country faces major social

Figure 1.1. **Annual GDP growth rates in South Africa, 1961-2003**

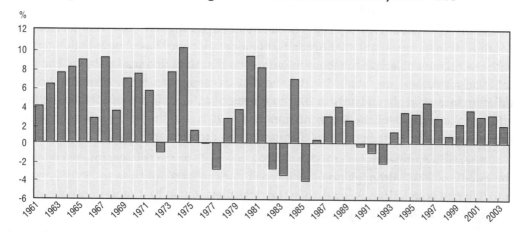

Source: World Development Indicators CD-ROM, World Bank, 2004.

Table 1.1. **Selected macroeconomic indicators for South Africa, 1994-2003**

		1994	1995	1996	1997	1998	1999	2000	2001	2002	2003
GDP	USD billion	135.8	151.1	143.7	148.8	133.7	131.1	128.0	114.2	106.3	159.9
GDP growth	Annual %	3	3.1	4.3	2.6	0.8	2.0	3.5	2.8	3.6	1.9
Inflation, consumer prices	Annual %	8.9	8.7	7.4	8.6	6.9	5.2	5.3	5.7	8.9	6.0
Unemployment[1]	% of total labour force	4.4	4.5	5.1	5.4	25.2	25.3	n.a.	29.5	n.a.	n.a.
Exports of goods and services	% of GDP	22	23	25	25	26	26	29	31	34	28.2
Total exports of goods and services	USD billion	30.1	34.7	35.3	36.5	34.4	33.7	36.6	35.0	35.4	n.a.
Imports of goods and services	% of GDP	20	22	23	23	25	23	26	27	30	26.4
Total imports of goods and services	USD billion	27.0	33.4	33.3	34.9	32.9	30.3	33.1	30.9	31.8	n.a.
Trade	% of GDP	42	45	48	48	50	49	54	58	56	48.5
External debt, total	USD billion	21.7	25.4	26.1	25.3	24.8	23.9	24.9	24.1	25.0	27.8
External balance on goods and services	% of GDP	2.3	0.9	1.4	1.1	1.2	2.6	2.8	3.6	3.4	n.a.
Exchange rate	ZAR/USD	3.6	3.3	4.3	4.6	5.6	6.1	7.0	8.6	10.5	7.6

n.a.: not available.

1. The data for 1994-1997 is not comparable with the data for 1998-2003 due to the change in the definition of unemployment.

Source: World Development Indicators CD-ROM, World Bank 2004; Development Bank of Southern Africa (unemployment); South Africa Reserve Bank *Quarterly Bulletins* (exchange rate).

challenges including poor management of social and educational systems, a high prevalence of HIV/Aids infection (20% of adult population), and a high level of crime.

A more stable economy

Since the start of the democratisation process, South Africa's macroeconomic policy has been directed towards the stabilisation of the macroeconomic environment, with the government attaching high importance to the confidence of domestic entrepreneurs and the international community. Since 1994/95, when the budget deficit was about 5.5% of GDP, public finance has been substantially consolidated, resulting in fiscal contraction in real terms. However, since 2001/02, there has been a gradual transition from fiscal austerity to a growth-oriented policy. Despite growing emphasis on reducing poverty and increasing social spending, enormous social needs remain unmet and a large segment of the population is excluded from the formal economy – as highlighted by very high unemployment rates – and has limited access to social services (AfDB/OECD 2004).

In the 1980s, South Africa experienced double-digit inflation. Since February 2000, the South African Reserve Bank (SARB) conducts monetary policy based on inflation targeting with the primary objective to reduce inflation and maintain financial stability. The rate of inflation for 2000-01 was about 5% and the 2002-04 target was set at 3% to 6%. However, inflation increased significantly in 2002 to a peak of 11%, mainly propelled by the lagged effect of the collapse of the South African *rand* in 2001 and the poor performance of the agricultural sector. By the end of 2003, inflation had dropped again to 4%.

After rising interest rates in 2001 and 2002, the SARB began to lower interest rates from the middle of 2003. Although nominal interest rates in 2004 are close to 1980s' levels, the inflation rate is significantly lower than the rates prevalent at that time. Consequently, the real interest rate is much higher today than in the early 1980s (Figure 1.2).

During the 1990s, the *rand* was weakening against the US dollar and other currencies and at the end of the decade the depreciation has accelerated. Currently, SARB implements a floating exchange rate policy and there are no exchange rate targets. The period 2001-03 has been characterised by important variations in the exchange rate, and particularly a strong weakening of the *rand* during the second half of 2001. During 2003 and 2004 the *rand* was strengthening and approached its mid-2001 level (Figure 1.3).

Trade liberalisation

During the 1980s, various countries imposed trade and investment sanctions on South Africa. The announcement by the State president early in 1990 that apartheid would be abolished, political prisoners freed and negotiations started for a new dispensation, brought in its wake a more lenient attitude regarding trade with and investment in South Africa. Sanctions were discontinued after the democratic elections in 1994.

As far as South Africa's own policies are concerned, the policies in the 1980s were oriented towards market and trade controls and increasing self-sufficiency. In the early 1990s, a gradual shift to market liberalisation and opening of the economy to world trade occurred mainly as a result of the international political acceptability of South Africa

Figure 1.2. **Inflation and interest rates in South Africa, 1980-2004**

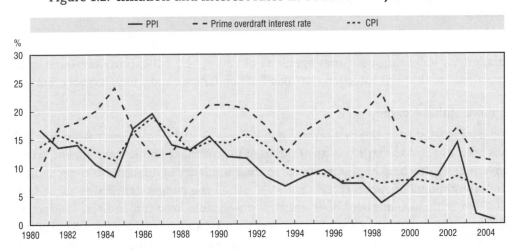

Source: Statistics South Africa (Stats Online at *www.statssa.gov.za*).

Figure 1.3. **Exchange rates of the South African Rand against selected currencies, 1990-2004**

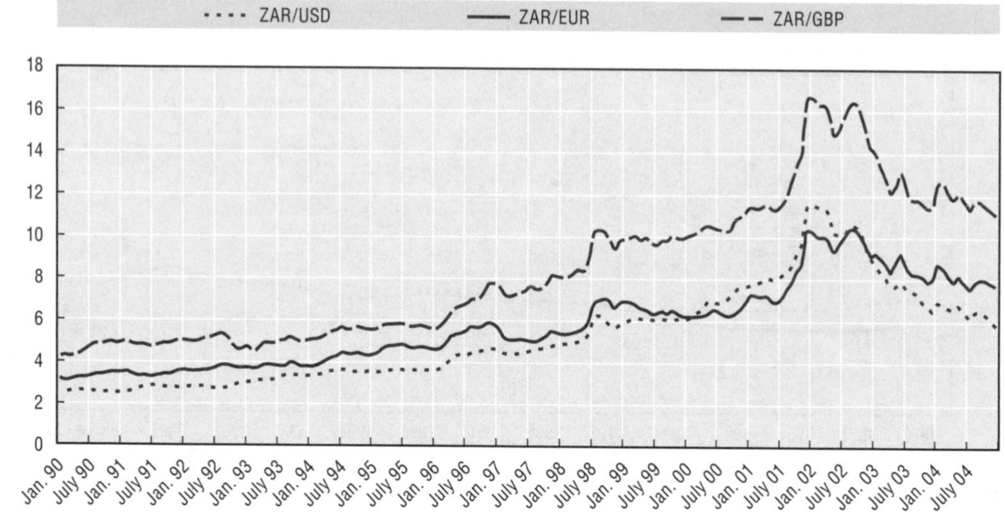

Source: South African Reserve Bank, *www.reservebank.co.za*.

but also after South Africa signed the 1994 Marrakech Agreement. South Africa was a founding member of the GATT.

In the spirit of the Marrakech Agreement, South Africa fast tracked the process of trade liberalisation and simplified its system of border measures. Quantitative restrictions, specific duties, and price controls, import and export permits and other regulations were replaced by tariffs. Initial progress in rationalising the tariff regime and lowering nominal and effective protection was rapid (Table 1.2). The maximum existing tariff was reduced from almost 1400% to 55% and the average economy-wide tariff fell from 28% to 7.1%.

Overall, the South African economy is increasingly oriented towards world markets both in terms of exports and imports. The share of exports of goods and services of total GDP increased from 22.2% in 1994 to 34% in 2002 and that of imports from 19.9% to 30.5% over the same period. However, after the peak in 2002, these shares declined somewhat in 2003 and 2004 (Figure 1.4).

Table 1.2. **Changes in the South African tariff structure**

	All rates			Positives rates[1]
	1990	1996	1999	1999
Number of lines	12 500	8 250	7 743	2 463
Number of bands	200	49	47	45
Minimum rate, %	0	0	0	1
Maximum rate, %	1 389	61	55	55
Unweighted mean rate, %	27.5	9.5	7.1	16.5
Standard deviation, %	n.a.	n.a.	10.0	8.6
Coefficient of variation, %	159.8	134.0	140.3	52.2

1. Exlcuding 0 rates.

Source: Lewis (2001).

Figure 1.4. **South Africa: Total exports, imports and trade of goods as % of GDP, 1990-2004**

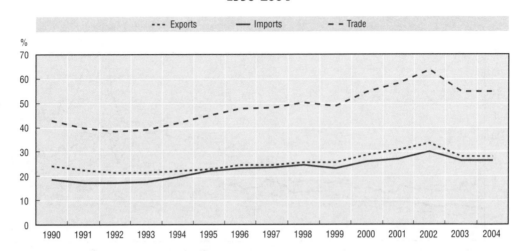

Source: World Development Indicators CD-ROM, World Bank, 2004.

Continuing high unemployment

Some of the most stringent measures of apartheid applied to labour. The natural operation of economic forces in the labour market was superseded by ideologically inspired measures aimed at minimising black participation in the "white" economy. The mobility of Blacks, who were relegated to perform mostly unskilled work, was severely restricted. Urban influx controls were used to restrict migratory growth of black urban populations. One effect was a geographical segmentation of black labour.

These discriminatory measures created an artificial shortage of unskilled labour, and increased wages in urban centres. Average real wages of black workers in the non-primary sectors rose by 2.9% per annum between 1975 and 1990 (Hofmeyr, 1994). However, these measures were not extended to farming areas.[4] For many black workers, work on commercial farms of the white community presented the only income opportunity besides the very limited opportunities available in the "homelands".

Low skills and illiteracy present serious problems in terms of employment and productivity. According to Wilson and Ramphele (1989) more than 5 million Blacks, 20 years and older, were illiterate in 1980. In general, illiteracy is more prevalent among older age groups. In the 1970s and 1980s, the number of black children attending school grew although real government expenditure per black pupil enrolled decreased by a massive 50.5% (Bromberger, 1982). Although declining, after 1994, the overall rate of illiteracy was estimated at 14% in 2002 (AfDB/OECD, 2004).

South Africa adopted a much broader definition of unemployment in 1998. The unemployment status no longer requires active job search by the unemployed (i.e. it includes those in the labour force not actively searching employment). This change in definition increased the official figure of unemployment rate from 5.4% in 1997 to 25.2% in 1998. While not comparable with earlier estimates, the new figure provides a more realistic picture of the situation. The 8.4 million persons in the labour force who are "economically non-active" reflects to a large part the hidden unemployment in rural areas and is a cause of serious concern (Table 1.3).

Table 1.3. **Composition of South African labour force, 2002-04**

Million

	2002	2003	2004
Total employment	12.0	11.7	12.0
Formal employment	6.8	7.5	7.8
Informal employment	5.2	4.2	4.2
Total workforce	26.3	29.9	30.4
Economically active	18.5	20.0	20.4
Economically non-active	7.8	9.9	10.0
Expanded unemployed	6.5	8.3	8.4

Source: Bruggemans (2004).

High unemployment is a principal cause of food insecurity and malnutrition for many households and a serious problem in South Africa. The quantity of total calories may be available, but the quantity of protein and nutrients, the diversity of foods, and the stability of access to food throughout the year are a source of concern. Estimates suggest that approximately 1.5 million South African children suffer from malnutrition, with 24% of the children stunted and 9% underweight. On the other side, recent nutrition surveys indicate that a growing proportion of South Africa's population faces "excessive" calorie intake leading to health problems such as diabetes and heart diseases. (These issues are more developed in Section 3.5.)

Growing burden of HIV/Aids

No policy review of South Africa can ignore the socio-economic impact of HIV/Aids because it has a significant effect on labour productivity and hence the competitiveness of the South African economy. HIV/Aids infection (20% of the adult population) represents a huge cost to a business, whose competitiveness may be adversely affected by low productivity and high labour costs. The United Nations Development Programme has estimated that the Human Development Index of South Africa will be 15% lower in 2010 due to HIV/Aids (Joint United Nations Programme on HIV/Aids and United Nations Development Programme, 2000).

The impact of HIV/Aids is particularly acute in rural areas and the labour-intensive agricultural sector where it destroys human capital, weakens institutions and exacerbates the problem of poverty. Labour turnover rates, labour productivity and production costs on commercial farms are adversely affected by the deaths and poor health of workers with HIV/Aids. The capacity of small-scale farming households to cultivate their land is also adversely affected because infected members are too weak to perform farming tasks and members with farming skills die from the disease.

1.2. The agriculture and food sector in South Africa

Declining but still economically important

South African agriculture is of a dualistic nature, with a well-developed commercial sector comprising about 45 000 commercial farms (mostly owner-operated and using hired labour), which occupy 86% of agricultural land. This commercial sector is capital-intensive, using hired labour, and strongly linked to global markets. However, in terms of revenue most of these farms are relatively small and the owners are often relying on off farm incomes. Subsistence and sub-subsistence (communal) farms (operated by family labour)

Table 1.4. **Principal statistics on farm structure in South African commercial agriculture by group of farms according to economic size**

Income (farm turnover)	Number of farming units	Employment		Employee remuneration	Gross farming income	Expenditure		Farming debt	Market value of assets
		Proprietors and tenants	Paid employees	Salaries and wages		Current	Capital		
		Number		Million ZAR					
Less than ZAR 299 999	23 428	25 101	241 124	1 136	7 404	6 160	752	7 628	28 025
ZAR 300 000-ZAR 999 999	11 805	4 755	137 028	671	5 336	4 241	312	3 985	11 802
ZAR 1 000 000-ZAR 1 999 999	5 214	3 340	128 835	891	7 351	5 946	363	4 324	13 022
ZAR 2 000 000-ZAR 3 999 999	3 041	10 038	124 956	658	5 057	4 035	434	4 567	15 133
ZAR 4 000 000-ZAR 9 999 999	1 657	2 089	148 366	1 167	10 330	8 242	440	5 024	14 188
ZAR 10 000 000 and more	673	704	160 511	1 693	17 850	13 468	647	5 330	16 258
Total	45 818	46 026	940 820	6 216	53 329	42 092	2 947	30 858	98 428

Source: Stats SA 2005, Census of Commercial Agriculture 2002, p. 17.

occupy the remaining 14% of farmland. Past government policies, which restricted Blacks to certain regions (homelands) and therefore excluded them from entering mainstream agriculture, was a major factor in promoting the dualistic nature of agriculture in South Africa that exists today.

The commercial sector is similar to most OECD countries in that the top 20% produce about 80% of the total value of production (Table 1.4). The fact that 23 000 commercial farms (or 51%) earn less than ZAR 300 000 (USD 36 800) per annum is an indication that most of South Africa's commercial farms are in fact rather small economic units.

The importance of agriculture in the overall economy has declined from around 6% in the 1980s to 3.6% in 2001-02. However, it remains an important sector in terms of employment, accounting for around 10% of the country's official employment. Commercial agricultural production in South Africa was valued at ZAR 68 billion in 2003, while its contribution to the total gross domestic product was ZAR 35.6 billion or 3.1% of GDP.

According to the 2002 Census, formal agriculture provides employment for about 481 000 full-time farm workers (with total annual incomes of ZAR 5.2 billion) and 459 000 seasonal and casual workers (total incomes ZAR 1 billion). The smallholder sector provides mostly part-time employment for at least an additional 1.3 million households. In total, it is estimated that about 6 million people rely on agriculture for a livelihood. With such a large labour force, average labour productivity in South African agriculture is relatively low compared with other countries (Figures 1.6 and 1.5). However, the fact that a large number of commercial farms rely on non farm incomes, and the existence of a large number of subsistence and semi-subsistence farmers (for which there is a lack of data) implies that sector-wide averages should be interpreted with caution.

The agro-food sector is increasingly export oriented, with net exports of agricultural products constituting some 22% of the sector's contribution to GDP in 2002, compared to 15.5% in 1994 (Abstracts, 2005). The share of agro-food exports in total exports during this period fluctuated between 8% and 10%, while the share of total imports after an increase from 4% to 8% in the early 1900s, had declined to around 6% (Figure 1.7). (The developments in agriculture trade are described in Section 1.4.)

Figure 1.5. **Agriculture's share of GDP, 2000-02 average**

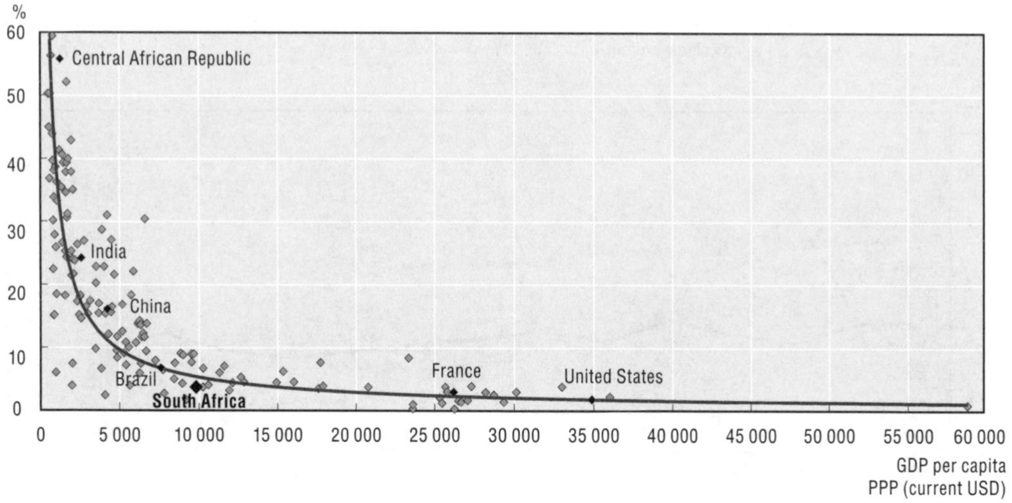

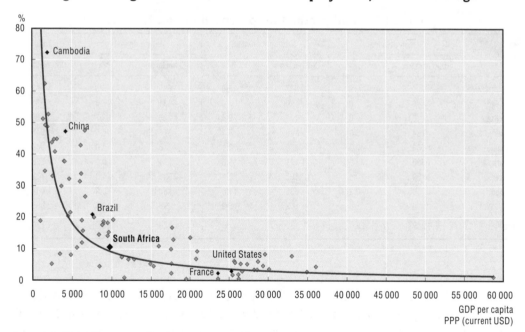

Source: World Development Indicators CD-ROM, World Bank, 2004.

Figure 1.6. **Agriculture's share of total employment, 2000-02 average**

Source: World Development Indicators CD-ROM, World Bank, 2004.

Limited natural endowments for agriculture

About 82% of total land area in South Africa is classified as farmland. However, 84% of this farmland can be only used as extensive pasture. Potentially arable land represents only 16% of the total and is unevenly distributed across the country (Table 1.5). Nature conservation areas (natural parks) cover 10.5% of the land area while forests represent 1.1%. (The challenges in addressing agri-environmental problems are described in Section 5.2.)

Figure 1.7. **Share of agriculture[1] in GDP, agricultural exports and imports, 1990-2004**

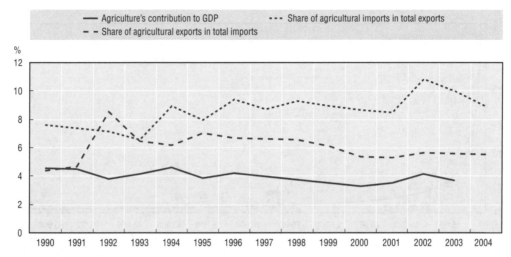

1. Agriculture includes agriculture, hunting, forestry and fishing.
Source: Abstract of Agricultural Statistics, South Africa Department of Agriculture, 2005; Comtrade Database, 2005.

Table 1.5. **Land production potential in South Africa**

Province	High potential		Medium potential		Low potential		Total
	000 hectares	%	000 hectares	%	000 hectares	%	000 hectares
Western Cape	0	0	897	12.5	639	15	1 537
Northern Cape	0	0	0	0	331	7.8	331
Free State	0	0	2 133	29.6	1 220	28.7	3 353
Eastern Cape	284	8.8	388	5.4	376	8.8	1 048
Kwazulu-Natal	1 539	47.9	440	6.1	70	1.0	2 049
Mpumalanga	1 360	42.3	1 171	16.3	34	0.8	2 565
Limpopo	20	10.6	157	2.1	596	14.0	773
Gauteng	6	0.2	835	11.6	166	3.9	1 007
North West	0	0	1 162	16.2	896	19.0	2 058
Total	3 209	22.0	7 182	49	4 329	29.0	14 720

Source: Soil and Irrigation Research Institute, South Africa, 1986.

Although the scope for expansion of field crops and horticulture in South Africa is limited overall, the regional situation is more diverse. For example, the Western Cape has more or less reached the limits of its potential area expansion while Limpopo Province uses less than 50% of its available arable land. The potential for production growth depends heavily on productivity improvements. There is considerable scope for yield increases in commercial farming areas, as well as the former homeland areas. This is especially true for horticultural products, which are relatively less land-intensive compared to crop or livestock production.

Water resources are also scarce and unevenly distributed across the country. The international benchmark for chronic water scarcity is 1 000 m^3 per capita per year of renewable freshwater resources. With an annual per capita availability of 1 200 m^3 per annum, South Africa is close to this threshold. As a consequence of the topography and the nature of rainfall distribution, the natural availability of water across the country is very uneven, with more than 60% of the river flow coming from only 20% of the land area. Because of the highly variable nature of river flow and the infrequent occurrence of large floods, greater regulation to limit spillage is not economically viable, since much of the flood waters which may be stored would be lost to evaporation.

Most of the water drainage is in the eastern and south-eastern parts of the country, while the greatest need for water is in the central region and adjoining areas. In some parts the use of water already significantly exceeds the local resource potential. Supply and needs have thus had to be balanced by intensive interbasin transfers of water. Total storage capacity of about 27 billion m^3 has been created by the construction of large dams, holding more than half of the mean annual runoff for the country. The main irrigated areas are the drier parts of the country, such as the Orange basin, the Crocodile (Limpopo) basin, the lower Vaal basin, the Sundays/Fish basins and the Western Cape area.

A diverse and dynamic sector

The volume of agricultural output has increased by almost 20% between 1990 and 2003. The year-to-year changes demonstrate that horticultural production is less vulnerable to annual fluctuations compared to the field crops (Figure 1.8). Field crops, horticulture and livestock products accounted respectively for 33%, 27% and 40% of total agricultural output in 2001-03, with the horticultural sector gaining its relative importance over livestock production during the past decade (Figure 1.9).

Overall, the agricultural sector is well diversified. However, due to specific soil, water and market conditions, farmers often have little scope to diversify within a region. The southern and western interior (semi-arid area) is suitable for extensive livestock production (sheep, cattle). Intensive livestock farming (dairy, poultry and pork production) is practised in the arable areas of the country, generally closer to the major metropolitan markets or on the coast where access to imported feed is easier. The country is a net importer of meat, most of imports being from neighbouring countries, Botswana and Namibia.

Figure 1.8. **Agricultural output indices, 1990-2004**

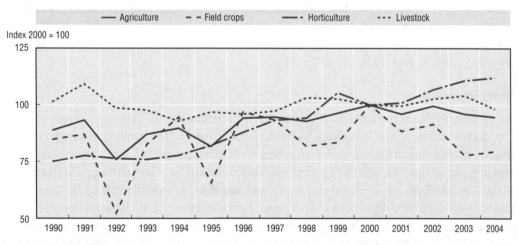

Note: Preliminary data for 2004.

Source: Abstract of Agricultural Statistics, South Africa Department of Agriculture, 2005.

Figure 1.9. **Structure of the gross value of agricultural production, 1990-92 and 2001-03**

%

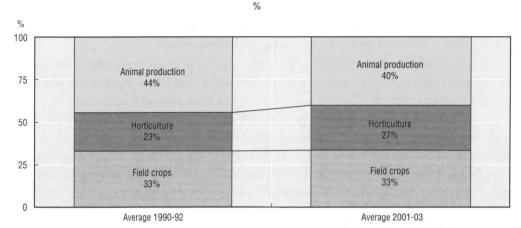

Note: Data from 2002 to 2003 are preliminary.

Source: Abstract of Agricultural Statistics, South Africa Department of Agriculture, 2005.

Field crops

The most important field crops grown in South Africa are maize followed by sugar cane, sunflower and wheat. The country has traditionally been a net exporter of maize and sugar, and a net importer of wheat. Maize is mostly produced in the *Highveld* regions of the interior of the country (Free State, North West, Limpopo and Mpumalanga), sugar cane in the KwaZulu-Natal coastal areas and in the *Lowveld* areas of Mpumalanga. Summer wheat is produced in the Free State and winter wheat in the Western Cape.

Field crop production is extensive and mostly without irrigation.[5] Thus, field crop yields are relatively low (compared with the US or European levels) but also more variable due to low and erratic rainfall. Maize is the most important grain crop in South Africa, being both the major feed grain (yellow maize) and the staple food for the majority of the South African population (white maize), mainly in rural areas. With an area of 3.5 to 4 million hectares, maize is cultivated on around 25% of total arable land. The other important field crops are wheat, sunflower and sugar cane. Wheat is produced mainly for human consumption with only small quantities of lower quality wheat marketed as feed. Sunflower seed is the most important oilseed crop. Sugar cane area is relatively stable with a slight increase in area from 1996. Around one-half of the sugar production is exported (Figures 1.10, 1.11 and 1.12).

Horticulture

South Africa's horticultural production consists of all the major fruit groups (deciduous, citrus and subtropical), vegetables and flowers. The main types of deciduous fruits are table grapes (grown under irrigation along the Orange River in the Northern Cape, and in parts of the Western Cape), wine grapes (cultivated in select winter rainfall regions of the Western Cape), apples and stone fruit (produced under irrigation mostly in the winter rainfall regions). Some deciduous fruit is grown in the interior (*e.g.* in the eastern parts of the Free State province). Citrus fruit is grown in the Olifants River valley along the west coast of the Western Cape province, and in the *Lowveld* areas of the Limpopo and Mpumalanga provinces; subtropical fruit is grown in those areas as well, and in KwaZulu-Natal. A large

Figure 1.10. **Field crop plantings, 1990-2004**

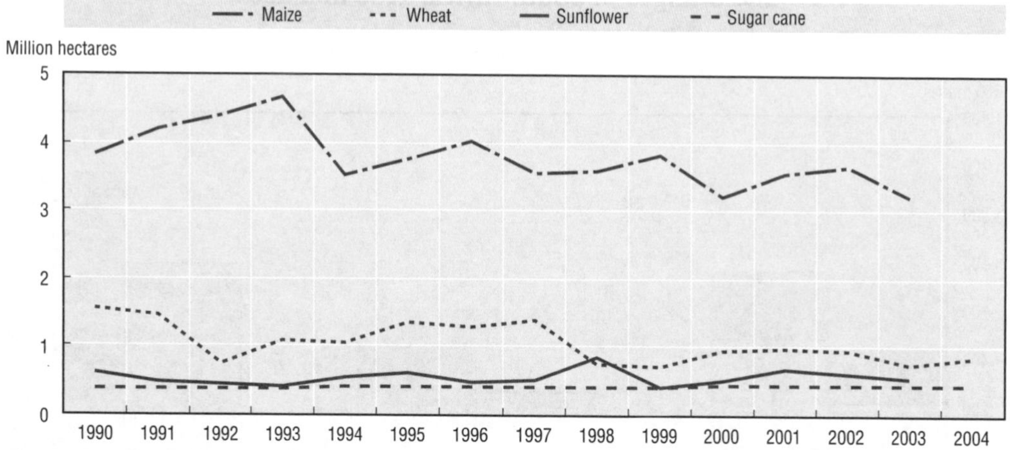

Maize
Wheat
Sunflower
Sugar cane
Million hectares
5
4
3
2
1
0
1990
1991
1992
1993
1994
1995
1996
1997
1998
1999
2000
2001
2002
2003
2004

Source: Abstract of Agricultural Statistics, South Africa Department of Agriculture, 2005.

Figure 1.11. **Field crop production, 1990-2004**

Maize
Wheat
Sunflower
Sugar cane
Million tonnes
25
20
15
10
5
0
1990
1991
1992
1993
1994
1995
1996
1997
1998
1999
2000
2001
2002
2003
2004

Source: Abstract of Agricultural Statistics, South Africa Department of Agriculture, 2005.

Figure 1.12. **Field crop yield, 1990-2004**

Maize
Wheat
Sunflower
Sugar cane (right scale)
Tonnes per hectare
Tonnes per hectare
8
6
4
2
0
60
45
30
15
0
1990
1991
1992
1993
1994
1995
1996
1997
1998
1999
2000
2001
2002
2003
2004

Source: Abstract of Agricultural Statistics, South Africa Department of Agriculture, 2005.

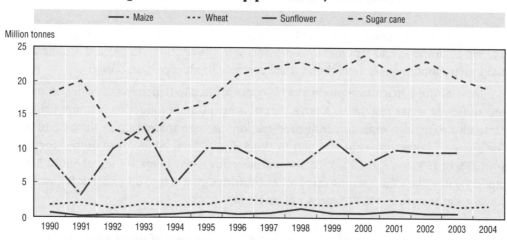

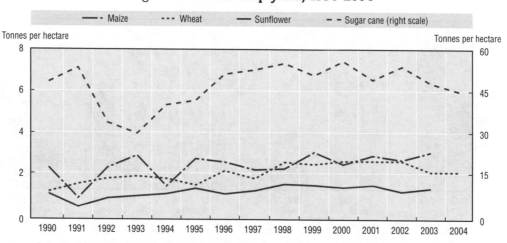

Figure 1.13. **Domestic consumption and exports of apples, table grapes and oranges in South Africa, 1990 and 2004**

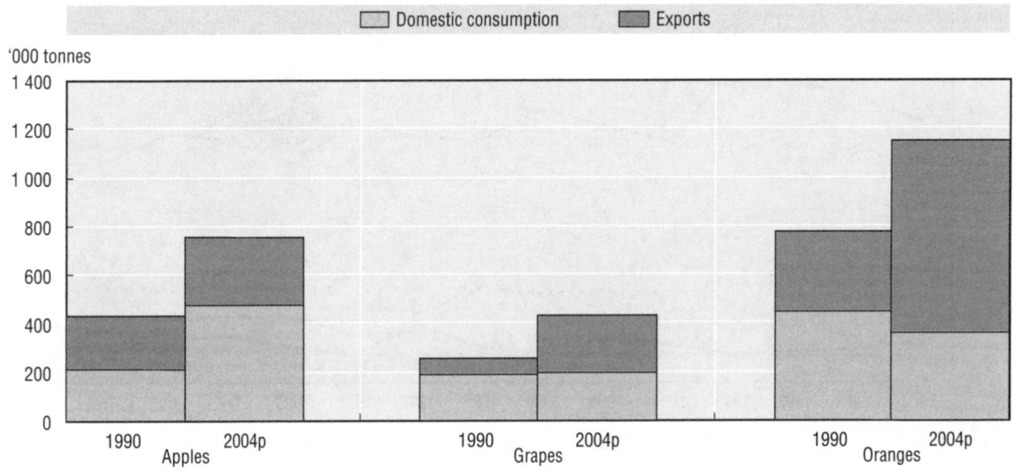

Domestic consumption ☐   Exports ■

'000 tonnes

p: Preliminary.

Source: Abstract of Agricultural Statistics, Department of Agriculture, 2005.

share of fruits produced is exported, fresh or processed. Vegetables are grown in the *Lowveld* of Limpopo and Mpumalanga provinces, in the southern Cape, and around all the main metropolitan areas. Less than 5% of vegetable production is exported.

Most of the horticulture production is concentrated in regions with high quality land and sufficient water resources. A large part of horticultural production is under irrigation. Horticulture, mainly wine and fruit production, has been increasing in the last 10 years. The share of horticultural production in the value of total agricultural output increased from 21% in 1990 to 27% in 2003. This was largely due to the liberalisation of South Africa's export regimes and the opening up of other countries' markets to SA exports, following the move to democracy in 1994 (Figures 1.13 and 1.14).

Figure 1.14. **Domestic consumption and exports of other main fruit in South Africa, 1990 and 2004**

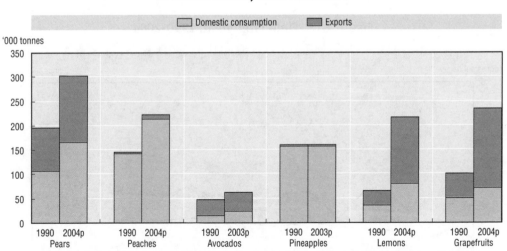

Domestic consumption ☐   Exports ■

p: Preliminary.

Source: Abstract of Agricultural Statistics, Department of Agriculture, 2005.

The most important categories of fruit produced are citrus fruits (mainly oranges), apples, pears, peaches, table grapes and avocados. The fruit sector is the most export oriented. Around 85% of table grapes and 70% of avocado production is exported, while for the citrus fruits and apples these shares are around 50% and 33% respectively. The most important vegetable produced in South Africa are potatoes (41% of vegetable area), followed by cabbage, onions and tomatoes. Vegetable production is more oriented towards domestic consumption. Although its area is increasing, the horticultural sector occupies a relatively small share of arable land. However, it is a labour intensive sector and provides important labour opportunities. Overall, the number of workers (permanent equivalent) in fruit production is estimated at nearly 300 000, with the number of their dependents reaching more than one million.

Livestock

Poultry meat, beef, milk and wool are the most important livestock products. There are two main patterns of production. The extensive production of cattle, sheep and goats occurs on most of the pasture land in the arid and semi-arid areas, as it is the only possible production. The more intensive production of poultry, milk and pigmeat is located in areas with field production and closer to the main consumption centres and the ports.

Livestock remains the most important category of agricultural production although its share in total agricultural output declined from 44% in 1990 to 39% in 2003. Poultry meat, beef, milk and dairy are the most important livestock products. In 2003 their share was 70% of the total value of livestock production. Other livestock products are eggs, sheep meat, wool and mohair, and pork (Table 1.6).

Production of most livestock products was declining in the early 1990s but stabilised from 1995. The only notable exception was poultry meat for which production has been

Table 1.6. **Livestock numbers and slaughterings, 1990 to 2004**
Thousand heads

	Cattle		Pigs		Sheep and goats	
	Number[1]	Slaughterings[2]	Number[1]	Slaughterings[2]	Number[1]	Slaughterings[2]
1990	13 500	2 843	1 665	2 360	32 753	9 098
1991	13 500	2 968	1 654	2 189	31 084	8 505
1992	13 100	2 959	1 653	2 267	29 733	7 787
1993	12 500	2 628	1 570	2 101	27 829	7 694
1994	12 600	2 111	1 585	1 973	28 204	5 203
1995	13 000	2 171	1 707	2 194	27 746	5 904
1996	13 400	2 118	1 699	2 172	27 874	5 685
1997	13 700	2 095	1 736	2 062	27 308	5 536
1998	13 800	2 197	1 780	2 006	27 343	5 905
1999	13 600	2 666	1 647	2 145	26 630	6 115
2000	13 500	2 247	1 678	1 816	25 848	5 964
2001	13 500	2 452	1 710	1 914	25 425	5 964
2002	13 600	2 479	1 663	1 931	24 943	6 012
2003	13 500	2 506	1 663	1 950	25 019	6 117
2004p	13 500	2 601	1 651	2 038	24 466	5 042

p: Preliminary.
1. Numbers at 31 August. For the category sheep and goat, the numbers include only animals on commercial farms.
2. Cattle and Pigs: Total numbers slaughtered at registered auction and non-auction markets and for own consumption. Sheep and Goats: From 1993/94 slaughterings at registered abattoirs.
Source: Abstract of Agricultural Statistics, Department of Agriculture, 2005.

Figure 1.15. **Production of main livestock products in South Africa, 1990-2004**

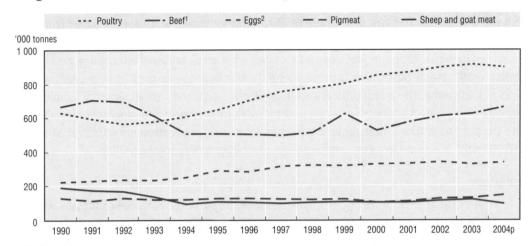

p: Preliminary.
1. Beef from South African origin.
2. Eggs include eggs for hatching.
Source: *Abstract of Agricultural Statistics*, Department of Agriculture, 2005.

steadily increasing. Between 1990 and 2003, production of poultry meat increased by 60%, while sheep and goat production halved within the same period (Figure 1.15).

Addressing agri-environmental problems

Agri-environmental problems are moving up the policy agenda in South Africa with the recognition that environmental problems, both those created by agriculture and those imposed externally on agriculture, are serious limiting factors to sustainable production and increased productivity. The main concerns are soil degradation and water pollution.

Soil degradation

Soil scientists generally regard *soil acidification* as one of the most serious factors reducing the productivity of South African soils. Excessive application of nitrogen fertilisers is the main reason. Rectification will be expensive, as close to 100% of crop land is likely to be affected. On average, approximately 2 tonnes of lime per hectare will have to be applied (Du Toit *et al.*, 1994; Beukes, 1995). Correct handling of soil acidity will be crucial in developing agriculture in the previous "homelands", where there is much potential provided acidity is properly addressed and high-yielding pastures are introduced into livestock systems. Improved livestock management will be a crucial component (Goodland, 1995; Van der Merwe and de Villiers, 1998). This is a major challenge because such management has in the past largely been lacking and will be very difficult to implement under communal land tenure systems.

In South Africa, *soil organic matter* has been seriously deteriorated, mainly because of monoculture cereal production, short fallow periods, the absence of effective crop rotation systems and intensive tillage (Van der Merwe and de Villiers, 1998; Du Toit *et al.*, 1994). There is a need to introduce cultivation systems (*e.g.* minimum tillage, grass cover, legume systems, conservation of crop residues and directed fertilisation) that will promote the uptake of reduced forms of nitrogen and cut down on the oxidation of reduced forms of nitrogen.

Runoff and erosion is another concern. About 20% of South Africa's total land area is highly susceptible to soil erosion and it is estimated that roughly 30% of South Africa's farm land has already been significantly affected. The annual soil loss due to erosion is approximately 2.5 tonnes per hectare with the estimated rate of soil formation much lower at 0.31 tonnes per hectare (Lombard *et al.*, 1996). Table 1.7 shows the extent of annual wind and water erosion in South Africa.

Table 1.7. **Extent of wind and water erosion of agricultural land in South Africa, 1998**
Thousand hectares

	Serious	Moderate	Non-significant	Total
Wind erosion	985	3 026	9 360	13 370
Cultivated land	415	1 326	1 427	3 168
Pastures	570	1 700	7 933	10 203
Water erosion	1 732	5 387	9 860	16 979
Cultivated land	931	2 258	2 887	6 076
Pastures	801	3 129	6 973	10 903
Total	2 717	8 413	19 220	30 349

Source: Van der Merwe and de Villiers (1998).

Desertification threatens more than 50% of South Africa's surface area. Fragile dryland ecosystems are degenerating through misapplication of technology, inappropriate land use selection and poor management. *Salinisation and alkalisation* are the result of water logging and/or pollution. Approximately 54 000 hectares of cultivated agricultural land in South Africa is seriously and 128 000 hectares moderately affected by alkalinity and water logging (Van der Merwe and de Villiers, 1998).

The extent of environmental damage caused by *fertiliser and pesticide usage* is unclear. At least one irrigation scheme has been shown to have significant negative effects on water quality (Aihoon *et al.*, 1997). In the early to mid-1980s, farmers (particularly grain farmers) began reducing fertiliser use as it became increasingly clear that rates of application were excessive. There has been some decline in the use of phosphorus and an increase in nitrogen applications in recent years (Table 1.8).

Table 1.8. **Total application of nitrate, phosphorus, and potassium in South African agriculture, 1987-2003**
Thousand tonnes

	Nitrate	Phosphorus	Potassium
1987-89	354	119	105
1990-94	368	104	104
1995-99	404	103	118
2000-03	428	90	111

Source: President's report: The Fertilizer Society of South Africa. FSSA Journal 1996, 2001 and 2004.

Water resources

South Africa has *limited water resources* and an increasing demand for water. Lombard *et al.* (1996) project that South Africa's per capita availability of renewable water will decline from 1 200 m^3 in 1992 to 760 m^3 in 2010 – a decline of 37% over the period, or 2.5% per annum. The Water Research Council warned in 1993 that water needs could exceed supply

Table 1.9. **Agricultural water needs in South Africa, 10-year averages and projections for 2000 and 2010**

	Irrigation		Stock watering	
	Million cubic metres	% of total	Million cubic metres	% of total
1980	8 504	52.2	262	1.6
1990	9 695	50.9	288	1.5
2000[1]	10 974	48.9	316	1.4
2010[1]	11 885	45.9	358	1.4

1. Projected data (1996).

Source: Lombard *et al.*, The physical-biological environment. In: Spies. P.H. (ed.) Agrifutura 1995/96. Stellenbosch: University of Stellenbosch, 1996.

by 2020-30. Construction of new dams will become increasingly costly as the suitability of sites in surplus water areas is limited. Irrigation is the largest single use of water with needs projected to increase but at a rate less than total needs (Table 1.9).

In some parts of South Africa, the availability of fresh water for all uses, including agriculture, is seriously threatened by large areas covered by alien *invader vegetation* that uses up large quantities of water, and *afforestation*. There are areas where stream flow stopped completely or has been seriously reduced. The clearing of such vegetation results in considerable increases in stream flow and a "Work for Water" project of the Department of Water Affairs and Forestry has addressed the problem to a very limited extent.

The quality of many water resources in South Africa is deteriorating as a result of *salinisation* and to a lesser degree because of *eutrophication* and *pollution by trace elements*. The water in some dams has become unsuitable for irrigation of the main crops grown in those areas (Lombard *et al.*, 1996). *Sewerage pollution,* caused by poor systems run by some municipalities, has become a serious problem in some areas. For example, in the Bree River irrigation area in the Western Cape – a valley producing high quality fruit and wine – the authorities recently acted only after public pressure and threats of legal court action. In another area in Gauteng, litigation between land owners and a large steel manufacturer is pending over the pollution of ground water.

Agriculture in South Africa is generally on the receiving end of water pollution, but has in some instances also added to the problem. Overuse of fertilisers for some crops and sewage from some forms of intensive livestock production have been the main culprits.

Acid rain from heavy industries is also a problem, especially in Mpumalanga Province, which is a main grain producing and an important livestock producing area. In this province, pH values of between 3.9 and 4.6 have been registered, and the sulphur dioxide concentration in the Mpumalanga Highveld air space is between five to ten times higher than that found in the most polluted cities in western countries (Tyson, 1988; Lombard *et al.*, 1996).

Declining farm employment but improving conditions

Under apartheid, employment on commercial farms of the white community was one of the only income opportunities for many black and coloured people in the homelands. This resulted in a large and cheap source of unskilled, sometimes functionally illiterate workers, for commercial agriculture. Those farms provided much more than employment. Most full-time farm worker families lived on the farm, while their children received education in on-farm schools. Commercial farms therefore provided livelihoods, housing and education to about 3 million family members of the 0.5 million full-time employees.

Before 1994, commercial agriculture was heavily supported through subsidised interest rates and tax concessions regarding the purchase of machinery. These factors stimulated labour/capital substitution in agriculture to such extent that it led to overcapitalisation and declining returns to capital, despite the huge pool of available, but low-skilled labour. The result was unemployment and underemployment of agricultural labour, coupled with wages lower than would have otherwise prevailed. Removal of these subsidies has coincided with an increase in casual but not regular labour.

In addition, there are also about 240 000 small-scale farmers who provide a livelihood to more than 1 million of their family members and occasional employment to another 500 000 people. They supply local and regional markets, often to informal traders. There are approximately another 3 million people in communal farming households, mostly in the former homelands that primarily produce for subsistence needs (DoA, Strategic plan 2001). More recent estimates of the number of agricultural households were based on the data from the project PROVIDE: based on a broad definition for agricultural households, the number for South Africa totalled some 2.7 million households supporting 14 million people. Using a more strict definition, the numbers added up to 0.8 million households and 3.3 million people respectively. By its very nature, subsistence agriculture – although it has provided a livelihood to many people – has not provided stable remunerated employment except for short periods of the year, normally at harvest time. Since "livelihood" in the case of subsistence agriculture generally implies severe poverty,[6] such conditions become an issue for social rather than sectoral policy.

The real level of employment in South African agriculture is difficult to estimate as statistics provide information only on employment on commercial farms. Figure 1.16 illustrates the long-term decline in employment on commercial farms since 1971. The brief increase in the 1980s is likely due to capital shortages and some increase in labour-intensive production. This labour-shedding added to unemployment in rural towns and to an influx of unemployed people seeking work in metropolitan areas.

Figure 1.16. **Number of farm employees and domestic servants on commercial farms, 1971-1996**

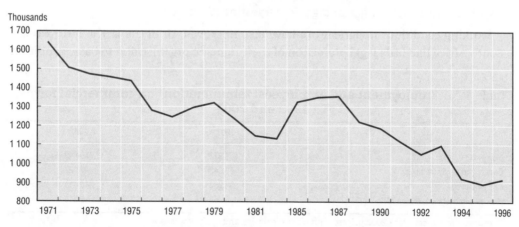

Source: Abstract of Agricultural Statistics, South Africa Department of Agriculture, 2004.

Table 1.10. **Farm employment in South Africa, 1985-2002**

Number of employees

	1985	1990	1991	1992	1993	1994	1995	1996	2002
Regular	807 341	728 414	702 323	656 772	647 839	625 244	628 925	605 451	481 375
Casual, seasonal	516 411	456 262	413 239	394 425	491 588	302 185	289 810	308 690	459 445
Total	1 323 752	1 184 676	1 115 562	1 051 197	1 139 427	927 429	918 735	914 141	940 820

Source: Stats SA: Agricultural Censuses and Surveys.

More recent data on the commercial farm employment in South Africa show that the sector shed 247 000 regular employees since 1990 (Table 1.10). The number of casual and seasonal workers has also been declining over the first half of this period, but has increased since the mid-1990s. The category of casual and seasonal employees is notoriously difficult to estimate. However, the large increase in exports of fruit (the sector that is the largest user of casual and seasonal labour) may explain this increase in employment.

There has been a substantial shift towards higher use of skilled labour. The employment of managers, for example, increased more than six-fold since 1970, and by almost 25 000 persons, or 370%, since 1995. The number of professionals and technicians has increased by 150% from 1970 to 1995. The 2002 Census data have not indicated any particular change since 1995. The number of managers, recorded in 2001, is somewhat lower, but corresponds to the reduction of the number of farms (on average every second farm is hiring a manager). This shift in the skill profile of farm workers has favoured male workers over female, and coloured workers over African workers. The number of male farm workers, for example, decreased by 38% from 1970 to 1995, while the number of female farm workers declined by 72%. Simultaneously, the number of African workers declined by 58.8%, while the number of coloured workers increased by 88.4% over the 25 year period.[7]

The most recent census data (2001) on employment and remuneration suggest that farm wages are rising (Table 1.11). A decline in the number of paid employees combined with an increase in aggregate remuneration implies that average real per capita remuneration rose by 2.5% to ZAR 6 216 (in constant 2002 prices). It would appear that structural changes, especially the risk management strategies of farmers, have resulted in an increased demand for fewer, more skilled workers and managers. These effects are felt more severely in the field crop and livestock sectors, where the demand for part-time workers is small, unlike the horticultural sector, where seasonal workers are hired for a range of activities including pruning and harvesting (Vink, 2003).

Working conditions in agriculture have also improved. Until the 1990s, farm workers in South Africa had little legal protection of their rights to organise and to basic conditions

Table 1.11. **Employment and employees' remuneration[1] on commercial farms, 1993 and 2002**

	1993	2002
Employment	1 161 912	986 842
Owners and family members	68 642	46 027
Paid employees	1 093 265	940 815
Employees' remuneration, million ZAR	5 782	6 216

1. Remuneration at constant 2002 prices: cash wages, salaries and cash bonuses.

Source: Abstract of Agricultural Statistics, South Africa Department of Agriculture, 2004.

of employment. The Agricultural Labour Act, No. 147 of 1993, addressed this shortcoming to some extent, but it was only after 1994 that farm worker rights were brought in line with workers elsewhere in the economy. Henceforth, the four major labour laws in South Africa, including the Labour Relations Act (1995), the Basic Conditions of Employment Act (1997), the Skills Development Act (1998) and the Employment Equity Act (1998), also applied to the agricultural sector. As from December 2002, new articles of the Basic Conditions of Employment Act apply specifically to farm workers and, among other things, determine minimum wages for farm workers. Only in practice since March 2003, the effect of these latest regulations on agricultural employment has not yet been determined. However, such regulations tend to increase the opportunity costs of employment and may lead to a reduction of employment.

Box 1.1. **Remuneration of hired farm labour**

Farm labour remuneration in South Africa has traditionally consisted of both cash and in-kind remuneration. In-kind remuneration can be very important and mainly consists of food rations, grazing rights for limited numbers of livestock and, in some regions, fields to be cultivated for own gain. There is a wide range of cash wages. In the research work which led up to the introduction of the minimum wage for hired farm labour, it was determined that for the highest paid group the average cash wage was ZAR 950 per month paid to 227 000 workers (35%). This is about one-third above the country average of ZAR 710 per month (1996 numbers). The lowest paid group average wage paid by farmers in certain districts is ZAR 450 per month (25% of all workers). With the introduction of the minimum wage, the regulations prescribe that only 20% of the minimum wage may be paid in the form of housing and food.

Increasing financial pressures

South African (commercial) agriculture is capital and intermediate input intensive. The relative share of inputs has not changed significantly since the 1980s, with intermediate inputs (excluding livestock) and capital representing almost 70% of the total input use (Table 1.12).

In real terms, the purchase of intermediate inputs rose by 1.59% per annum over the 1980-2003 period (Table 1.13). While purchases of packing materials and animal feeds increased over time, there seems to be a downward trend in the purchases of fuel and fertiliser (but not on chemicals). Higher fuel efficiency in newer farming machinery and a growing trend among farmers to move toward minimum tillage systems were probably the major factors dampening fuel purchases over time. Fertiliser purchases decreased after the

Table 1.12. **Input use structure in South African agriculture, 1947-96**

%

	Labour	Land	Intermediate inputs	Capital	Total
1947-1980	24.3	7.8	32.5	35.4	100
1980-1989	18.4	12.8	36.9	31.9	100
1990-1996	19.1	11.9	37.9	31.1	100

Source: Vink N., The use of inputs in South African commercial agriculture. In: Groenewald, J.A. (ed.), Median term economic review of the South African agricultural sector. Pretoria: National Department of Agriculture, 2005.

Table 1.13. **Intermediate input purchases in South African agriculture, 1980-2003**

Million ZAR at constant 2000 prices

	Packing material	Fuel	Fertilizer	Feed	Chemicals	All intermediate goods and services
1980-84	720	3 735	3 259	3 373	1 929	14 780
1985-89	883	4 051	2 794	3 715	1 550	18 518
1990-94	1 156	3 204	2 318	4 310	1 743	19 382
1995-99	1 588	3 650	2 655	5 545	1 951	22 947
2000-03	1 690	3 025	2 416	7 371	2 413	26 726
Period 1980 to 2003						
Annual growth, %	3.9	−1.1	−2.5	3.1	0.9	1.6
Annual price increase, %	9.6	10.9	11.5	11.5	10.3	11.1

Source: Calculated from data in Abstract of Agricultural Statistics, South Africa Department of Agriculture, 2005.

early 1980s. Some experts argue that many grain farmers exceeded economically viable fertilisation rates in the late 1970s and early 1980s, and that financial hardships that prevailed in grain farming areas during the 1980s caused grain farmers to reduce fertilisation of rain-fed plantings.

There are no data on the use of agricultural machinery (mainly tractors) by smallholder farmers. In the past, government-assisted tractor purchase schemes were available, particularly in the "homelands", and the smallholders depended heavily on these services. These schemes have been terminated and a number of farmers now rely on private contractors for ploughing and other tillage operations. In many cases, to improve their negotiating position, farmers are renting tractor and other machinery services through a co-operative. A large number of small-scale farms use animal traction (mostly oxen, although donkeys, horses and mules are also used).

In the commercial farm sector, the debt/asset ratio increased from 13.9% in 1980 to around 28% at present (Table 1.14). The high debt/asset ratio in South Africa coupled with high mortgage bond rates (which increased in real terms when taking into account the reduction in inflation), creates adverse cash flow problems as the return on investment is estimated at about 5%. However, on the other side this development reflects also the trend towards (more capital intensive) horticultural production.

The increase in the debt/asset ratio in South Africa is due to the investment driven by previous policies and declining capital asset values. The real value of capital assets (i.e. land and fixed improvements, machinery and livestock valued at 1995 prices) on

Table 1.14. **Capital assets and debt of commercial farmers, 1980-2003**

	Capital assets	Debt	Debt/Assets	Net income/Debt
	Million ZAR		Ratio	Ratio
1980-84	32 585	6 273	0.19	0.32
1985-89	47 605	12 936	0.27	0.38
1990-94	62 048	14 090	0.23	0.43
1995-99	82 684	22 935	0.28	0.36
2000-03	108 134	29 944	0.28	0.54

Source: Calculated from Abstract of Agricultural Statistics, South Africa Department of Agriculture, 2005.

commercial farms has fallen during the last two decades from ZAR 185 billion in 1980 to ZAR 64 billion in 2000. The value of land and fixed improvements as a proportion of the total value of capital assets fell from 78% in 1980 to 58% in 2000 (NDA: Agricultural Statistics, 2003). The declining real value of farm land in South Africa is mainly attributed to increased real interest rates during this period coupled with the reduced support to commercial farms.

Data on small-scale farmers' revenues, capital and indebtedness comparable to that presented for the commercial farming, do not exist. However, there have been surveys among communities of small-scale farmers. Results obtained in a survey in Limpopo (Spio, 2003) compared revenues between farmers who borrowed money from financial institutions, and those who did not. The borrowers obtained significantly higher per hectare yield values, used significantly more fertiliser, seed, labour and other inputs, and obtained higher revenues (Table 1.15).

Table 1.15. **Total incomes of small-scale farmers based on survey in Limpopo Province**

	Farm income	Non-farm income	Total income	Average cultivated area
	ZAR			Hectares
Borrowers	3 236	2 037	5 273	3
Non-borrowers	896	3 046	3 932	2

Source: Spio, The impact and accessibility of agricultural credit: A case study of small-scale farmers in the Northern Province of South Africa PhD thesis, University of Pretoria, 2003.

The traditional communal land tenure system practised in the former "homelands" presents a serious impediment to modernisation and development of commercialised agriculture in those areas due to land fragmentation and a lack of marketing skills, extension services, agricultural credit and tenure security. A lack of proper infrastructure, including communications, transport and other social services infrastructure aggravate the situation.

1.3. Deregulation of agricultural marketing and impacts on the agricultural markets

Agricultural marketing was controlled in South Africa for more than half a century. Under the 1937 Marketing Act and other legislation related to specific products, *e.g.* wine and sugar, different marketing schemes were applied for different products and product groups. The range of measures included compulsory one-channel marketing, fixed prices, fixed marketing margins, restrictive registration of traders and/or processors, compulsory pooling, production quotas, marketing quotas, compulsory centralised price bargaining and quantitative import control. Such schemes covered over 70% of the value of South African farm production resulting in a high degree of rigidity and inefficiencies in marketing.

The Marketing of Agricultural Products Act, introduced in 1996, was aimed at improving market access/efficiency and enhancing agricultural exports and foresaw a significant reduction of state involvement in agricultural markets.

A freer pricing system

The price and market deregulation prompted significant private sector response: new trade and market institutions began emerging and the number of traders increased.

In 1996/97, an Agricultural Markets Division (AMD) of the South African Futures Exchange (SAFEX) was created, to function as a major agricultural price discovery centre through its futures and options trade in white maize, yellow maize, wheat and sunflower. Futures and option prices serve as the benchmark for prices in the daily "spot" markets. However, a lack of publicly available market information hinders the potential gains from the functioning of this agricultural futures exchange.

Prices of products which are not traded on SAFEX (mainly livestock) are increasingly determined at various commodity auctions, as well as the traditional fresh produce markets in the main metropolitan areas. A large proportion of primary agricultural production (such as oilseeds, milk, fruit) is now sold directly to processing industries with prices negotiated within (sometimes long-term) delivery contracts. Many retailers do not buy their fresh fruit and vegetables at the large municipal fresh produce markets and prefer to purchase directly from the larger commercial producers through pre-season growing programmes.

Less reliance on state support and improved efficiency

Although many sectors experienced a difficult period of adjustment, the deregulation of markets opened opportunities for entrepreneurial farmers and led to a more efficient allocation of resources in agriculture. The net effect of these changes is that the South African agricultural industry has become less dependent on state support and more competitive internationally.

The impacts of market forces and policy reforms are well seen in the grain sector. The maize area declined from over 5 million hectares in 1986/87 to the present 3.5 million hectares, while that of wheat from over 2 million hectares to about 0.9 million hectares. These changes are largely attributable to the declines in real grain prices and expectations of significant reductions in the drought assistance to grain farmers.[8] As a result, farmers moved out of grain production in marginal cropping areas, where maize and wheat land was successfully converted into grazing. This improved cash flow and introduced more stability for farmers in relatively high-risk production areas.

A more competitive and less regulated food chain

The single channel schemes under the Marketing Act (1937) implied pure monopoly or pure monopsony markets. Products could not be traded through any channels other than the control board involved, or its appointed agent(s).[9] Some control boards also restricted the number of firms allowed to do business in certain products, such as the right to trade and process red meats, winter cereals, maize, sorghum, dry beans and dairy products. Cotton processors and representatives of farming groups were required to negotiate price arrangements for the crop under the auspices of the Cotton Board.

Restrictions on firm registrations caused high degrees of concentration in upstream and downstream sectors. The Commission of Enquiry into the Regulation of Monopolistic Conditions Act found intensive concentration e.g. in the abattoir, condensed milk, milk powder and cotton ginnery industries. Two major companies and one central co-operative had a joint market share of 84% and 94% in the beef and pork markets, respectively (Lubbe,

1992). The Board on Tariffs and Trade concluded in 1992 that the market concentration engendered by the Marketing Act made a large contribution to the high food marketing margins in South Africa.

The repeal of the Marketing Act did away with measures like one-channel marketing, marketing quotas and restrictive registration. The effects of deregulation differed by product sector, partly because of the different modes of production, and partly because the nature of control under the old Act differed across commodities (the changes in the market organisation of specific commodity sectors following the marketing reform is discussed in Chapter 2). One exemption to the market deregulation is the sugar market, where measures such as domestic marketing quotas, price pooling and one-channel export are still maintained.

Accelerated rationalisation of commercial farms

The structure of commercial farms in South Africa has been influenced by both market deregulation and by the land reform programme. In response to deregulation, commercial farmers (especially in the field crop sector) adopted a wide variety of risk management strategies to cope with the declining and fluctuating producer prices that resulted from deregulation. These strategies included both income diversification e.g. on-farm agro-tourism, off-farm employment; and farm diversification e.g. different products, different regions. The result has been the consolidation towards a smaller number of larger commercial farms, typical of the farm industry rationalisation prevalent in most developed and developing economies.

Developing small-scale commercial agriculture

Smallholder farming, still located mostly in the former homelands,[10] is an impoverished sector dominated by low-input, labour-intensive forms of production. Up to 2.5 million households subsist in this sector, having been relegated to farming on 13% of available agricultural land. Low productivity is a major challenge in the small-scale subsistence sector, attributable to past discriminatory policies coupled with such problems as tenure insecurity, very small land holdings and ineffective support services (e.g. extension, finance and marketing). The government policy guidelines now dictate that 80% of the efforts of the Department of Agriculture and the Environment directed at agriculture should be allocated to assist the small farm sector. Such general directives, however, are extremely difficult to interpret, implement and monitor.

The communal areas which form the bulk of the former "homelands" are still using the traditional system of communal land tenure under which local leaders (chiefs) allocate communal land to the members of the commune for cultivation and pasture for their animals (mostly sheep and goats). Efforts to reform this system have met strong resistance from local leaders who have vested interests in the status quo. However, as seen in Latin America, converting insecure tenure systems into a modern property rights system, with a transparent and accessible land market, is fundamental to good resource management, the provision of credit and increased productivity (Hernando de Soto, 1996). The black population in rural areas is the target of the land reform policies (see Chapter 2) and is expected to benefit from the development of the small-scale, market oriented farm sector. However, it is clear that adequate supporting infrastructure must also be in place if these new entrepreneurs are to survive.

It is essential for the development of small-scale farms and for the less developed regions of South Africa, to have a financial system able to mobilise savings, allocate capital and monitor farmers, business firms and micro-enterprises. The overall supply of credit to smallholder agriculture in not known with any degree of accuracy due to diversions of loan funds and the cyclical nature of many small-scale farming activities. Coetzee (2003) estimates that less than 2% of the Land Bank's loans portfolio in 2003 was for small-scale agriculture. He also notes the minor role of private sector and State lending and that the number of provincial parastatal credit institutions has declined as they were not financially sustainable. The problem is mostly that of high transaction costs and risk of default which render formal financial institutions unwilling to provide services to those who are not engaged in the formal economy. The property right deficiencies in communal farming are another serious impediment to financing agriculture in the communes.

Small-scale farmers still have limited access to markets for their products, be it for fresh produce, grains or livestock. Makhura and Mokoena (2003) outline the following constraints, based on regional studies in Limpopo and KwaZulu-Natal:

- *Transport:* As most small-scale farmers do not have their own means of transport, they usually have to rent transport, which is sometimes expensive (in terms of cost per unit transported) because of the small volumes involved. Transport contractors are sometimes not able to service certain rural areas because of the poor road condition. Many of these rural areas are poorly served with public transport.

- *Collection and storage:* In many rural areas, storage facilities are either non-existent or inadequate or unsuitable or centralised to such an extent that products have to be transported to long distances over bad roads.

- *Market infrastructure:* Marketing of fresh produce on centralised urban fresh product markets is difficult to small-scale farmers, not equipped with adequate transport facilities, as perishable products produce must be transported over long distances, at high costs and risks of quality deterioration.

- *Discrimination:* Some small-scale farmers experience discrimination, particularly at fresh produce markets and livestock auctions.

- *Market information:* A lack of market information, or information not available on timely basis, and also of means to disseminate such information is a severe stumbling block for many small-scale farmers.

- *Bargaining power:* Small-scale farmers lack organisation, bargaining power and knowledge to effectively use their membership of the marketing trusts that were formed when the control boards under the former Marketing Act were abolished (Kirsten and Vink, 2002).

- *Institutional responsibility:* There is a lack of institutional responsibility focussed at ensuring marketing access for small farmers, and those that do exist (*e.g.* the NAMC, DTI and provincial departments of agriculture) are poorly co-ordinated (Kirsten and Vink, 2002).

1.4. South Africa's trade in agricultural products

The South African economy, including agriculture, is an important and growing presence in world markets. Three major political and economic developments of the 1990s contributed to this process. The most important was the lifting of economic sanctions against South Africa following the establishment in 1994 of a democratic government. The

Figure 1.17. **South African agricultural exports and imports, 1992-2004**
Million USD

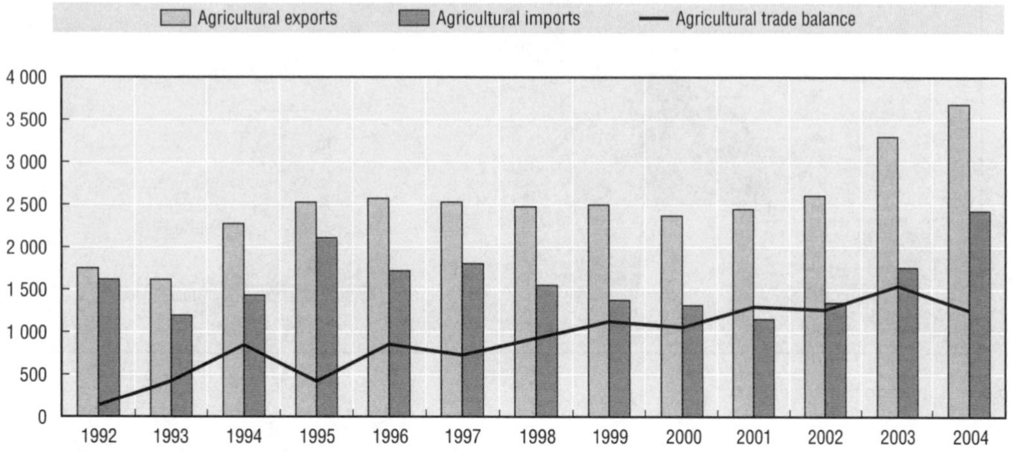

Source: Calculated based on the Department of Trade and Industry data.

next radical change was the repeal of the Marketing Act of 1937, which led to establishment of a much freer economic and entrepreneurial environment with major reductions in government interventions in domestic production, marketing and trade. Finally, on the international front, the Uruguay Round Agreement of Agriculture (URAA) introduced new disciplines governing agricultural trade.

This substantial opening of the agricultural sector placed South Africa among the world's leading exporters of such agro-food products as wine, fresh fruits and sugar. The country is also an important trader in the African region. Over the last decade, agricultural trade constantly registered a positive balance (Figure 1.17), with a tripling of exports and a doubling of imports in constant, terms resulting in a positive agricultural trade balance of around USD 1 billion per year[11] in the current decade (Table 1.16).

Table 1.16. **South Africa's agro-food trade,[1] 2000-2004**
Million USD

	2000	2001	2002	2003	2004	2002-04 average
Agro-food export	2 253	2 369	2 507	3 152	3 574	2 771
Agro-food import	1 423	1 286	1 483	1 936	2 652	1 756
Agro-food trade balance	830	1 083	1 024	1 216	922	1 015
Coverage rate of agro-food import by export, %	158	184	169	163	135	162
Share of agro food trade in total trade, %						
Export	9	8	11	10	9	9
Import	5	5	6	6	6	6

1. Agro-food trade as defined in Annex 1 of the URAA.
Source: Comtrade Database, 2005.

Sharp growth in agricultural exports

The beginning of the current decade witnessed particularly strong growth in agricultural exports, largely on the basis of the considerable depreciation of the *rand*. South Africa's agricultural export revenues reached nearly USD 3 billion in 2002-04, which constituted almost 9% of the total value of national exports (Table 1.16).

Figure 1.18. **South African agricultural exports by destination, 2002-04 average**

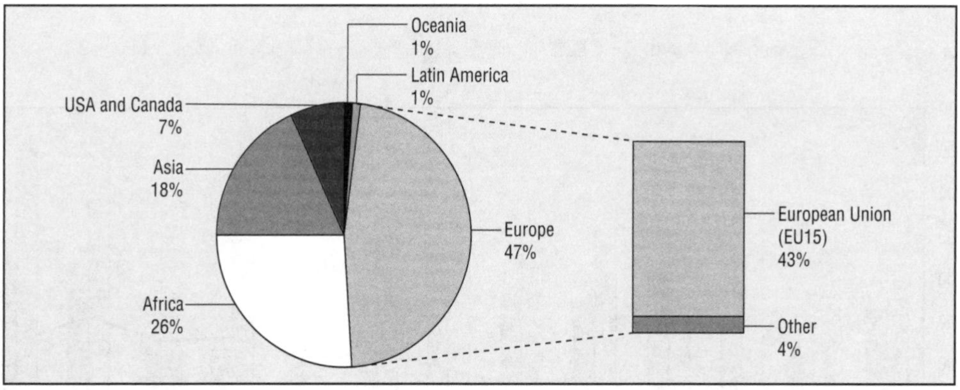

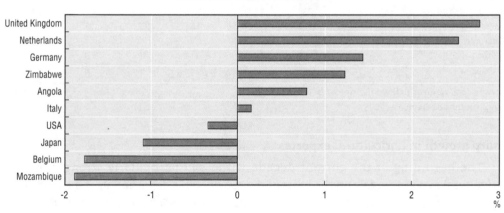

Source: Comtrade Database, 2005.

Europe is by far the largest importer of South Africa's agricultural products, absorbing almost one-half of the country's agricultural exports (Figure 1.18). The African market is the second most important, accounting for around 26% of exports, with the Asian market slightly less important with an 18% share. North America (the United States and Canada) plays a relatively modest role as an export destination, absorbing only around 7%, while exports to Latin America and Oceania are marginal.

Changes in export shares of the main trading partners in 2002-04 indicate the most recent geographic trends in South African agricultural trade. There has been a shift towards the EU market, notably the United Kingdom, Netherlands and Germany (Figure 1.19). The share of exports to the United States and Japan has declined from 2000 levels.

South Africa exports a wide variety of agricultural products with no one commodity dominating. Wine, fresh and processed fruits and sugar are South Africa's leading agricultural exports, together accounting for over 51% of total agricultural exports (Figure 1.20). Among livestock products, only wool has relatively important weight in exports.

Figure 1.19. **Changes in export shares to South Africa's main export destinations between 2000 and 2004**

Source: Comtrade Database, 2005.

Figure 1.20. **South Africa's agricultural exports by products, 2002-04 average**

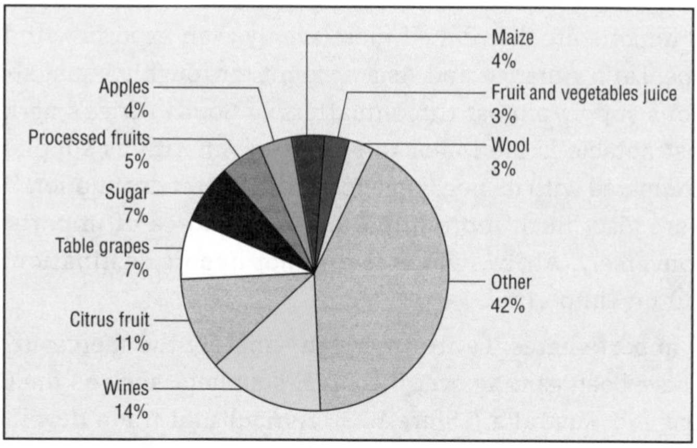

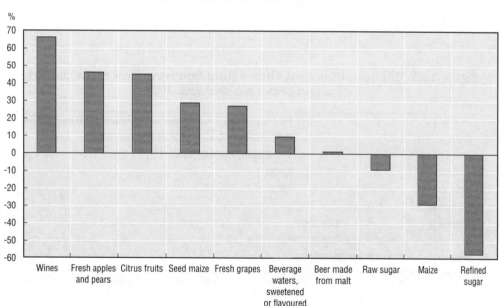

Note: Group "other" includes commodities with a share below 3% of the total.
Source: Comtrade Database, 2005.

There have been changes in the traded volumes of main export commodities between 2002 and 2004 (Figure 1.21). The volume of wine exports increased by over 60%; and by over 40% for major fruits. Maize and (mainly refined) sugar exhibited significant declines in export volumes.

Agricultural imports also on the rise

Agricultural imports are also growing but less rapidly than exports (Figure 1.17, Table 1.16). Agricultural imports have accounted for 5% to 6% of total imports on an annual basis since 2000. The trend to increased agricultural imports suggests rising consumer demand is outstripping any domestic increases in production which could lead to import

Figure 1.21. **Changes in export volume of South Africa's main exportables between 2002 and 2004**

Source: Comtrade Database, 2005.

replacement. While agricultural exports and imports are increasing, year-over-year fluctuations remain volatile for both.

Agricultural imports are distributed more evenly than exports with less dependence on Europe. Europe, Latin America and Asia account for roughly equal shares. Combined, these three regions supply almost three-quarters of South Africa's agricultural imports (Figure 1.22). Most notable is the major role of Latin America as supplier of agricultural products (24%) compared with its negligible role as an export destination (1%). Oceania and North America are also much more important as a source of imports than as export destinations. Conversely, Africa, which is a major export destination, is not a major supplier of agricultural imports.

In terms of import shares, Latin American – mainly the Mercosur members – and Asian suppliers have been gaining over the OECD suppliers, such as the United Kingdom, the United States and Australia (Figure 1.23). Agricultural trade developments are not generally symmetric. For example, since 2000 the United Kingdom registered the largest increase in share of South African exports while the UK share of South African imports registered the largest decline.

Figure 1.22. **South African agricultural imports by source, 2002-04 average**

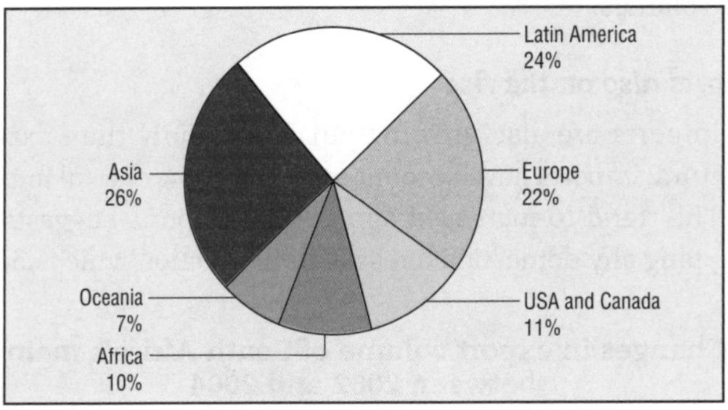

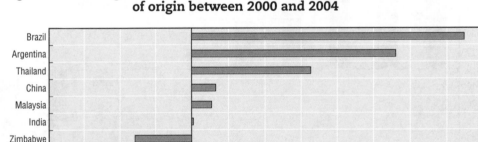

Source: Comtrade Database, 2005.

Figure 1.23. **Changes in import shares from South Africa's main countries of origin between 2000 and 2004**

Source: Comtrade Database, 2005.

OECD REVIEW OF AGRICULTURAL POLICIES – ISBN 92-64-03679-2 – © OECD 2006

Figure 1.24. **South Africa's agricultural imports by products, 2002-04 average**

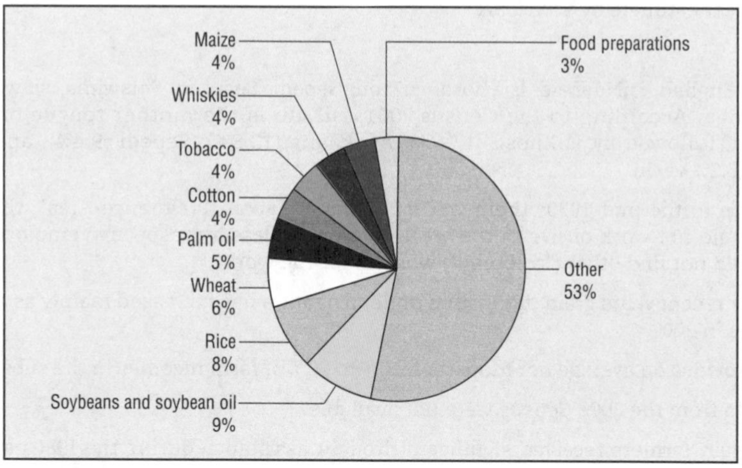

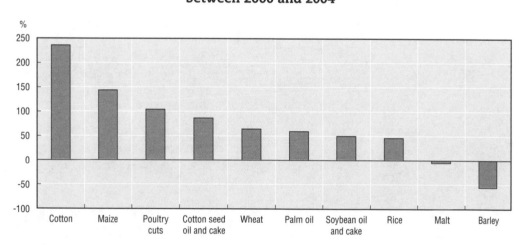

Note: Group "other" includes commodities with a share below 3% of the total.
Source: Comtrade Database, 2005.

The range of products imported is even more varied than exports. The main imported items being oils and oilseeds, grains, cotton and tobacco (Figure 1.24). Soybean/soybean oil, rice and wheat are the major imported agricultural products, representing almost one-quarter of total imports.

Changes in the volumes of imports by product have been more pronounced than for exports, and for the most part, positive. Cotton imports increased by over 200% over the 2000-04 period, while maize and poultry imports more than doubled. Import volumes of oils, rice and wheat each increased by about 50% (Figure 1.25).

Figure 1.25. **Changes in import volume of South Africa's main importables between 2000 and 2004**

Source: Comtrade Database, 2005.

Notes

1. 2005 mid-year estimate by STATS SA.

2. In 2003.

3. Afrikaans, English, isiNdebele, isiXhosa, isiZulu, Sepedi, Sesotho, Setswana, siSwati, Tshivenda and Xitsonga. According to the Census 2001, isiZulu is the mother tongue of 23.8% of the population, followed by isiXhosa (17.6%), Afrikaans (13.3%), Sepedi (9.4%), and English and Setswana (8.2% each).

4. However, up to the mid-1970s there was a "Coloured Labour Preference Area", that meant that Africans could not work or live in the Western Cape, unless a prospective employer could prove that he could not find other ("coloured") workers for the work.

5. However, in recent years grain production under irrigation has increased mainly as a result of high grain prices in 2002.

6. Farming provides on average not more then 10% to 20% of farm incomes in the subsistence sector.

7. Similar data from the 2002 Census were not available.

8. Summer grain farmers received significant drought assistance during the 1980s and once again in 1992.

9. Products, which were controlled through one-channel schemes, included maize, sorghum, wheat, barley, rye, oats, fresh milk, dairy products, oilseeds, tobacco, lucerne seed, rooibos tea, chicory, deciduous and citrus fruits, dried fruit, bananas, wool and mohair. Special legislation also enforced one-channel marketing of ostrich products and limited wine exports to one central co-operative.

10. "Homelands" were apartheid creations designated in the Native Land Act, No. 27 of 1913 and the Natives Trust and Land Act, No. 18 of 1936. These areas were "dumping grounds" for "surplus people" forcibly removed from urban centres and rural "black spots" – at least 3.5 million people were relocated between 1960 and 1983 (Surplus People Project, 1983).

11. The data on agricultural trade is based on the Comtrade data. The definition of agricultural trade adopted corresponds to the commodity nomenclature listed in Annex 1 of the Uruguay Round Agreement on Agriculture. This includes the following HS Chapters: 1 to 24 less fish and fish products, plus mannitol (2905.43), sorbitol (2905.44), essential oils (33.01), albuminoidal substances, modified starches, glues (35.01 to 35.05), finishing agents (3809.10), sorbitol n.e.p. (3823.60), hides and skins (41.01 to 41.03) raw furskins (43.01), raw silk and silk waste (50.01 to 50.03), wool and animal hair (51.01 to 51.03), raw cotton, waste and cotton carded or combed (52.01 to 52.03), raw flax (53.01), and raw hemp (53.02).

ISBN 92-64-03679-2
OECD Review of Agricultural Policies
South Africa
© OECD 2006

Chapter 2

Policy Evaluation

Chapter 2 of this report examines the agriculture, trade and related social policy reforms impacting on the sector. The first Section highlights the government's recent development strategies, policy objectives and institutional structure, which provide a framework for understanding and assessing subsequent policy reforms. Sections 2.2 and 2.3 describe current domestic and trade policies and institutions in detail, with a special focus on the fundamental government objective of land reform. Section 2.4 presents the government budgetary expenditures on agri-food policies while Section 2.5 provides a qualitative evaluation of key policy reforms and institutional arrangements affecting the agricultural sector. Finally, Section 2.6 estimates the level and composition of agricultural support in South Africa based on the same OECD methodology applied to all member countries and a growing number of countries outside the OECD area.

South African agriculture saw major policy changes in the past ten years. The centralised control of agricultural markets has been removed, trade has largely been liberalised and equitable access to services and resources for all groups of the population have been actively promoted.

Past reforms have pursued multiple objectives, in particular, the broadening of access to agriculture; reducing poverty; improving food security; and increasing productivity and profitability in the sector. The diversity of objectives and policies has to be seen against the background of the dualistic nature of the South African agricultural sector, where modern commercial agriculture with good institutional and physical infrastructure co-exists with an emerging black agriculture, marginalised and disenfranchised in the past, with little or no resources.

2.1. Agricultural policy framework

Strategic objectives

The government defined the main agricultural policy objectives in the context of the broad economic reforms in South Africa. The *White Paper on Agriculture* (1995) stated the following main policy objectives, which were later confirmed in the *Strategic Plan for South African Agriculture* (2001).

- To build an efficient and internationally competitive agricultural sector.
- To contribute to the objectives of the Growth, Employment and Redistribution (GEAR) Strategy, aimed at achievement of economic growth by reduction of income inequalities and elimination of poverty.
- To support the emergence of small and medium-sized farms side by side with large-scale commercial farms.
- To preserve agricultural natural resources and to develop supporting policies and institutions.

The emergence of the 2001 *Strategic Plan* was preceded by a number of government planning documents, which created a relevant framework for definition of the agricultural sector strategy. The government's vision for the sector implies sustained profitable participation in the South African agricultural economy by all stakeholders. It recognises the importance of maintaining and developing commercial production and strengthening international competitiveness, but at the same time it stresses the need to address the historical legacies and biases of apartheid. Overall, the main objectives defined in the 2001 *Strategic Plan* fall under the three main groups:

- Equitable access and participation: the objective is to stimulate equitable access to and participation in agricultural activity; to reduce racial inequity in land and enterprise ownership; and to unlock the entrepreneurial potential in the sector.

- Global competitiveness and profitability: the aim is to enhance profitability through sustained global competitiveness in the agricultural sector's input supply, primary production, agro-processing and agri-tourism industries.

- Sustainable resource management: the aim is to enhance farmers' capacities for sustainable management of natural resources.

Policy objectives

During the 1990s, a wide range of policy reforms were directed at achieving a stronger market orientation, firstly in the financial sector and then in agriculture itself. The *Marketing of Agricultural Products Act* (1996), which substantially reduced state intervention in agricultural marketing and product prices, replaced the Agricultural Marketing Act of 1937, which had been amended several times in the 1950s, 1960s and 1980s. The main objectives of the new Act were to provide free market access for all market participants; promote efficiency of the marketing of agricultural products; improve opportunities for export earnings; and enhance the viability of the agricultural sector. Under the Act, the National Agricultural Marketing Council (NAMC) is the main government body intervening in marketing of agricultural products.

The *White Paper on Land Policy* (1997), links land reform to the promotion of "… both equity and efficiency through a combined agrarian and industrial strategy in which land reform is a spark to the engine of growth". The main objectives of land reform are to redress past injustices, foster reconciliation and stability, support economic growth, improve household welfare and alleviate poverty. Land restitution, land redistribution and land tenure reform are the main elements of the land reform. The land reform accommodates a large series of demands from claiming land for settlement to the establishment of commercial farms.

The *Land Redistribution for Agricultural Development* (LRAD) programme (2000) was designed to provide financial assistance to black South African citizens to access land specifically for agricultural purposes. The strategic objectives of LRAD include: contributing to the redistribution of the country's agricultural land; improving nutrition and incomes of the rural poor who want to farm on any scale; reducing congestion in the overcrowded areas in the former homelands; and expanding opportunities for women and young people who live in rural areas. The *Comprehensive Agricultural Support Programme* (CASP) was introduced in 2004, and is currently being implemented at the provincial level. The aim of CASP is to enhance the provision of support services for agricultural development. CASP targets beneficiaries of the Land Reform and Agrarian Reforms programmes, dealing with the allocation of agricultural support to various groups of beneficiaries including the hungry and vulnerable, subsistence and household food producers, farmers, agri-business and entrepreneurs.

The *Reconstruction and Development programme* (RDP) and its specific application to agriculture under the *Broadening of Access to Agriculture Thrust* (BATAT), together with the White Paper on Agriculture (1995), address both agricultural and regional development objectives. South Africa's Constitution delegates certain regulatory competencies in some areas, including agriculture, to the provinces. The main objective of BATAT is to improve access to agriculture for those who were previously excluded by racial laws.

The overall focus of the *Integrated Sustainable Rural Development Strategy* (ISRDS) is to: "Attain socially cohesive and stable rural communities with viable institutions, sustainable economies and universal access to social amenities, able to attract and retain skilled and knowledgeable people, who are equipped to contribute to growth and development." More specifically, the ISRDS objectives are to: eradicate poverty and under-development; enhance local government capacity to deliver services; promote integrated planning and budgeting across the three levels of government (co-operative governance); and promote sustainable development.

By 2000, it became necessary to rationalise the overlapping of many food security programmes implemented by different government departments. The *Integrated Food Security and Nutrition Strategy* (IFSS) was designed to streamline, harmonise and integrate the diverse food security programmes existing at the time into a single framework. The stated objective was to attain universal physical, social and economic access to sufficient, safe and nutritious food by all South Africans at all times to meet their dietary and food preferences for an active and healthy life.

A broad-based *Black Economic Empowerment Framework for Agriculture* (AgriBEE) was introduced in 2006. The objectives of AgriBEE are to eliminate racial discrimination in the agricultural sector through implementing initiatives that mainstream black South Africans at all levels of agricultural activity and along the entire agricultural value chain. Monitoring of AgriBEE and Codes of good practise and monitoring criteria are outlined in the *Black Economic Empowerment* Act of 2003.

The main objectives of *trade policy* reform with respect to the agricultural sector, is to promote integration of the sector into the global economy in order to encourage competition and greater access to markets, technology and capital. More specifically, the reforms seek to increase market access for the country's agricultural products, and to increase supplies of competitive South African agricultural goods in international and domestic markets. The South African Government stated intention is to use the World Trade Organization (WTO) framework to improve market access for South African agricultural exports, and to protect local agricultural industries against unfair trade practices.

The transformation of the old *Water Act* was initiated by the Water Law Review. Important policy principles include the dissociation of water rights from parcels of land and the recognition that water is essentially a tradable commodity. Steps are also planned to enable participation of water users in water management on a local level. Water tariffs for bulk water supply are under review, but their scope and levels have not been yet finalised. The National Water Resource Strategy (NWRS) of 2002, which is currently under review, has as its main objectives establishment of a national framework for management of water resources, preparation of catchment management strategies, development of a water resource information system and identifying development opportunities and constraints.

Agricultural Research reforms envisage re-orientation of applied research towards the requirements of small farmers and the creation of incentives for the private sector to invest in agricultural research. Mechanisms are to be established for information sharing within the research system, both public and private. The main agency responsible for research and development, the Agricultural Research Council (ARC), has refocused its core activity towards: *a)* growth and modernisation of the developed commercial farming sector; *b)* meeting the challenges posed by the developing farming sector (small-scale, market oriented farms); and *c)* poverty alleviation through the building of social security nets.

Institutional structure

The key public institutions involved with agriculture are the Department of Agriculture and the Department of Land Affairs, with a lesser role attributed to the Departments of Water Affairs and Forestry, Environmental Affairs, and Trade and Industry. Other agricultural institutions involved in supplying products and services include the Agricultural Research Council (ARC), the National Agricultural Marketing Council (NAMC), financial institutions such as the Land and Agricultural Bank (Land Bank), Development Bank of South Africa (DBSA), commercial banks, and agricultural co-operatives. The main stakeholders representing the agro-food sector are Agri-SA, the National African Farmers Union (NAFU), Transvaal Agricultural union (TAU), and the Agricultural Business Chamber.

South Africa's approach to agriculture and rural development is built around the concept of developmental local government. The institutional framework has been constantly evolving. The democratisation of South Africa is associated with a policy of decentralisation in which services are increasingly being devolved to the local level.

The public sector "road map" (Annex Table 2.A1.1) depicts the complex web of departments serving agriculture. These departments are particularly affected by the often joint national and provincial legislative responsibilities. The government has adopted an inter-governmental planning system, which includes a Medium-Term Strategic Framework (MTSF) at the national level, Provincial Growth and Development Strategies (PGDSs) and municipal Integrated Development Plans (IDPs).

The PGDSs enable stakeholders from the public, private and parastatal sectors to jointly determine a plan for the sustainable growth and development of the provinces. Local authorities are also engaged in facilitating agricultural development. There were 284 local authorities, including the 47 district municipalities and 6 metropolitan councils established in 1995/96. By 2000, institutional and organisational reforms were initiated to reduce the number of municipalities, eliminate rural representative councils and merge rural and urban areas in the same municipality. Local municipalities were also expected to engage more in developmental activities, necessitating upgrading of capacity. Local authorities are required to draw up Integrated Development Plans (IDPs), Land Development Objectives (LDOs) and Local Economic Development Plans (LEDs).

2.2. Domestic policies

Price and income support measures

Important market intervention schemes providing support to farmers (commercial farms) were implemented for decades. The interventions were enabled by the Marketing Act which was one of the most controversial pieces of economic legislation in the history of South African agriculture. It was first enacted in 1937 (Act 27 of 1937) and amended in 1968. The Marketing Act was repealed in 1997, following the promulgation of the Marketing of Agricultural Products Act, Act 47 of 1996. The new Act involves much less state interference, regulation and state involvement in agricultural marketing and product prices.

The new Act also contains strict prescriptions and procedures to be followed for any proposed intervention and, in any event, all interventions have to be reviewed every two years. All new interventionist measures have to promote the objectives of the Act and all "directly affected groups" (a register of which is to be kept by the NAMC) are given an opportunity to comment on the proposed intervention. The measures by which the NAMC can intervene on markets are limited to:

- Imposition of statutory levies (see below).

- Approval of marketing pools.

- Compulsory registration required from those selling on markets.

- Records and returns have to be submitted to the NAMC by all market agents.

The main differences between the previous Marketing Act, 1968 and the Marketing of Agricultural Products Act, 1996 is summarised in Table 2.1.

Table 2.1. **Differences in Marketing Acts of 1968 and 1996**

Act of 1968	Act of 1996
Increased productivity	Increased marketing efficiency
Reduction of marketing margins	Optimum export earnings
Increased consumption and food self-sufficiency	Food security at household level
Maximum commercial producers on land	More accent on small-scale farmers
Economic farming units; minimum farm size	Increased sustainability of agriculture
Non participative and bureaucratic introduction of intervention	Participative, transparent and all-inclusive
Stabilising product prices	Producers must themselves stabilise income
Intervention based on single channel; pools, surplus removal, fixed prices, quotas; price support; promotion; general and special levies, registration, records and returns	Limited to levies; export control; pools; registration; records and returns
Requested by producers or introduced by Minister	Requested by any directly affected group of provinces
Consultation not always necessary although certain quantified producer support required	Consultation process prescribed by Act inclusive of all directly affected groups
No political process to approve levies apart from Minister	Levies need to be approved by both portfolio committees and the Minister
No maximum period and no interim testing of intervention	All statutory measures to be introduced for fixed period and tested at least every two years

Source: Van Schalkwyk, et al. (2003).

In 1970, there were 23 Control Boards administering the various schemes established under the Marketing Act of 1968. By 1998, all Control Boards had ceased operation.[1] The assets of the Boards at the time of closure were transferred to newly created Industry Trusts. The Industry Trusts management includes representatives of all stakeholders and includes also three members appointed by the Ministry of Agriculture. Apart from the initial transfer of resources, Trust activities are financed from voluntary levies paid by all stakeholders. The Industry Trusts can request the NAMC to impose statutory levies in cases where there is no agreement on voluntary contributions, with the final decision resting with the Minister of Agriculture. All statutory levies must be reviewed at least every three years. The activities on which the trusts may spend their financial resources are clearly defined by law and limited to general services: administration (maximum 10% of expenditures), industry-related research, information gathering, product promotion, and assistance to emerging farmers within the industry.

The government has abolished sugar cane quotas. The South African Sugar Association (SASA) no longer has statutory marketing powers, and is no longer the sole statutory sugar exporter. However, the Sugar Agreement of 2000 still permits raw sugar to be exported only through a single channel industry arrangement, and allocates quotas to individual producers for sugar sold on the domestic market. Also the sugar agreement, which divides proceeds between growers and millers, is still in place.

Land reform

The strongest imperative driving the government is the need to redress the inequitable land allocation of the past (Principal National Land Reform Acts are summarised in Box 2.1). The main objectives of land reform are:

- Redress past injustices.
- Foster reconciliation and stability.
- Support economic growth.
- Improve household welfare and alleviate poverty.

The Land Reform Programme forms part of the structural adjustment programme of the government and is implemented through three main programmes:

- *Land restitution:* Restoring land to people dispossessed in the past by racially discriminatory legislation. The Land Claims Commission and Land Claims Court deal with such cases.
- *Land redistribution:* Providing the poor and previously disadvantaged population with land to improve their livelihoods, use the land for settlement purposes or to establish farming enterprises.
- *Land tenure reform:* Ensuring security of tenure for different forms of land occupation, which enables individuals or groups to earn the benefit of their property and enjoy recognition and protection, without fear of arbitrary action by the State or landowners.

Box 2.1. **Principal National Land Reform Acts**

The Restitution of Land Rights Act (No. 22 of 1994) which provides for the restitution of rights in land to those dispossessed of land by the racially based policies of 1913.

The Provision of Certain Land and Assistance for Settlement Act (No. 126 of 1993) provides for the designation of land for settlement purposes and financial assistance for the acquisition of agricultural land and to secure tenure rights settlement support.

The Development Facilitation Act (No. 67 of 1995) provides a mechanism to facilitate land development for settlement.

The Upgrading of Land Tenure Rights Act (No. 112 of 1993), as amended, provides for the upgrading of various forms of tenure into ownership. The Act provides for assistance in identifying the rightful holder, mediating disputes, and surveying and transferring land.

The Land Administration Act (No. 2 of 1995) makes provision for the assignment and delegation of powers to the appropriate authorities.

The Land Reform (Labour Tenants) Act 3 of 1996 protects the land rights of labour tenants on privately owned farms and provides a process whereby such tenants can acquire full ownership of the land they occupy. Labour tenants are largely concentrated in provinces of Mpumalanga and KwaZulu-Natal.

The Communal Property Association Act 8 of 1996 enables groups of people to acquire and hold land in common, with all the rights of full private ownership. Communal Property Associations (CPAs) have been established by groups receiving land under both the restitution and redistribution programmes. By August 2000, a total of 239 CPAs had been registered.

The Extension of Security of Tenure Act 62 of 1997 (ESTA) was enacted as required in Section 25(6) of the Constitution and protects occupants of privately owned land from arbitrary eviction and provides mechanisms for the acquisition of long-term tenure security.

Land restitution

The land restitution programme is aimed at the restitution of land rights to those forcibly removed from their land since 1913. The Land Claims Commission deals with land claims and compensation of the present owners and restitution to the claimants. Within the process of restitution the dispossessed person or community is either given back their original property (or similar property), or receive an equivalent financial compensation. The legislation governing this programme is the *Restitution of Land Rights Act* 22 of 1994. The restitution targets people who were dispossessed of their land as from 19 June 1913. The *White Paper on land policy* identifies two key institutions besides the Department of Land Affairs (DLA) for the implementation of the programme:

● The *Commission for Restitution of Land Rights* (CRLR) under a chief Land Claims Commissioner and four (later five) Regional Commissioners was established as a mandate of the Restitution of Land Rights Act. While the CRLR was originally envisaged as an independent body, it now falls under the control of the DLA, on which it depends for funds, administrative support, and research expertise and policy direction. The function of the Commissioner is to receive the claims lodged by claimants, to inform the claimants about the progress of their claims and to inform the public about their rights to claim land. The commission is required to investigate the validity of claims and facilitate negotiations between the claimant and the present landowner.

● The *Land Claims Court* – if no settlement is reached, the commission takes the matter to the Land Claims Court. The Land Claims Court has the status of a High Court and consequently appeals are heard in the constitutional court or in the Supreme Court of Appeal.

According to the Chief Land Claims Commissioner (Gwanya, 2004), restitution contributed directly to immediate poverty alleviation during the past ten years of democracy. Some ZAR 1.6 billion has been provided as financial compensation, and the restitution beneficiaries have spent this compensation mostly on home improvements, education and other livelihood projects. These funds have boosted local economic status of beneficiaries, and helped to restore their dignity. Restitutions of land were most important in provinces of Mpumalanga, Northern Cape and KwaZulu/Natal (Figure 2.1). While the number of settled claims has increased, the processing of rural claims, where in many cases there is a large number of beneficiaries per claim, remains the greatest challenge faced by the commission (Table 2.2).

Figure 2.1. **Restitution of agricultural land, by 31 March 2004**

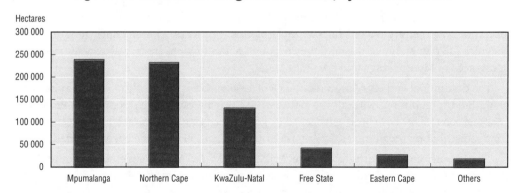

Source: Annual Report 2003-2004, Commission on Restitution of Land Rights.

Table 2.2. **Cumulative statistics on settled restitution claims, as of 31 March 2004**

	Land restoration	Financial compensation	Alternative remedy	Total number of claims settled	Beneficiaries involved
Urban claims settled	14 758	25 477	2 477	42 712	264 480
Rural claims settled	2 873	3 234	6	6 113	397 827
Total	17 631	28 711	2 483	48 825	662 307

Source: Annual Report 2003-2004, Commission on Restitution of Land Rights.

Figure 2.2. **Settled rural claims by type of compensation, as of 31 March 2004**

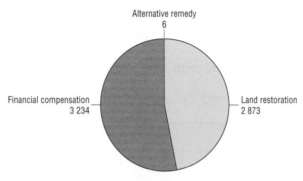

Source: Annual Report 2003-2004, Commission on Restitution of Land Rights.

The restitution process required a further injection of capital to ensure sustainable settlement of restitution claims. Another issue is the administration of the restitution process. The Commission has a staff complement of 390 out of 511 funded posts. There was high staff turnover recently linked to the fact that staff members have five-year contracts ending December 2005.

Land redistribution

Land redistribution is aimed at providing people with access to land for either settlement or agricultural purposes. The aim is *inter alia* to settle small and emerging farmers on viable farming operations in the commercial farming areas. The LRAD aims to transfer 30% of all white-owned agricultural land in 15 years to previously disadvantaged individuals. In contrast with the land restitution, the land reform programme in South Africa has performed below its expectations (Figures 2.3 and 2.4). The ambitious targets are difficult to achieve within the financial, institutional, educational and technical constraints. A variety of constraints have impeded the speed of land delivery, amongst others, institutional capacity, financial deficiencies, inadequate agricultural support services, and the lack of co-ordination.

Structure of the land redistribution programme

The redistribution programme was initially introduced as a pilot programme in each province. It was aimed at poor black communities who lacked any or sufficient land. Through the use of a state grant package, the Settlement/Land Acquisition grant (SLAG) of ZAR 15 000 (later increased to ZAR 16 000), eligible households could buy land on the market, either for settlement or agricultural purposes. A Settlement Planning Grant was

Figure 2.3. **Progress with land restitution since 1994**

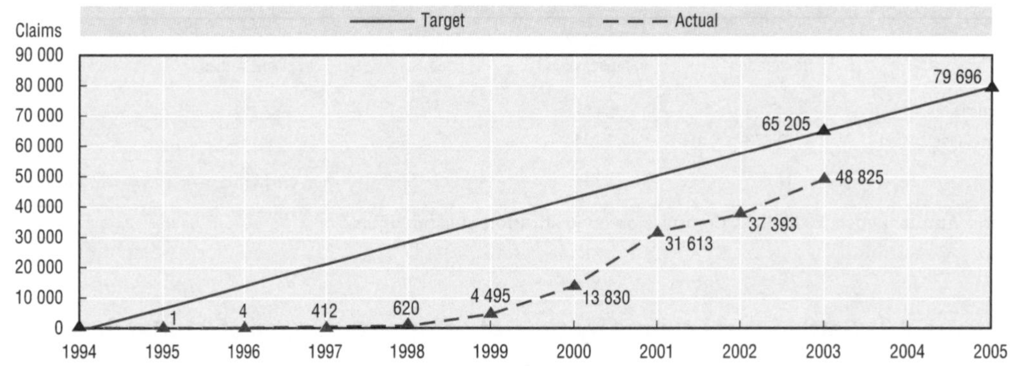

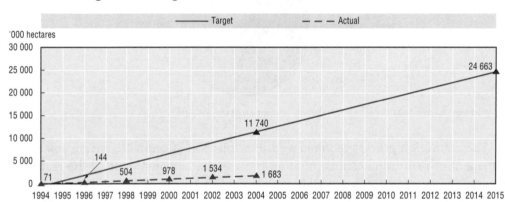

Source: Annual Report 2003-2004, Commission on Restitution of Land Rights.

Figure 2.4. **Progress with land redistribution since 1994**

Source: Department of Land Affairs.

also made available to enlist the services of planners and other professionals who would assist beneficiaries in preparing project proposals and settlement plans (Department of Land Affairs, 1995).

A separate initiative, a grant for the acquisition and development of municipal commonage, has also been made available to municipalities wanting to provide communal land for use (typically for livestock grazing) by the peri-urban and rural poor. By the end of 1999, a total of 77 municipal commonage projects had been implemented and 75 were in a preparatory phase.

The redistribution programme has different components, or sub-programmes:

● Agricultural Development – to make land available to people for agricultural purposes.

● Settlement – provision of land for settlement purposes.

● Non-agricultural enterprises – provision of land to non-agricultural enterprises, for example eco-tourism projects.

The SLAG programme was reviewed in 1999 and is now only applicable to settlement aspects of land reform. The LRAD programme discussed below, was developed to cater for agricultural purposes and is the main vehicle for settling commercial farmers (small, medium and large-scale).

The Land Redistribution for Agricultural Development sub-programme (LRAD)

The LRAD sub-programme has two distinct parts. The first deals with transfer of agricultural land to specific individuals or groups. The second dealing with commonage projects, which aim to improve people's access to municipal and tribal land primarily for grazing purposes. Both parts deal with agricultural land redistribution. However, they operate according to different financial mechanisms, different targets groups, and different delivery systems. The following description of the LRAD mechanisms deals only with the first part of the sub-programme.[2]

LRAD is designed to provide grants to black South African citizens to access land specifically for agricultural purposes. The strategic objective of the sub-programme include: contributing to the redistribution of 30% of the country's agricultural land over 15 years; improving nutrition and incomes of the rural poor who want to farm on any scale; decongesting over-crowded former homeland areas; and expanding opportunities for women and young people who stay in rural areas.

LRAD provides opportunity to participants to design individual projects reflecting their situation and objectives. Beneficiaries have access to a range of grants (from ZAR 20 000 to ZAR 100 000) depending on the amount of their own contribution in kind, labour and/or cash. Beneficiaries must provide an own contribution of at least ZAR 5 000. The grant and own contribution are calculated on a per individual adult basis (18 years and older). If people choose to apply as a group, the required own contribution and the total grant are both scaled up by the number of individuals represented in the group. The approval of the grant is based on the viability of the proposed project, which takes into account total project costs and projected profitability.

The LRAD is flexible enough to accommodate a number of types of projects. Purely residential projects would not be supported under LRAD unless beneficiaries seek to establish household gardens at their new residences, and unless funds for top-structure are sourced from elsewhere (e.g. Department of Housing). Since the launch of the LRAD programme in 2001, a total of just over 23 000 beneficiaries have been assisted to acquire land, and some 436 000 hectares have been delivered.

The types of projects that can be catered for under LRAD include, but are not limited to, the following:

- *Food safety-net projects* – Many participants may wish to access the Programme to acquire land for food crop and/or livestock production to improve household food security. This can be done on an individual or group basis. Many of these projects will be at the smallest end of scale, because poor families may be able to mobilise only the minimum own contribution in cash, labour and materials.

- *Equity schemes* – Participants can receive equity in an agricultural enterprise corresponding to the value of the grant plus their own contribution. Under the terms of LRAD, the grant is intended for people actively and directly engaged in agriculture. The purchased equity is marketable in order to retain its value.

- *Production for markets* – Some participants will enter LRAD to engage in commercial agricultural activities. They will access the grant and combine it with normal bank loans, approved under standard banking procedures, and their own assets and cash to purchase a farm. These farmers will typically have more farming experience and expertise than those accessing land for subsistence or food safety-net type activities.

- *Agriculture in communal areas* – Many people living in communal areas already have secure access to agricultural land, but may not have the means to make productive use of that land. Such people are eligible to apply for assistance for productive investment in their land such as infrastructure or land improvements. These projects may take on the character of food safety-net projects, or may be more commercially oriented.

Financial assistance to the Land Redistribution Programme

To achieve land reform objectives the Department of Land Affairs (DLA) makes available the following land reform grants:

- *LRAD Grant:* The LRAD grant allows for black South African citizens to access land specifically for agricultural purposes. This grant can be accessed, on an individual basis, per sliding scale from a minimum of ZAR 20 000 to a maximum of ZAR 100 000, depending on the participants' own contribution. The grant would be used to cover expenses such as land acquisition, land improvements, agricultural infrastructure investments, capital assets, short-term agricultural inputs and lease options.

- *LRAD Planning Grant:* This grant provides financial assistance for project planning to applicants.

- *Settlement/Land Acquisition Grant:* This grant is currently set at a maximum of ZAR 16 000 per qualifying household, to be used for land acquisition for settlement purposes, enhancement of tenure rights, and investments in infrastructure, home improvements.

- *Grant for the Acquisition and Development of Land for Municipal Commonage:* This grant is to enable primary municipalities to acquire land in order to extend or create commonage and provide infrastructure on the land to be acquired or on existing commonage for the use of qualifying persons.

- *Restitution Discretionary Grant:* This grant is set at a maximum of ZAR 3 000 per restitution beneficiary household where the original land is to be restored or where compensatory land is to be granted, through means of a negotiated settlement of the restitution claim. The grant is awarded to enable the successful claimants to take charge of their land upon transfer.

Land tenure reform

The process of land restitution and redistribution is complemented with a land tenure reform. Land tenure reform is a complex issue that deals with the entitlement of those that have various forms of land use. It aims to provide legal security of tenure on communal areas by transferring communal land to communities and providing for a unitary validated system of landholding in the country. Land tenure reform is implemented through a new legislation, which aims to protect or strengthen the rights of residents on privately owned farms and state land, together with the reform of the system of communal tenure prevailing in the former Homelands.

Progress under the land reform

Progress during the first few years of the land reform implementation was very slow but the pace began to quicken in 1998/99. By December 1999, a total of 667 825 hectares of land (representing less than 1% of the country's commercial farmland) had been redistributed and about 60 000 households were allocated grants.

By February 2004, 1.05 million hectares of land were redistributed and, together with the 0.5 million hectares redistributed under the LRAD programmes, represented 47% of the total national land reform output. The other contributions have been the 146 856 ha of land allocated under land tenure reform (4.5%), 772 626 ha in State land (23.7%) and 810 292 ha in restitution (24.8%) (National Treasury, 2004). During the financial year 2003/4, ZAR 839 million was made available for land restitution and ZAR 933 million is budgeted for 2004/5, growing to ZAR 1.37 billion by 2006/7. The DLA expenditure on the Land Redistribution Programme was ZAR 426 million in 2003/4 with ZAR 448 million budgeted for 2004/5 and ZAR 700 million for 2006/7.

Broad Based Black Economic Empowerment for Agriculture (AgriBEE)

The South African Government has set in place a general framework called Broad Based Black Economic Empowerment (BBBEE) to guide a targeted national equity drive as part of a comprehensive social and economic transformation policy. BBBEE represents a paradigm shift away from economic policies in which productive assets become ever more concentrated in fewer and fewer hands, and the gap between the rich and the poor becomes wider and wider. Through BBBEE a private, free market economy is envisioned that genuinely could empower every citizen by offering ways to ensure that all people become actively involved in the new wealth created through entrepreneurship and more sustainable economic expansion. To better focus the broad BBBEE approach within sectors of the economy and also promote closer co-operation between business, labour and government, sector charters have lately been developed for several industries.

In the case of agriculture an Agricultural Black Economic Empowerment (AgriBEE) framework has been developed. The AgriBEE framework is the Department's response to improving equitable access to and participating in agricultural opportunities, deracialising land and enterprise ownership and unlocking the full entrepreneurial potential in the sector. This framework was launched in July 2004 by the Minister of Agriculture and Land Affairs with the purpose of stimulating stakeholder consultations towards the establishment of an agriculture sector charter.

The process of finalising the Agricultural Sector Charter gained new momentum with the release of the Department of Trade and Industry's revised BEE Codes of Good Practice in June 2005. The AgriBEE steering committee has aligned a draft AgriBEE charter with the codes. The resulting draft Charter was presented for discussion at an AgriBEE *Indaba* (stakeholders meeting) in December 2005. A big spectrum of key agricultural value chains stakeholders and disempowered groups' representatives participated in the *Indaba*. The general thrust of the *Indaba* was aimed at all stakeholders to support the draft Transformation Charter for Agriculture. The final outcome of the *Indaba* was the endorsement of the draft as the basis for the conclusion of the final AgriBEE Charter by March 2006, taking into account inputs and issues raised at the *Indaba*. Agreement was also reached that the Minister of Agriculture and Land Affairs will launch the Final AgriBEE Charter with stakeholders once it has been approved by the Minister of Trade and Industry in terms of the BBBEE Act.

The immediate focus of AgriBEE implementation is to support skills development in the sector which is still largely characterised by illiteracy and inadequate skills levels. This limits black people to take full advantage of any economic opportunity in the agricultural sector. Empowerment initiatives will largely be geared towards specific designated interested groups such as women, youth and disabled persons, and promoting investment in the nodal land areas in South Africa. AgriBEE implementation mechanisms will be one of a range of government mechanisms (together with CASP, LRAD, MAFISA, etc.) forming part of a comprehensive support towards the economic integration of black people in the agro-food sector.

Policies related to input use and financing of agriculture

Agricultural Credit Board

Before 1994, the Agricultural Credit Board (ACB) catered to the resource and debt needs of the smaller commercial farmers[3] and provided credit well bellow market rates. It was funded by the Agricultural Credit Fund, which was replenished annually from the Department of Agriculture's budget. In line with the recommendations of the Strauss Commission, the ACB was closed in 1997.[4] The Agricultural Debt Management Act (45 of 2001) replaced the Agricultural Credit Act (28 of 1966). The new Act deals with the collection, management and disbursement of agricultural debt, primarily from loans granted by the former Agricultural Credit Board. After the liquidation of the ACB, the outstanding debt was ZAR 1.1 billion, declining to ZAR 680 million in 2005 with ZAR 1.1 billion accumulated in the account. The current legislation enables the government to reinvest the monies collected in the agricultural sector. It is from these funds that Micro-Agricultural Schemes for South Africa was established with ZAR 150 million in 2005 to provide micro-credit (see below).

Land Bank

The Land Bank has been heavily involved in lending to agriculture with its main clients being the co-operatives, commodity organisations, marketing boards and private farmers.[5] The Land Bank is an established institution with a long and, in terms of its past mandate, successful track record of lending to commercial farmers. It is also both a wholesaler and retailer of funds. The Land Bank does not receive any financial subsidy from the government but gets its money from the financial markets. The Land Bank does not pay tax and dividends to the government but uses some of its revenues to support development. Implicitly, at least some of the lending to agriculture could be provided at lower interest rates than from other commercial banks.[6]

The new role of the Land Bank is governed by the Land and Agricultural Development Bank Act of 2002 (Act No. 15 of 2002). This Act formed the basis for continued existence of the Land Bank, but with a renewed focus on providing financial services to promote and facilitate "equitable ownership of land, in particular the increase in ownership of agricultural land by historically disadvantaged persons".

The Land Bank provides financial services on a purely commercial basis to a diverse range of clients, including rural entrepreneurs who have traditionally been denied access to credit. As a specialist financier the Land Bank is guided by a new mandate, which requires it to promote rural development and support projects of the Comprehensive Agricultural Support Programme (CASP). Historically disadvantaged people have access to the Land Bank's Special Mortgage Bond. The Land Bank, besides financing commercial agriculture and agricultural industry, has made progress in loan financing for land redistribution (LRAD) projects.

As part of its targeting of small-scale farmers, the Land Bank provides a range of financial products at special interest rates for these individuals. Small-scale farmers wanting to buy farmland for the first time can apply for a special loan product whereby they can borrow up to 80% of the market value of the land purchased, at a special interest rate of 10% for 24 months. The Land Bank also provides incentives for clients for initiation of projects for the benefit of previously disadvantaged individual residents on their farm or in surrounding rural communities. Such incentives are in the form of discounts on the interest rates on existing or new loans held with the Land Bank. However, despite its rather successful funding strategy, the Land Bank is not able to provide financial services to the increasing number of small farmers who established their businesses during the land reform.

Micro-Agricultural Finance Schemes for South Africa

Micro-Agricultural Finance Schemes of South Africa (MAFISA), is a newly established state-owned scheme to provide micro and retail agricultural financial services on a large, accessible, cost effective and sustainable basis in the rural areas. MAFISA was approved by the government in January 2005. The scheme provides capital to support agricultural activities in the communal land areas as well as other small-scale agriculture. This will allow the Land Bank to focus on the commercial sector only. The services to be provided are: extension of credit; savings and insurance; and payment facilities for targeted beneficiaries such as communal land farmers, small landholders, tenants, household producers, food garden producers and rural micro-entrepreneurs. In 2005, MAFISA has been implemented as a pilot project in selected areas in three provinces, with ZAR 150 million allocated for the year. To date, ZAR 106 million in special mortgage loans have been approved (240 accounts).

Government investment grants

The government provided direct payments to finance (fully or partly) the costs of specific investments in agriculture, such as building fences, installing irrigation facilities and establishing farm infrastructure. These payments were dramatically reduced at the beginning of the 1990s and the last payments of around ZAR 1.4 million were most probably made in 1995/96: ZAR 388 000 for dam construction and infield works; ZAR 290 000 for soil conservation works; ZAR 684 000 for farm labour housing; ZAR 60 000 for pipelines for drinking water; and ZAR 22 000 for boreholes.

In 2005, the government introduced a Comprehensive Agricultural Support Programme (CASP), which is targeted to the beneficiaries of land reform willing to establish commercial farms. The support is to be provided mainly through investment grants allocated to viable projects.

Tax concessions

The Diesel Refund System, introduced in 2000, provides a refund on the tax and road accident fund levies paid on diesel fuel. The concession applies to farming, mining and forestry and comprises 31.6% of the fuel levy and 100% of the road accident fund levy on qualifying consumption (80% of the total eligible purchases used in primary production qualify for the refund).

In the mid-1990s, the government amended the tax treatment for agriculture, whereby capital purchases could now be written off over three years at rates of 50%, 30% and 20% per annum respectively, instead of over one year, thereby reducing the implicit subsidy for capital equipment.

Disaster relief

In the past, the government provided a three-tiered drought assistance programme for agriculture that included *ad hoc* emergency funds for crop producers (usually in the form of short-term debt consolidation), support to irrigation farms whose water quotas were cut due to reduced dam levels, and longer term assistance to protect the veldt and livestock grazing lands. This complex and expensive programme was replaced with a national disaster management system in which areas can be declared natural disaster areas by the President (similar to the US system), with the level, beneficiaries and means of support based on the nature and scope of the disaster. The DoA is responsible for assessing and managing any drought relief.

Water use policies

Given South African climatic and soil conditions, water use policies are a key determinant of agricultural productivity in specific areas. The promulgation of the new National Water Act (Act No. 36 of 1998) brought about changes in access to water by different users, including farmers. This followed the signing of the Water Services Act (Act No. 108 of 1997). The new legislation redefines water access such that all water is for public use. Changes that impact agriculture include:

- Higher priority afforded to water used by humans, including preferential access for small farmers.
- Authorised water use through compulsory licensing.
- Termination of the riparian principle of water rights.
- Implementation of an integrated catchments management system.
- Decentralisation of water management through Catchments Management Associations.
- Termination of water price subsidies.

The new Water Act addresses specifically the situation of small-scale farmers by advocating intensified provision and basic free delivery of on-site water to previously disadvantaged households. This has the potential to impact positively on household food security due to possible improved sanitation and food safety (Vink, 2003).

Agricultural research

The Agricultural Research Council (ARC) is the primary organ of the state charged with agricultural research and development. The ARC was created in 1990 through the Agricultural Research Council Act. It was founded through the amalgamation of 15 government specialised institutes some of them dating back to 1902. In 1992, the ARC was formally separated from the Department of Agriculture (DoA) and established as a publicly owned and funded agency charged with basic research, technology development and technology transfer.

One of the key challenges facing the ARC is responding to the needs of the emerging farmer sector. It has established the Sustainable Rural Livelihood Division, a cross-cutting division to link the various thematic research programmes. To this end the ARC co-operates with the National Department for Agriculture (NDA) and the departments of agriculture in the provinces to identify and support strategic research interventions.

As a shared functional competency between national and provincial spheres of government, provincial departments of agriculture also perform research and development functions. Technology research and development services make up on aggregate 9.6% of provincial agricultural budgets. Renewed efforts are underway to improve the co-ordination between the ARC and provincially based research and extension services to reduce duplication of efforts, better target research objectives and enhance the dissemination of technology.

Furthermore, the DoA's Programme *Economic Research and Analysis* provides the necessary information for developing and monitoring the agricultural sector. The programme provides timely, accurate and pertinent agricultural, economic and statistical information on a quarterly basis in order to support decision-making by all participants in the agricultural sector. Recently improvements to the crop forecasting system are also being addressed through a contract awarded to a consortium led by the Agricultural Research Council.

Agricultural research at universities focuses on basic research and university outreach programmes. Universities including agricultural and biological science faculties are funded under the Department of Education budget vote and are totally separated from the Agriculture budget. Moreover, the National Research Foundation, a parastatal reporting to the Department of Science and Technology, funds research projects at higher education institutions. The budgetary expenditure on agricultural related research is difficult to determine as it is not distinguished separately in the respective departmental budgets.

Extension, education and training

In South Africa, extension programmes are designed to facilitate and promote productive use of land by providing services such as training on production methods; marketing; and organising farmers into groups for purchasing inputs, marketing outputs and accessing finance. These services are a competency of the provincial departments of agriculture and are mostly oriented towards small-scale farming.

Agricultural education and training is geared to promote and develop environmentally and economically sustainable agriculture. Agricultural education and training is provided by various statuary and non-statuary institutions at the national and provincial level.

Some 11 colleges of agriculture, 6 universities of technology and 9 universities have offered various higher education and training programmes that are nationally accredited. At present the Department of Education is in the process, nearing finalisation, of rationalising and merging the tertiary institutions falling under its governance into a more unified system for education. Some of the agricultural colleges in certain provinces fall under the provincial departments of agriculture and are funded from their budget. The Intergovernmental Fiscal Review reflected the following percentage spread in provincial spending (Table 2.3).

Table 2.3. **Provincial spending on structured training**

Province	% of provincial budget
Eastern Cape	16.8
Free State	6.4
Gauteng	0
KwaZulu-Natal	10.4
Limpopo	33.3
Mpumalanga	11.4
Northern Cape	0
North West	11.8
Western Cape	9.9

Source: Intergovernmental Fiscal Review.

The spending in provinces reflects the number of colleges offering agricultural training and probably indicates that needs for such services vary across provinces. Limpopo has two colleges of agricultural training; Gauteng and Northern Cape have none, while the rest have a single college each. Colleges offer education and training in practical agricultural production on crops and livestock with some specialisation, based on regional specific agro-ecological production domains. Elements of agricultural extension are also included in the curriculum. With the recent introduction of a Bachelor of Technology degree, more theoretical components are included. Universities offer a broad and diversified range of agricultural sciences as well as agricultural engineering and business leadership.

The Department of Labour has introduced through the Skills Development Act and the Skills Development Levies Act a national system of Sectoral Education and Training Authorities (SETAs). The broad goal of the SETAs is the upgrading of skills and knowledge for employees and employers in their respective sectors. The Skills Development Act makes provision for the payment of grants to those employers who are contributing through the skills development levy (1% of total wage and salary bill). Employers can get up to 70% of their contribution back if they fulfil certain skills development requirements. The SETAs are responsible for the management and administration of these funds, and control the quality of training and development in the sector through the accreditation of training providers. SETA also plays a supportive role for the training and development actions (i.e. the development and registration of learnerships and skills programmes.

The Primary Agriculture Education and Training Authority (PAETA) also serves the primary agricultural sector. The scope of PAETAs development actions is targeted to farm workers, estimated at 45 000 commercial farmers; 400 000 permanent workers (on commercial farms); 350 000 seasonal workers; and 400 000 emerging farmers.

National regulatory services

The DoA programme, National Regulatory System (NRS), focuses on managing risks associated with animal and plant diseases; food safety, including the use of genetic resources and the importing and exporting of food; and bio-safety legislation pertaining to agricultural products entering South Africa and genetically modified products. The programme develops policy and legislation, and implements compliance and operational support systems. The various regulatory measures linked with these issues are described in a separate section below. Within the Department of Agriculture, the national regulatory services are organised in four main areas.

The Directorate for Food Safety and Quality Assurance regulates and promotes the production and sale of safe and quality agricultural food products of animal and plant origin. In this respect, the directorate provides leadership in the development of food safety and quality norms and standards to prevent, minimise and reduce the incidence of food-borne diseases, protect public health and life and facilitate trade. The directorate engages in the following activities:

● To determine food safety and quality norms and standards for import, export and local markets with regard to fruit, flowers, grains, vegetables, animal, and processed products and liquor products in terms of Agricultural Product Standards Act, 1990 (Act No. 119 of 1990) and the Liquor Products Act, 1989 (Act No. 60 of 1989).

- Effective registration, administration and control of agricultural enhancement agents (APEA) by applying proper and effective registration procedures, norms and standards to conform to approved requirements of safety, efficacy and quality in terms of the Fertilisers, Farm Feeds, Agricultural Remedies and Stock Remedies Act, 1947 (Act No. 36 of 1947).

- Develop food safety and quality norms and standards for agricultural products from animal origin in terms of the Meat Safety Act, 2000 (Act No. 40 of 2000).

- Develop and facilitate education and awareness programmes to promote food safety and quality assurance among the clients and the general public.

The Plant Health Directorate is responsible for policy, legislative norms and standards as well as guidelines to manage plant health risk, and to ensure compliance with international plant health obligations and responsibilities. The specific functions are to:

- Provide a national contact point for South Africa with regard to the WTO-SPS and IPPC responsibilities and obligations.

- Manage bilateral and multilateral plant health agreements and standards.

- Manage plant health export programmes and protocols.

- Manage an effective plant health system to support agricultural marketing and international trade for South African plants and plant products.

- Manage an effective plant health import permit system through Pest Risk Analysis.

- Render plant health quarantine and diagnostic services.

- Manage an Early Warning System for the early detection of the introduction and spread of exotic and quarantine plant pests and diseases.

- Manage plant health awareness and education programmes.

- Manage information in support of a national data bank for plant health early warning systems, policies and standards.

The activities of the Directorate of Plant Health are mandated mainly by the Agricultural Pests Act, 1983 (Act No. 36 of 1983) and relevant regulations. Other legislation has also relevance to the activities of the directorate and links to the Agricultural Pests Act of 1983, such as:

- National Environmental Management Act, 1998 (Act No. 107 of 1998) has reference with regard to the importation of biological control agents.

- Fertilisers, Farm feeds, Agricultural remedies and Stock remedies Act, 1947 (Act No. 36 of 1947) has reference with regard to the importation of biological control agents and treatment for wood packaging material.

- National Environmental Management Biodiversity Bill will have reference to the importation of alien species, listed invasive species and threatened or protected species and will be synchronised with the Agricultural Pests Act of 1983.

The Animal Health Directorate has the mandate to set legislation, policy and standards regarding all functions relating to animal health and veterinary services. The nine provinces execute all regulatory functions within their own area, in co-operation with both the national directorate and other provincial directorates. The National Directorate Veterinary Services ensure effective biological risk management in terms of animal diseases, food safety, as well as veterinary control of animal imports, by providing information, legislation, policy, standards, capacity building, certification, control and audits. The Animal Health Directorate has four sub-directorates, namely:

- *Animal Disease Policy Unit* that administers the Animal Diseases Act, 1984 and exercises border control, it also administers the Abattoir Hygiene Act and associated standards and norms.

- *Animal Health Import and Export Policy* controls veterinary import permits and ports of entry as well as export abattoirs and certification.

- *Animal Health Epidemiology Unit* is responsible for disease surveillance, reporting, data collection, training and liaison.

- *Animal Health Development in Rural Areas.*

The Agricultural Food, Quarantine and Inspection Services Directorate monitors risk management strategies, policies and legislation for food safety and the control of animal and plant diseases. The directorate staff carries inspection services/audits at official ports of entry on plants, animals and their products as well on national plant and plant products with regard to plant health, quality and food hygiene on plants and plant products.

The Perishable Product Export Control Board (PPECB) is the control body for all exports of perishable products. About 90% of the controlled products are fruit, 5% are vegetables and the rest comprises maize, rice, groundnuts, dairy products and meat. PPECB is assigned by the DoA to implement mandatory regulations and standards.

Agricultural and rural infrastructure

Infrastructure is a crucial element of agrarian production and marketing systems. Rural production infrastructure is supported by the governments of all levels through a variety of government departments and statutory bodies. According to an Intergovernmental Fiscal Review, two-thirds of agriculture spending on infrastructure is for capital projects and one-third for maintenance.

Specific agricultural related infrastructure includes government spending on on-farm and communal land infrastructure such as dipping tanks, replacement and upgrading of existing structures, and fencing. This expenditure is financed from provincial department budgets under farmer support programmes and at the national level through conditional grant transfers to provinces under the terms of the Comprehensive Agricultural Support Programme (CASP).

Agricultural infrastructure, more broadly defined, includes large dams and bulk water conveyance systems to farms or project borders. Agricultural irrigation accounts for almost 60% of water used in South Africa. Water services and water resource management is a competency of the Department of Water Affairs and Forestry (DWAF). The National Water Act of 1998 deals with the management of water resources to ensure sufficient water for basic human needs and environmental sustainability. The National Water Resources Strategy provides the framework within which water resources are managed in all parts of the country. It also assists in the establishment of catchment management agencies, and provides for compulsory licensing of agricultural water use. DWAF delivers water services through Water Users Associations, co-operative associations of individual water users undertaking water-related activities at a local level for their mutual benefit.

Marketing and promotion

The DoA Agricultural Trade and Business Development programme develops policies governing access to national and international markets, and promote Black economic empowerment (AgriBEE) in the sector. The Department of Agriculture is supported by the National Agricultural Marketing Council (NAMC), which regulates the marketing of agricultural products. The transfer payment to the National Agricultural Marketing Council to cover its operating cost is planned to grow from ZAR 6.7 million in 2000/01 to an expected ZAR 11.6 million in 2006/07, an annual average increase of 9.7%.

Vital elements of a competitive sector include the transmission of information on subjects ranging from market locations to packaging, labelling and meeting certain technical requirements, the provision of quality control services, and the development of infrastructure. Although marketing is generally a private-sector function, the government plays a role by:

● Strengthening measures on export production and marketing such as research and extension; provision of training facilities and courses focusing on, amongst others, developing export marketing expertise; pest and disease control and inspection services.

● Facilitating access of farming sector and agro-industries to economy wide measures implemented by the Department of Trade and Industry (DTI), such as: the Export Marketing and Investment Assistance Scheme; shipment financing through the Credit Guarantee Insurance Corporation and export promotion support through trade fairs, trade missions and diplomatic missions.

● Implementing new measures for promoting exports, such as:

❖ Providing assistance to the agricultural sector to develop markets by facilitating the sector's participation in trade missions, exhibitions, fairs and other activities that increase international awareness of South African agricultural products.

❖ Availability of market intelligence and market information based on publicly and privately funded research into market and global trade trends research.

Agri-environmental measures

Agri-environmental measures are applied in South Africa within diverse environmental (non-agriculture specific) regulations. The Agricultural Policy Discussion Document of 1998 (Ministry of Agriculture and Land Affairs, 1998) endorsed a number of pre-1994 regulations concerning conservation of natural resources. These are supported, in part, by the post-1994 Development Facilitation Act (Act No. 67 of 1995) and the National Environment Management Act (Act No. 107 of 1998). The agri-environmental measures mainly concern water, land use and biodiversity issues.

Water protection

National legislation (the Conservation of Agricultural Resources Act 43 of 1983, and the National Water Act 36 of 1998) is in place to deal with adverse effects of agriculture on water quality. Specific control measures have been drafted giving detail on how intensive-farming systems should handle the problem of water pollution. The agricultural research councils undertake research on this problem and are able to provide practical information and technical guidelines to farmers.

The National Water Policy for South Africa and the National Water Act 36 of 1998 make provision for water to be protected, used, developed, conserved, managed and controlled in a sustainable and equitable manner. This provision has implications for the development of irrigation works and the application of water in agricultural production. A water conservation and water demand strategy is in the process of being developed. A water pricing strategy is being implemented, and will be progressively extended to include the small-scale farmers.

Land protection

To ensure sustainable use of agricultural natural resources, while recognising that the main responsibility lies with the farmers and their communities, the national Land Care programme was introduced. The Land Care programme aims to create a conservation ethic by means of education and the monitoring of sustainable land management. Its core element is that it will encourage people to take responsibility for their own environments with the support of the government at the national and provincial level. The Land Care programme consists of five elements:

- Major programmes for *resource conservation* – for each province the major concerns about sustainable resource use are identified and specific projects developed to address these needs. These projects are also designed to create employment in rural areas.
- *Capacity building* of local communities and support staff. The purpose of this programme element is to provide capacity building for local communities and support staff.
- *Awareness programme* – is a communication and information strategy geared primarily for the farmers and secondarily for the broader land-user communities and also young people.
- *Policy and legislation* programme is geared for the formulation of policy and legislation that deal with *incentives* and *disincentives* in meeting the targets set in natural resource management.
- *Research and evaluation* is aimed at establishing and implementation of a continuing monitoring/evaluation system to monitor progress, assess emerging and changing needs, and to provide a basis for planning and research.

Biodiversity

In respect of the conservation of plant and animal species and the protection of endangered ecosystems, the principal emphasis is on meeting internationally agreed standards and commitments and translating these into national programmes.

Social measures

Agricultural policies that contribute to broader social goals include land reform, various types of support to small farmers, food security and AgriBEE. Social measures being undertaken to transform the sector to be more socially just and equitable are focussed on the previously disenfranchised black agriculture but the range of beneficiaries is much broader, including:

- Previously disadvantaged people who wish to engage in farming as a fulltime activity.
- Landless people or people with limited access to land.
- Farm workers and their families.

- Labour tenants, their families and other persons who need long-term security of tenure.
- Individuals and communities who wish to secure tenure.
- Successful claimants of land restitution.

Consumer measures

Certain basic consumer foodstuffs, such as brown bread, eggs, milk, maize meal and rice (mostly imported) are exempt from the Value Added Tax (VAT). This policy is implicitly targeted at poor households, since food purchases form the largest share of their household expenditure.

Food price increases during 2002, prompted policy makers to take action in a bid to shield the poor from the effects of such increases. The first action taken in this regard was the commitment of ZAR 230 million by parliament to the National Food Emergency Scheme (NFES) in 2002. The NFES, created in 2003, is the safety-net component of the country's Integrated Food Security Strategy (IFSS). The NFES activities include:

- Immediate provision of *food parcels* for three months. The process involves identifying poor households and providing them in their localities with food parcels (all food parcels are the same in terms of contents and quantity).

- Increased *access to social security safety nets:* The NFES aims at enhancing access by poor people to social security benefits. Those recipients of food parcels who qualify but have not yet accessed social security grants are supposed to be linked with the social security division.

- Providing *agricultural households with gardening starter packs.* The Department of Agriculture is responsible for designing and implementing the starter pack component of the NFES. The process involves designing a plan, selecting the beneficiaries for the starter packs and assisting them with inputs such as seeds, tools and advice on the process of food production. The primary goal of this service is to ensure household food security.

Regulatory requirements

The main areas where the state applies its regulatory functions is food safety (Sanitary and phytosanitary measures, Veterinary measures), animal improvement (*e.g.* Animal breeding, registration, animal disease control, animal welfare), plants quality and protection (legislation on plants, seeds – including genetically modified organisms, plant protection and plant quality control, etc.). Effective measures are needed to maintain such standards through, for example, prevention and control of epidemic diseases and effective inspection and diagnostic services.

Food safety

The responsibility for setting food safety standards and enforcing them lies with the Department of Agriculture and other government institutions, particularly the Department of Health. As a general principle, food safety and quality regulations are applied in accordance with the provisions of the WTO SPS Agreement and other international conventions. South Africa is an active participant in the Codex Alimentarius Commission, International Plant Protection Convention, International Office of Epizootics and International Institute of Agricultural Co-operation. The relevant international standards, guidelines and recommendations of the Codex Alimentarius are used as quantitative benchmarks. The NDA ensures strong participation from the agricultural sector (including legal and scientific contributions) against unfair standards set by importing countries.

On the domestic market, the hygienic production of food of animal origin is governed by Veterinary Public Health (VPH) policy. Meat hygiene legislation is currently controlled under the Abattoir Hygiene Act (Act No. 121 of 1992), and a new Meat Safety Bill will cover all commercial animal slaughter facilities. However, VPH also covers milk hygiene (which falls under the Department of Health and local authority jurisdiction) as well as eggs and fish (which lack a proper VPH policy framework at present). As a consequence, VPH matters will be brought under the National Food Safety Act.

Technical Barriers to Trade

South Africa is a signatory to the WTO Agreement on Technical Barriers to Trade (TBT) and uses this agreement and its trade remedies as instruments to address any attempt to restrict its exports through technical barriers. The role of the Department of Agriculture is to ensure that standards applied are non-discriminatory and transparent and are least trade distorting.

Inspection

The government is responsible for setting standards and also for an effective inspection system that enforces compliance with a large variety of commodity-specific and country-specific regulations. However, the government is increasingly outsourcing the delivery of some inspection functions where it has confidence in the existing private sector institutions. There are several pieces of legislation providing the legal framework for inspection services, which are administered through different government departments and directorates.

The removal of interdepartmental duplication in areas such as enforcement, risk management, laboratory services, information systems and communication is expected to lead to a more efficient use of scarce resources. The Minister of Agriculture has appointed a team to review organisational options and examine the feasibility of a single Food and Agricultural Commodities Inspection Agency (FACIA).

Animal improvement

Livestock operations include a wide variety of production systems from large-scale extensive beef, wool, mutton, and mohair production to intensive dairy, pig and poultry systems. The purpose of regulation in respect of breeding is primarily to support the industry through steps which encourage investment in improved stock and provide confidence for those engaged in the purchase and sale of breeding stock. The limitations of the previous Livestock Improvement Act, 1977 (Act No. 25 of 1977) was that it:

● Restricted the importation of genetic material to registered stud breeders.

● Protected the local artificial insemination industry and put restrictions on the local collection and sale of semen.

● Provided insufficient control over embryo collection and transfer activities.

● Did not allow equal access to information and to genetic material for smaller, disadvantaged stock owners.

A new Animal Improvement Act attempts to remove such distortions and ensure that importers and suppliers of animals and genetic material are bound by standards that will maintain or improve production efficiency. The Bill proposes to retain certain valuable regulatory aspects of the existing Act, such as the identification and use of genetic material that could be used to the advantage of the national herd; the provision of animal reproduction services; and the establishment and maintenance of animal breeders' societies. However, the Bill also makes provision for the following important changes:

- Deregulation of the artificial insemination industry.
- Removal of restrictions on imports or exports of breeding animals or genetic material.
- Protection of South Africa's indigenous and locally-developed livestock breeds.
- Registration of embryo collectors.

Animal registration

The system of registration, identification and performance monitoring of animals has largely been confined to the white commercial sector. The costs of this system have increasingly been borne by livestock owners, through registration by breeders' societies, for example, and through charges for the cost of services rendered by the Stud Book and Livestock Improvement Association. The widening of benefits to emergent farmers and stock owners in commercial areas is a government priority.

Animal welfare

The responsibility for animal welfare services has been transferred from the Department of Justice to the Department of Agriculture. Minimum standards for services and for the training of inspectors are defined. The focus is on promoting humane behaviour to avoid unnecessary pain and distress to animals, rather than reacting to individual acts of cruelty. Legislation and codes of conduct are still to be developed in this area and will draw on international experience in the field of animal welfare and animal rights, while recognising the specific challenges of South Africa arising from the cultural diversity and poverty.

Animal disease control

The Constitution provides a framework for the government's livestock and animal health services. Animal health control and diseases are a joint national and provincial competency. A number of veterinary-related spheres of the government have also been derogated as provincial and local competencies. They include veterinary services (excluding regulation of the profession); facilities for the accommodation, care and burial of animals; the licensing and control of undertakings that sell food to the public; and municipal abattoirs and pounds. The Animal Diseases Act of 1984 (Act No. 35 of 1984) governs the infectious animal diseases and parasites that pose a treat to agriculture in South Africa and the Southern African region as a whole.

Plants and plant quality

The aim of policy regarding plants and plant quality is not only to ensure that the agricultural industry is provided with a consistent and transparent service that allows for the application of known standards, but also to install confidence in South African plant products in international markets. Legislation on plants, seeds, plant protection and plant quality control is necessary for both farmers and consumers, and is becoming increasingly important in the field of international trade where SPS and TBT measures, if inadequately managed, can seriously jeopardise export prospects. The main legislation currently in place covers:

- Plant improvement, giving legal recognition to propagating material which meets purity and germination requirements.

- Plant breeders' rights, providing protection for those engaged in developing improved plant varieties and allowing them to derive financial benefits from their efforts.

- Plant protection, giving powers to prevent the importation and spread of plant pests and diseases.

- Product standards, covering the sale and export of all agricultural plant products.

In the area of product standards, the government has already delegated certain functions to industry-based organisations to carry out some of the tasks of regulation. The underlining principles will be the integrity of assignees in both the domestic and international arenas; the need for an efficient and economic delivery system; and transparency and other criteria that may emanate from South Africa's membership to conventions.

2.3. Agro-food trade policies

Recent trade policy developments

The overall process of trade liberalisation in South Africa is characterised by a lowering of the average tariff level by one-third over five years. There was a notable progress in tariff liberalisation for the whole economy. In the 1990s, tariff liberalisation was more rapid prior to 1996, while a modest reduction in the number of tariff lines, as well as in the maximum rates applied, has occurred up to 1999.

In spite of reforms to the South African tariff regime, the tariff schedule remains complex, and for some products the applied tariffs are changing frequently. This creates uncertainty for businesses that frequently import goods. This state of affairs is also echoed by Cassim *et al.* (2002) who state that less progress has been made to create greater uniformity in the range and number of tariffs that exist in South Africa. Cassim *et al.* (2002) furthermore state that a highly dispersed and cumbersome tariff structure may mean that protection remains uneven and gains from openness may be limited, since with considerable tariff peaks, trade reform may not be completely successful in encouraging exports especially for those sectors that rely on internationally competitive inputs.

Agricultural trade policies

South Africa's agro-food trade regime had been characterised by numerous quantitative restrictions, a multitude of tariff lines, a wide distribution of tariffs, and various other forms of protection such as formulae, specific and *ad valorem* duties and surcharges. These restrictions, a maze of price controls and other regulations, often eliminated any foreign competition. The situation changed considerably after South Africa became a signatory of the URAA and promulgated the Marketing of Agricultural Products Act, 1996. These events represented a turning point in the marketing of agricultural products in South Africa.

The agricultural trade reforms have complemented the deregulation of domestic agricultural policies. South Africa's trade liberalisation under the WTO has depended on the reduction of tariff lines as well as tariff levels. As a result of the tariff schedule rationalisation which was implemented in 1997, the agricultural tariff levels declined by 38%. Licenses and quotas are restricted to quota administration in respect of trade agreements, and non-tariff import controls remain only for sanitary and phytosanitary measures accepted by the WTO. Also as a result of the signing of the Marrakech Agreement, the process of tariff reduction and the lowering of effective and nominal protection have been relatively fast. Direct export subsidies, previously provided under the General Export Incentive Scheme (GEIS), were also discontinued in 1997.

Import measures

South Africa's import protection for agricultural and food products is based mostly on specific and *ad valorem* tariffs. It also provides for *tariff rate quotas,* which are country and product specific, as well as anti-dumping and countervailing duties. The levels of agricultural tariffs are investigated by the International Trade Administration Commission (ITAC) within the same framework as for all other products. Both the National Agricultural Marketing Council and the National Department of Agriculture advise the Minister on the tariff reports received from ITAC, which are then approved by the Minister for Agriculture and Land Affairs. It is not government policy to use customs duties as a means for generating budgetary revenue. Under the Southern Africa Customs Union (SACU) Agreement, in which South Africa plays a leading role, import duty revenues of the members are accumulated in a common fund, most part of which is destined to other, less-developed, members of the Customs Union, so any unilateral action by the South African government has implications for these countries.

Tariffs: As a member of SACU, South Africa applies common external tariffs set for all members of SACU. Average rate of duty applied is 9.7%, well below the commitment levels of the bound rates (39.7% on average). For most agro-food products, *ad valorem* tariffs or specific duties (or a combination of both) are applied. *Tariff quotas* exist for a range of agricultural products under the minimum market access commitments, at tariffs of 20% of the bound rates.

The level of protection for main agricultural products varies considerably:

- For maize, a specific import duty (ZAR/tonne) is applied, calculated according to a formula based on world price and the relevant exchange rate. Between 1998 and 2005, the *ad valorem* equivalent of the duty fluctuated between 0 to 28%. Until July 2005, similar formula tariff also existed for wheat, fluctuating in *ad valorem* terms between 0 to 30%. In July 2005, the formula tariff for wheat was replaced by an *ad valorem* tariff of 2% (Annex Table 2.A1.2).

- For sugar and sugar products import tariffs range from zero on cane molasses, and fructose syrup to 25% on sugar and sugar confectionery. Additional duty level adjustment (ZAR/tonne) is applied based on a trigger price system. Hence, the *ad valorem* equivalent of the duty ranged from 12% to 85% between 2001 and 2005 (*ad valorem* equivalents of the duty are not available for the previous years) (Annex Table 2.A1.3).

- For soybeans the applied tariff ranges between 8% and 10%, and for sunflower it is set at 3.5%.

- Average tariff for fruits is 7.3% (Chapter 8 of the HS System), while that for vegetables is 10.6%.

- Live animals are imported duty free, while for meat and edible meat offal import tariffs are set up to 40%, and for meat products up to 50%.

- Dairy products are mostly subject to specific tariffs; generally *ad valorem* equivalents for dairy products are well above the average agricultural tariff level.

- Imports of wool and fine or coarse animal hair are mostly subject to a zero tariff.

Safeguard measures: Although South Africa reserved the right to use special agricultural safeguards for a number of products, these were not used in the course of the implementation period as they were not deemed necessary, mainly because of the substantial margin between bound and applied tariffs which made it possible to raise tariffs when deemed necessary.

Import quotas and licences: Licenses and quotas now only apply to quotas foreseen by the trade agreements.

Import permits: Under the Import and Export Control Act of 1963, the Minister of Trade and Industry may limit the import of certain goods into South Africa. For those goods subject to import control measures, importers must apply for import permits. The list of restricted goods requiring import permits has been substantially reduced as the result of phasing out of import permits in favour of tariffs.

Export measures

Export subsidies: In 1995, the government initiated a three-year programme to eliminate the General Export Incentive Scheme (GEIS), as envisaged under the commitments to the WTO. In June 1995, the GEIS benefits became taxable and the number of export categories eligible for the subsidy was reduced, while the level of subsidy was also cut. In March 1996, a programme to accelerate the phasing out of the GEIS was announced. In April, the GEIS subsidy for processed products was cut from 14% of the export value to 12% and was scheduled to decline further to 6% in July. The GEIS subsidy for raw materials was cut from 3% of the export value to 2% in April 1996, and was phased out in July 1996, effectively limiting the GEIS to fully manufactured products. Since July 1997, when the GEIS was abolished, no export subsidies are applied for agro-food products. However, the price pooling regime for sugar is effectively subsidising sugar exports, while the costs are born by local sugar consumers.

Export permits: For those products that need to comply with certain EU or US quota arrangements, the South African government requires an export permit to ensure that small and medium enterprises, as well as disadvantaged communities get a fair chance to export under certain quota windows.

Standards and regulations

Various government departments and parastatals set and police standards affecting the trade of agricultural products, most notably the Department of Agriculture, the Department of Health, Department of Trade and Industry (DTI), the South African Bureau of Standards (SABS) and the Council for Scientific and Industrial Research (CSIR). Most standards conform, or are in close conformity with international standards.

Trade agreements

South Africa was a founding member of the General Agreement on Tariffs and Trade (GATT) and the subsequent World Trade Organisation (WTO). South Africa is involved in several regional trade agreements of which the Trade, Development and Co-operation Agreement with the European Union was the most recently signed (11 October 1999). The

Southern African Customs Union (SACU) and the Southern African Development Community (SADC) are related to international trade involving South Africa. The bilateral treaty with Zimbabwe is also very important to agriculture.

Southern African Customs Union

The Southern African Customs Union (SACU), whose members are South Africa, Botswana, Lesotho, Namibia and Swaziland (BLNS countries), has been in existence since 1910 and was renegotiated in 2002, introducing new provisions:

● SACU becomes an international judicial body.

● Formation of six new institutions: a Council of Ministers; Customs Union Commission; Secretariat; Tariff Board; Technical Liaison Committees (i.e. Agriculture, Customs technical, Trade and Industry and Transport); and a Tribunal.

● Co-operation on customs issues, industrial development, competition issues, agriculture, unfair trade practices and dispute settlement.

● Introduction of a new revenue-sharing arrangement, favouring the less-developed SACU – BLNS countries.

The new institutional framework provides a basis for greater autonomy in respect of economic development for BLNS countries and can play an important role in ensuring that South Africa provides political and economic leadership in the region to implement mutually beneficial policies. The new Tariff Board effectively removes South Africa's control over tariff-setting for SACU as a whole. Greater integration should also entail increased investment in sectors that hold a comparative advantage in BLNS countries.

Southern African Development Community

In 1994, South Africa became a member of the 14-member Southern African Development Community (SADC).[7] The SADC free trade agreement is to be implemented between 2000 and 2008. A very important feature of the SADC is the trade protocol intended to stimulate trade between member countries through the reduction in tariffs. SADC incorporated the principle of asymmetry: a phase-down of SACU tariffs in five years (by 2005 which has been implemented); and those of other countries in 12 years by 2012. Each non-SACU SADC country prepared two offers: one to South Africa and the other to the rest of SADC. In order to compensate the less-developed SACU members that would liberalise their imports faster than non-SACU countries, the SACU offer was made conditional upon BLNS being able to maintain all the preferences they had enjoyed in trading with the non-SACU SADC states, for example, enhanced market access for selected products of export significance. Under the principle of asymmetry, there was a general understanding that the "developing" non-SACU states (Mauritius and Zimbabwe) would mid-load their tariff reductions while the Least Developing Countries (LDCs) would backload. Zimbabwe has not yet started its tariff phase down due to the prevailing political and economic situation.

South Africa-EU Trade, Development and Cooperation Agreement

The Trade, Development and Cooperation Agreement (TDCA) between South Africa and the European Union and its member states was signed in October 1999 and implemented on 1 January 2000. Under this agreement, a free trade area between the two parties will be established by the end of the transition period in 2012. The area will cover approximately 90% of total trade between the two parties. The agreement has been notified to the WTO in terms of GATT Article XXIV. The TDCA will be reviewed during the course of 2006. The aim would be to further liberalise trade amongst the parties, while also addressing market access issues other than goods. The amended agreement is expected to come into force during 2007.

SACU-EFTA Free Trade Agreement

SACU (Botswana, Lesotho, Namibia, South Africa and Swaziland) has recently concluded a free trade agreement with the European Free Trade Association (EFTA) (Liechtenstein, Iceland, Norway and Switzerland). The agreement covers both agricultural and non-industrial market access. It also includes some evolutionary clauses that would allow the future inclusion of other aspects into the agreement, *e.g.* trade in services. The agreement is expected to come into force on 1 July 2006.

Other agreements

Apart from the existing Free Trade Agreements (FTAs), South Africa with other SACU partners is currently negotiating a FTA with the United States and with MERCOSUR. Negotiations towards a comprehensive FTA with the United States started in 2003, and are still underway. The target date for completion is December 2006. SACU negotiated a Fixed Preferences Agreement, as a first step towards a FTA, with MERCOSUR. This agreement grants fixed margins of preferences in a limited number of tariff lines to either party. The agricultural offers cover approximately 33% of agricultural trade both ways. The agreement also has annexes on Safeguard Measures and on Dispute Settlement. At present, work continues to finalise some aspects of the agreement, including Rules of Origin, customs co-operation, and SPS measures. Implementation is envisaged for 2006. Further negotiations with Nigeria, Africa's most populated country and second largest economy, and the giant Asian markets of India and China, have been planned as well but negotiations are not yet underway.

South Africa is also a beneficiary of several preferential trade agreements such as: the US initiative African Growth and Opportunity Act (AGOA); and a Generalised System of Preferences (GSP) status with Canada, Norway, United States, Japan, Switzerland, and the European Union. The latter rejected South Africa's application to join the African Caribbean and Pacific (ACP) group, which implies that South Africa can participate in/ qualify for only tendering and procurement but not market access to the European Union.

2.4. Government expenditures on agro-food policies

This section gives an overview of government expenditure trends at the national and provincial level. The tables below are taken from the Intergovernmental Fiscal Review 2004, published by the Treasury with reference to financing agriculture. Concerning the financing of wider rural economic infrastructure, the expenditures provided are only estimates, as the line item budgetary reporting system does not disaggregate infrastructure for agriculture (*e.g.* rural roads are used for many economic and social services, water from dams is used as potable water, for industry, environment and irrigation.)

The combined budgets for the national and provincial departments of agriculture increased steadily between 2000/01 and 2003/04, rising from ZAR 3 billion to a projected ZAR 4.4 billion (Table 2.4). The combined budgets are expected to continue to grow over the Medium Term Expenditure Framework (MTEF), rising to ZAR 5.5 billion in 2006/07, an

Table 2.4. **Provincial and national agriculture expenditure, 2000/01 to 2006/07**

Million ZAR

	2000/01	2001/02	2002/03	2003/04[1]	2004/05[2]	2005/06[2]	2006/07[2]
Eastern Cape	451	563	572	752	898	781	822
Free State	118	120	146	210	211	226	243
Gauteng	66	50	70	62	81	92	104
KwaZulu-Natal	372	432	475	549	641	693	743
Limpopo	656	581	718	786	905	1 046	1 117
Mpumalanga	200	204	246	258	324	403	433
Northern Cape	55	58	71	75	93	104	112
North West	279	294	309	325	342	360	378
Western Cape	98	119	137	182	242	246	254
Total provinces	2 295	2 421	2 744	3 199	3 738	3 951	4 204
National[3]	705	843	893	1 198	1 079	1 195	1 287
Total	3 000	3 264	3 638	4 396	4 817	5 146	5 492

1. Preliminary.
2. Medium term estimates.
3. Excludes the Land Care projects and Comprehensive Agriculture Support Programme conditional grants which are included in the provinces.

Sources: National Treasury provincial database; 2004 Estimates of National Expenditure.

annual average increase over the seven-year period of 10.6%. Provinces account for 80% of total sector spending.

Remuneration of employees remained the largest share of budgetary spending, but declined from 72% in 2000/01 to 60% in 20002/03, and is forecast to fall further to 57% in 2006/07. Expenditures to enhance farmer support programmes, including infrastructure development, are increasing. Additional funds are allocated through the conditional grant scheme (ZAR 750 million above the 2004 MTEF) to implement the new framework for farmer support under the Comprehensive Agricultural Support Programme.

Table 2.5 and Figure 2.5 show provincial expenditures by programme and as a percentage of the total. The farmer support programme is currently the largest expenditure and is expected to register the largest absolute growth in coming years.

Table 2.5. **Provincial agriculture expenditure by programme, 2000/01 to 2006/07**

Million ZAR

	2000/01	2001/02	2002/03	2003/04[1]	2004/05[2]	2005/06[2]	2006/07[2]
Administration	658	593	663	736	843	886	931
Sustainable resource management	146	193	200	227	259	350	383
Farmer support and development	892	1 028	1 200	1 487	1 695	1 720	1 843
Veterinary services	293	255	279	303	361	389	411
Technology research and development services	209	247	292	308	339	345	360
Agricultural economics	15	17	20	30	60	65	68
Structured agricultural training	81	87	91	108	181	196	207
Total	2 295	2 421	2 744	3 199	3 738	3 951	4 204

1. Preliminary.
2. Medium term estimates.

Source: National Treasury provincial database; 2004 Estimates of National Expenditure.

Figure 2.5. **Composition of total provincial agriculture expenditure by programme, 2000/01 to 2006/07**

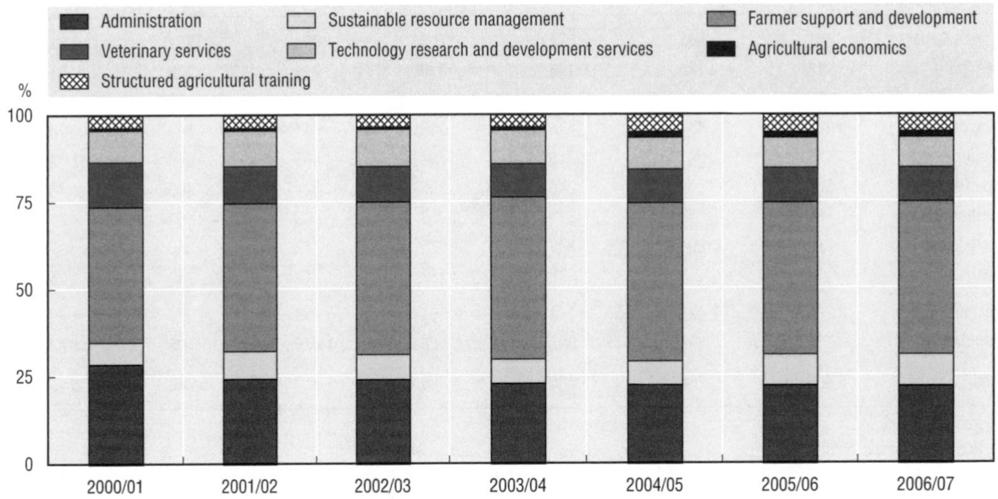

Source: National Treasury provincial database; 2004 Estimates of National Expenditure.

In general, the programme expenditure patterns of provinces differ considerably (Table 2.6 and Figure 2.6). However, it is not clear whether all provinces follow the same criteria and principles to allocate cost to administration and other individual programmes.

Table 2.7 presents national agriculture expenditures over the period 2000/01 to 2003/04, with budgetary estimates for the period 2004/05 to 2006/07. Farmer support and development is the largest programme and shows the most significant increase in expenditure. About 87% of the budgetary spending associated with this programme is allocated by the provinces with the remaining 13% at the National level.

Table 2.6. **Provincial agriculture expenditure by programme, 2004/05**

Million ZAR

	Administration	Sustainable resource management	Farmer support and development	Veterinary services	Technology research and development services	Agricultural economics	Structured agricultural training	Total
Eastern Cape	347	47	316	91	55	11	31	898
Free State	76	26	52	23	20	2 1	2	211
Gauteng	20	7	30	24	n.a.	n.a.	n.a.	81
KwaZulu-Natal	106	35	342	72	66	n.a.	19	641
Limpopo	140	53	591	21	22	17	60	905
Mpumalanga	44	37	95	47	66	13	21	324
Northern Cape	22	9	37	10	14	1	n.a.	93
North West	59	18	158	48	31	8	21	342
Western Cape	30	27	74	23	63	7	18	242
Total	843	259	1 695	361	339	60	181	3 738

n.a.: not available.

Source: Provincial Departments of Agriculture.

Figure 2.6. **Shares of provinces in aggregate provincial-level expenditures on agricultural programmes, 2004/05**

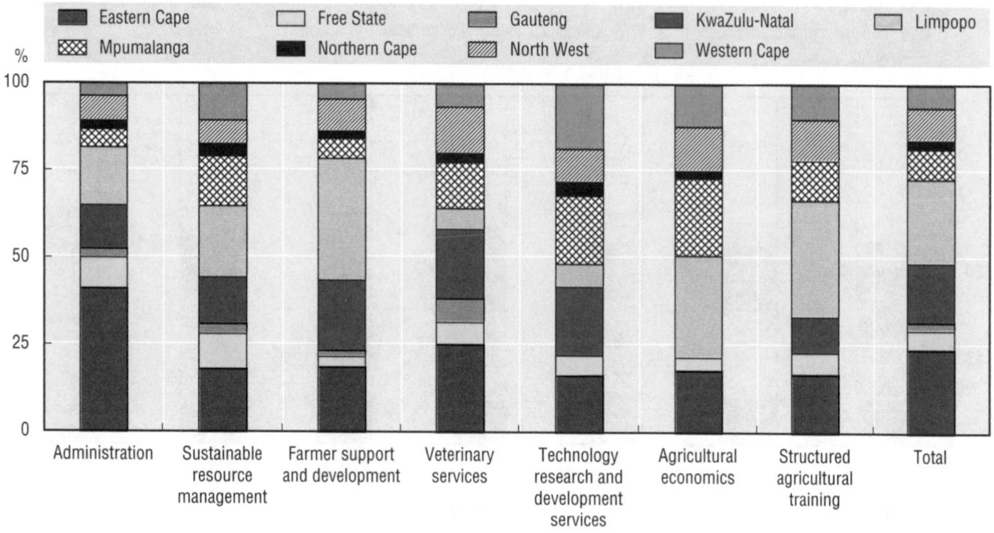

Source: Provincial Departments of Agriculture.

Table 2.7. **National agriculture expenditure by programme, 2000/01 to 2006/07**

Million ZAR

	2000/01	2001/02	2002/03	2003/04[1]	2004/05[2]	2005/06[2]	2006/07[2]
Administration	94	114	137	151	158	167	177
Farmer support and development	14	101	123	287	261	328	383
Sustainable resources management and use	125	123	122	135	165	180	196
National regulatory services	139	157	152	198	195	241	256
Communication and information management	50	60	75	81	83	87	92
Other programmes	302	315	309	382	445	481	529
Total	723	871	917	1 234	1 306	1 485	1 632

1. Preliminary.
2. Medium term estimates.
Source: National Treasury, 2004 Estimates of National Expenditure.

Apart from the budget expenditures of the National Department of Agriculture described above, increasing budgetary expenditures were linked with the implementation of the land reform programmes in South Africa (Table 2.8). While the overhead costs of the implementation of the land reform programme (personnel wages, administration, equipment, etc.) were increasing, especially in the first years of operation, the transfers to beneficiaries of land reform has been the most important expenditure component since 1997. Annual transfers show important year-to-year variations.

Figure 2.7. **Composition of total national agriculture expenditure by programme, 2000/01 to 2006/07**

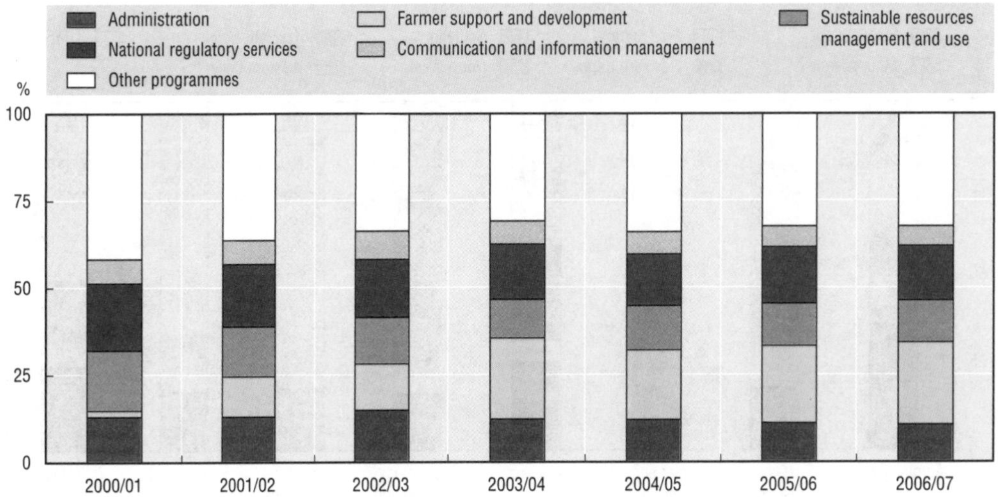

Source: National Treasury, 2004 Estimates of National Expenditure.

Table 2.8. **Budgetary expenditure on Land reform**

Million ZAR

	1994	1995	1996	1997	1998	1999	2000	2001	2002	2003
Personnel	2.2	4.4	9.0	15.1	28.2	37.6	42.0	42.7	46.7	47.1
Other administrative costs	0.4	3.0	4.2	27.7	21.8	27.6	29.2	28.2	28.3	32.6
Transfer payments	0.0	0.0	80.8	122.3	312.7	202.9	158.5	277.1	308.4	346.4
Total	2.7	7.5	94.1	165.2	362.8	268.1	229.6	348.0	383.4	426.1

Source: Department of Land Affairs.

2.5. Evaluation of policy instruments and institutional arrangements

Government intervention in agricultural marketing and trade prior to the beginning of the 1990s had severe distorting effects on agriculture. In the post-Second World War period, up to the 1980s, key sectors of agriculture were supported through prices maintained above the border parity, various subsidies, including preferential interest rates, and relatively favourable taxation rules. Agricultural policy reforms were initiated in the early 1980s as a response to the growing awareness that previous policies were fiscally unsustainable. The process was accelerated by political changes after 1994.

The institutional and policy reforms implemented by the South African government since 1994 have included the closure of the marketing boards and the agricultural credit board; abolition of certain tax concessions; reduction in direct input subsidies; introduction of new labour legislation in the sector; launch of a land reform (land restitution and redistribution) and programmes supporting the farmers benefiting from land reforms; and implementation of development programmes providing research and development services to the emerging farming sector.

Market support

There have been no interventions on domestic markets to support producer prices in South Africa since 1996. Although there is no longer direct state intervention, the sugar market remains a regulated market, and the mechanism applied[8] is implicitly taxing the consumers of sugar in South Africa.

A recent DoA discussion document on agricultural marketing identifies some ongoing frustration with the current marketing act, which fails to create a level playing field on which black farmers can compete effectively with their white counterparts in the marketing and selling of produce. The NAMC is seen by some as the instrument that should address this problem but it has no legislative power to act on the issue and there are no instruments, compatible with a market economy, which can enforce market access for a specific group of producers. However, the various market access facilitation activities described above, which are provided as a general service to the farming sector, could be more targeted to the emerging small-scale farming sector producing for domestic markets.

Some observations on the impacts of changes in market support on specific commodities sectors are presented below.

Field crops

The most important changes included the abolition of pan-territorial and pan-seasonal pricing mechanisms, with concomitant changes to physical access to the market, and to the food processing sector, and a range of institutional impacts. With deregulation, the major grain (maize, wheat) processing industries become more differentiated as the location of production shifted in response to differential prices across regions and over time. One of the first manifestations was that an increasing proportion of the maize crop is now milled by small-scale millers, both on- and off-farm (industry estimates suggest this can be as high as 30% of the crop).

The abolition of pan-territorial and pan-seasonal pricing has also had consequences for the rural finance sector. Under the control schemes, the control boards appointed agents, mostly farmer co-operatives, to carry out the physical functions of receipt of the crop, payment, storage, and onward consignment to the processors. These input supply co-operatives therefore became effective regional monopolies, which enabled them to become preferred suppliers of seasonal credit to farmers. They generally used the Land Bank loans as their source of funds. With deregulation, however, the commercial banks have been able to expand their share of this market.

Livestock products

There has been increased vertical integration in the supply chain, mainly fuelled by the large feedlots that own their own abattoirs and in some cases, also retail outlets. Some abattoirs are linked to feedlots or wholesalers or are owned by municipalities. Others belong to individual farmers, co-operatives or small to medium enterprises. Deregulation has also resulted in a rapid increase in the number of smaller abattoirs in the rural areas, mostly on-farm facilities that are combined with retail outlets or that supply directly to retailers in the formal market. One result is that the large metropolitan abattoirs are all running at less than a third of capacity, leading to severe financial problems for the holding company, ABACOR. Packaged meat is now generally transported to metropolitan areas.

There has also been movement away from auctions to less transparent negotiated prices between sellers and buyers.

The proportion of red meat sold in the informal sector directly onto poor urban and peri-urban communities has also increased. Live sheep and cattle are bought on the farm, or even delivered to these townships, and slaughtered at the roadside where the meat is sold raw or cooked in various forms. While it is known that this trade makes up a substantial proportion of total red meat sales, its exact magnitude has not been estimated. Similarly, there is an active market in pig and poultry by-products such as offal, chicken heads and feet.

Horticulture products

In the horticultural sector the recent reforms have the greatest impact on export markets. Previously, fresh deciduous and citrus fruit exports were marketed under "single channel pool" schemes, whereby producers were required to channel their produce into a pool operated by a statutory monopoly. The main impact of the reforms was an increase in the quality and quantities exported, as well as more destinations of exports, as literally hundreds of marketing and exporting agents entered the market, although only ten firms handle 85% of exports (Louw and Fourie, 2005).

The majority of vegetables are still sold on urban fresh produce markets, despite the increasing trend by the major retailers to source their fresh produce directly from contracted growers. Fresh produce agents operate on these markets and compete for both suppliers (vegetable producers) and buyers. Between 1994 and 2002, 32% of potatoes, 59% of tomatoes and 73% of onions were sold through these markets (Jooste and Dempers, 2005).

Input subsidies

Large-scale drought relief is no longer provided by the government. Instead, farmers are encouraged to use risk insurance for protection in case of natural disasters. The government's role consists of providing timely information on climate and market trends, to assist farmers in reducing risks. The state is narrowing its intervention and advocates for a stronger role of the private sector, including the provision of risk insurance. The Department of Agriculture is in the process of implementation of risk management strategies to reduce vulnerability of farmers to natural disasters and to alleviate poverty. Limited support is provided in the form of *ad hoc* disaster payments.

Under the reform of public spending and the fiscal regime in agriculture, several tax concessions were abolished or reduced, in particular the tax preferences related to capital investments where the one-year accelerated depreciation rule was lengthened to three years. This reduced the implicit subsidy for capital equipment although there is still a tax concession to agriculture as capital purchases in the other sectors have a five-year write-off period. In addition, capital improvements on farms are fully tax deductible and from 2001, a fuel tax rebate has also been applied on 80% of fuel consumption in agriculture.

Farm credit

Under reforms of agricultural financing, the Agricultural Credit Board ceased its operations and all interest rate subsidies were removed. The government is promoting the availability of financial services to small-scale and resource-poor farmers in obtaining access to formal financial markets, while ensuring that measures which assist poorer farmers to gain access to credit and other financial services do not inhibit the development of commercial, competitive financial services in the rural areas. Government action is mostly limited to measures to reduce both transaction costs and the high risk of lending.

The Micro-Agricultural Finance Schemes of South Africa (MAFISA) was established to provide micro credit and related services to the rural poor, leaving the Land Bank to deal with commercial agriculture. In principle, MAFISA is targeting those, who with the help of the loan, are able to establish a viable business and escape poverty. In this respect, careful client targeting and development/application of transparent selection criteria are of utmost importance to secure longer term financial viability of the programme.

Agri-environmental measures

The new agri-environmental policy initiatives are based on the recognition that not enough attention was being paid in the past to the promotion of farming methods that enhance soil and water conservation, whether in dry land crop production, irrigation farming or in the use of natural vegetation for animal production. The Agricultural Policy Discussion Document of 1998 recognised the possibility to use incentives to promote sustainable resource use through environmentally friendly farming practices. However, the underlying concept was that farmers must take primary responsibility for resource conservation at their own costs. It also suggested that existing tax incentives to promote soil conservation, which are in conflict with this principle, should be withdrawn. It is, however, unclear how these undertakings have been implemented.

Trade policy

The main objective of trade policy reform with respect to the agricultural sector, is to promote the integration of the sector into the global economy in order to encourage competition and greater access to markets, technology and capital. More specifically, the recent reforms seek to increase market access for the country's agricultural products, and to increase the trade in competitive South African agricultural goods in international and domestic markets. The South African government regards the World Trade Organization (WTO) framework as a means to improve market access for South African agricultural exports, and to protect local agricultural industries against unfair trade practices.

In general, the tariffs regime has been simplified and the level of tariffs reduced during the 1990s. In most cases the applied tariffs are well bellow the bound rates. However, for some products (maize, wheat, sugar) tariff schedule remains complex (formula tariffs), and applied tariffs are changing frequently (for more detailed information on tariffs see Section 2.3). This may create uncertainty for businesses that frequently import goods and isolate the domestic markets from price changes on world markets.

No export subsidies have been applied since the 1996 reforms, but the regime applied on the sugar cane/sugar market is effectively subsidising sugar exports and taxes implicitly the domestic sugar consumers. The government assists the private sector by providing financial support for the development of general services to exporters, such as maintaining information systems, marketing and research activities, and provision of training to develop export marketing expertise. Pest and disease control and inspection services also contribute to the enhancement of export activities, as well as access to the general schemes supporting exports applied by the Department of Trade and Industry (DTI) such as: the Export Marketing and Investment Assistance Scheme; shipment financing through the Credit Guarantee Insurance Corporation; and export promotion support through trade fairs, trade missions and diplomatic missions.

Infrastructure developments

While the agricultural budget was reduced, public investments in critical areas, such as infrastructure and health, are increasing. Rural economic infrastructure developments, such as rural transport, telecommunication and information technologies, are crucial for agricultural markets. Not all farmers in South Africa have access to the telecommunication and/or electricity networks. Transport and communications have been singled out as the most obvious infrastructural barriers to boosting the agricultural and rural market economy. Rural entrepreneurs who are in touch with product, input and financial markets, can invest resources in rural areas more effectively, thereby promoting economic growth.

Equally important are the provision of social services and investments in infrastructure that will provide a knowledgeable, skilled, healthy, economically active society in rural areas. Just as transport and communication are the priority drivers for economic activity, education, skills development and health are the priority drivers for human capital development and welfare. These issues are key to agricultural productivity and economic growth as well as to the development of rural areas and addressing the issues of poverty and underdevelopment in rural areas.

Institutional reforms

All three tiers of government are involved in agriculture (central, provincial, and municipal). According to the present Constitution of South Africa, agriculture is classified as a concurrent national and provincial function, which includes specified legislative competencies. The stated process of restructuring of the public sector includes the "provincialisation" of various state institutions, the restructuring of important statutory bodies with a development mandate in the rural areas (e.g. the Development Bank of Southern Africa and the Land Bank), and the reorientation of the Agricultural Research Council (ARC). The government has taken a number of measures to restructure rural financial markets with the objective of building, from the bottom up, a system of financial services that provides broader access for all. The central government has embarked on a programme of privatisation of state-owned enterprises, and closing those which are considered non-viable.

In contrast with the previous dispensation local (municipal) government boundaries have been extended to include also rural farm land. Local government has however also been given a very strong economic development mandate that is inter alia embodied in integrated economic development plans (IDPs), which must cover all economic sectors including agriculture. Besides taxes (property) and services, local government has a much more direct impact on farming than in the past. Local communities are taking over the responsibility for projects currently managed by the state. Local governance policy is aimed at the creation of administrative efficiency and financially viable structures with local governments used as delivery vehicles for Local Economic Development (LED). The implementation of policies closer to the local levels provide an opportunity for better targeting and tailoring of policy measures to local needs and conditions.

Regulatory system

The deregulation of domestic agricultural markets and the liberalisation of agricultural trade have increased, rather than decreased, the need for an effective system of food safety and quality standards for agriculture and food products. As a member of the WTO and signatory to the SPS and TBT Agreements, South Africa has a well developed and transparent set of regulatory requirements for agricultural production and trade based on internationally agreed standards. The government is moving to greater industry self-regulation with user fees for government provided services.

Research and development

The government is investing in on-farm and communal land infrastructure. However, the reduction in funding in real terms has had serious repercussion for the implementation of land reform programmes and for the funding of agricultural research. One of the serious consequences of the declining agricultural research budget has been the loss of senior research staff. About 80% of doctoral level research staff have left for the private sector. For budgetary reasons, the Agricultural Research Council is increasingly undertaking contract research for private sector entities that may not be aligned to the strategic research requirements of the policy makers. The limited public resources financing agricultural research and development are increasingly targeted to the needs of the farmers benefiting from the land reform and willing to set viable commercial businesses in agriculture.

Training and education

Given the low skill levels in rural areas, agricultural extension services are critical to any development strategy. Extension is the most important part of agricultural services budget in most of the provinces, especially in those provinces with underdeveloped rural areas: Limpopo (76%), North West Province (60%), and Eastern Cape (59%). These provinces inherited the former homelands and had to amalgamate various departments and agriculture schemes into a single provincial department. The majority of their personnel lack appropriate skills to provide the necessary support services to farmers. One of the challenges facing the provincial agriculture departments is reducing their share of expenditure on salaries (i.e. reduce the numbers), while simultaneously expanding their skills base. A 1997 study, commissioned by the DoA, found that whereas in other countries expenditure on salaries were, on average, 55%, expenditures for extension staff in some South African provinces was as high as 95%, leaving very little budget for running costs.

Critics of the formal education system identify as a major shortcoming of the present national agricultural education and training programme the lack of public accountability, policy formulation and co-ordination and strategic guidance. The DoA has recently introduced a National Strategy for Education and Training for Agriculture and Rural Development in South Africa to address these issues.

Consumer support

There is no implicit support to consumers through regulated food prices. In fact, consumers are implicitly taxed through import tariffs. However, some basic foods are exempt from the VAT, and there is a programme financing the distribution of food parcels to poor households. Additional measures link recipients of food parcels to social safety nets and provide poor agricultural households with gardening supplies. These two measures have the potential to provide a longer term and more sustainable solution to food security in rural areas, while the distribution of food parcels is viewed as an emergency measure.

Land reform

Under the land reform programme, the land restitution programme is well advanced and the main challenge has been land redistribution. Redistribution was initially aimed at poor black communities, who had no or insufficient land, and provided state grants, initially under *the Settlement/Land Acquisition grant* (SLAG). From 2000, support was under the *Land Redistribution for Agricultural Development* (LRAD) programme, which also provides grants for those intending to establish commercial farms. The *Comprehensive Agricultural Support Programme* (CASP) programme (introduced in 2004) provides support and development services.

There is a broad-based consensus emerging among the various stakeholders that South Africa needs to resolve its outstanding land issues as a matter of urgency, though much controversy surrounds the specifics of how this should be done. The key issues are how to a) harness market forces to redistribute land from the rich to the poor; b) improve the processes of land acquisition and resettlement; and c) create stakeholder consensus around the implementation strategy. If agreement can be reached on a policy framework which allows a menu of options to be pursued, the results can then be monitored, evaluated and modified as the programme proceeds.

The government needs to engage stakeholders in dialogue around policy implementation. Stakeholders, including local government structures, farmers associations, NGOs, and churches, can assist in a number of ways. They can identify programme priorities, support applicants in accessing the various land reform programmes, and provide follow-up technical assistance to successful beneficiaries. NGOs and research institutions can provide valuable monitoring and evaluation services, and assist in policy development. The World Bank has examined the situation closely and provides the following recommendations.

Developing a menu of land acquisition options

The overall policy objective would be to have a ready set of complementary land acquisition methods that have been tested and made operational. An improved policy framework would thus consist of a package of at least three options for land acquisition: compulsory acquisition, market-assisted or community-driven land acquisition, or negotiated land transfers. Governments should add variants, adapted to local circumstances, of these options to their policy "tool kit" and start a "learning-by-doing" process, flexible enough to be scaled up when good results are obtained. Legal mechanisms which transfer the ownership directly, or almost directly, from the former owner to the beneficiaries, may be considered to avoid a lengthy transfer of ownership during which the state has to ensure the security of the asset "in transit".

Simplifying acquisition of sub-divisions

Land acquisition options need to include the acquisition of subdivisions, rather than whole farms. In such a case, the state will not be interested in acquiring the whole farm for redistribution, but rather a part of it, provided that the rest of the farm remains commercially viable. Under South African conditions, this method should be considered for various reasons:

● It avoids costly experiments by beneficiaries to attempt keeping the commercial parts running under collective farming arrangements.

● It saves on acquisition costs, by not acquiring what is probably the most expensive part of the farm, and also the part of the farm initially least likely to be effectively used for production purposes by small-scale farmers.

● Acquiring subdivisions would create new farm "neighbourhoods" in which the new neighbours may be able to work together and help each other (the tutorial role of the skilled farmers is an important vehicle to bring the existing human potential into the land reform process).

Decentralise decision-making

South Africa's experience with land redistribution since 1994 confirms the international lessons that underline the need to decentralise and make programmes more community-driven. South Africa's flagship redistribution programme, LRAD, made the important step of decentralising decision-making down to the provincial level, and reaped immediate benefits in terms of speed and the quantity of projects implemented. The logical next step is to decentralise even further to the district level, followed by further decentralisation down to the municipal level. Redistribution would become more in-line with local conditions and the capacities and needs of the beneficiaries. As vertical accountability is relaxed, horizontal and downward accountability, and integration between programmes should be strengthened. The land reform programmes could then become an integral part of the local development plans, which in South Africa are the basis for local development budgeting and implementation.

2.6. Evaluation of support to South African agriculture

This Section presents a quantitative evaluation of support provided to South African agriculture through its agricultural policies, which were described in Sections 2.2 and 2.3. The evaluation is based on the standard method developed by the OECD Secretariat to asses the levels of support in member countries, and consists of a series of agricultural support indicators such as the Producer Support Estimate (PSE), Consumer Support Estimate (CSE), Total Support Estimate (TSE) and General Services Support Estimate (GSSE) (see Box 2.2 for definitions). Such assessment is also done for a widening range of non-member economies which are large players on world agro-food markets (*e.g.* Brazil, China, Russia, and Ukraine), and now for the first time, for South Africa.

An overall evaluation of support is presented first, followed by a commodity-specific focus on South Africa's main agricultural commodities. The evaluation covers the period 1994-2003 and is based on 14 commodities,[9] which account for about 74% of the total value of agricultural output in South Africa.

Box 2.2. **OECD indicators of support to agriculture: Definitions**

Producer Support Estimate (PSE): An indicator of the annual monetary value of gross transfers from consumers and taxpayers to support agricultural producers, measured at farm gate level, arising from policy measures, regardless of their nature, objectives or impacts on farm production or income. The PSE measures support arising from policies targeted to agriculture relative to a situation without such policies – i.e. when producers are subject only to general policies (including economic, social, environmental and tax policies) of the country. The PSE is a **gross** notion implying that any costs associated with those policies and incurred by individual producers are not deducted. It is also a **nominal assistance** notion meaning that increased costs associated with import duties on inputs are not deducted. But it is an indicator **net** of producer contributions to help finance the policy measure (e.g. producer levies) providing a given transfer to producers. The PSE includes implicit and explicit transfers. The **%PSE** is the ratio of the PSE to the value of total gross farm receipts, measured by the value of total production (at farm gate prices), plus budgetary support.

Producer Nominal Assistance Coefficient (NACp): An indicator of the nominal rate of assistance to producers measuring the ratio between the value of gross farm receipts including support and gross farm receipts valued at world market prices without support.

Producer Nominal Assistance Coefficient (NPCp): An indicator of the nominal rate of protection for producers measuring the ratio between the average price received by producers (at farm gate), including payments per ton of current output, and the border price (measured at farm gate level).

Consumer Support Estimate (CSE): An indicator of the annual monetary value of gross transfers to (from) consumers of agricultural commodities, measured at the farm gate (first consumer) level, arising from policy measures which support agriculture, regardless of their nature, objectives or impact on consumption of farm products. The CSE includes explicit and implicit transfers from consumers associated with: market price support on domestically produced consumption (transfers to producers from consumers); transfers to the budget and/or importers on the share of consumption that is imported (other transfers from consumers). It is **net** of any payment to consumers to compensate them for their contribution to market price support of a specific commodity (consumer subsidy from taxpayers); and the producer contribution (as consumers of domestically produced crops) to the market price support on crops used in animal feed (**excess feed cost**). When negative, transfers from consumers measure the implicit tax on consumption associated with policies to the agricultural sector. Although consumption expenditure is increased/reduced by the amount of the implicit tax/subsidy, this indicator is not in itself an estimate of the impacts on consumption expenditure. The **%CSE** is the ratio of the CSE to the total value of consumption expenditure on commodities domestically produced, measured by the value of total consumption (at farm gate prices) minus budgetary support to consumers (consumer subsidies).

Consumer Nominal Assistance Coefficient (NACc): An indicator of the nominal rate of assistance to consumers measuring the ratio between the value of consumption expenditure on agricultural commodities domestically produced including support to producers and that valued at world market prices without support to consumers.

Consumer Nominal Assistance Coefficient NPCc): An indicator of the nominal rate of protection for consumers measuring the ratio between the average price paid by consumers (at farm gate) and the border price (measured at farm gate level).

Box 2.2. **OECD indicators of support to agriculture: Definitions** *(cont.)*

General Services Support Estimate (GSSE): An indicator of the annual monetary value of gross transfers to services provided collectively to agriculture and arising from policy measures which support agriculture, regardless of their nature, objectives and impacts on farm production, income, or consumption of farm products. It includes taxpayer transfers to: improve agricultural production (research and development); agricultural training and education (agricultural schools); control of quality and safety of food, agricultural inputs, and the environment (inspection services); improving off-farm collective infrastructures, including downstream and upstream industry (infrastructures); assist marketing and promotion (marketing and promotion); meet the costs of depreciation and disposal of public storage of agricultural products (public stockholding); and other general services that cannot be disaggregated and allocated to the above categories due, for example, to a lack of information (miscellaneous). Unlike the PSE and CSE transfers, these transfers are not received by producers or consumers individually and do not affect farm receipts (revenue) or consumption expenditure by their amount, although they may affect production and consumption of agricultural commodities. The **%GSSE** is the ratio of the GSSE to the *Total Support Estimate*.

Total Support Estimate (TSE): An indicator of the annual monetary value of all gross transfers from taxpayers and consumers arising from policy measures which support agriculture, net of the associated budgetary receipts, regardless of their objectives and impact on farm production and income, or consumption of farm products. The TSE is the sum of the explicit and implicit gross transfers from consumers of agricultural commodities to agricultural producers net of producer financial contributions (in MPS and CSE); the gross transfers from taxpayers to agricultural producers (in PSE); the gross transfers from taxpayers to general services provided to agriculture (GSSE); and the gross transfers from taxpayers to consumers of agricultural commodities (in CSE). As the transfers from consumers to producers are included in the MPS, the TSE is also the sum of the PSE, the GSSE, and the transfers from taxpayers to consumers (in CSE). The TSE measures the overall transfers associated with agricultural support, financed by consumers (transfers from consumers) and taxpayers (transfers from taxpayers) net of import receipts (budget revenues). The **%TSE** is the ratio of the TSE to GDP.

Aggregate results

Producer Support Estimate

As measured by the aggregate percentage PSE, producer support in South Africa equalled 5% of the gross farm receipts in 2000-03, indicating a relatively moderate degree of policy interventions at the agricultural producer level (Table 2.9).[10]

Table 2.9. **South Africa: Percentage PSEs and CSEs, 1994-2003**

	1994	1995	1996	1997	1998	1999	2000	2001	2002	2003	2000-03 average
Percentage PSE	10	16	8	12	8	9	5	2	8	5	5
Percentage CSE	−11	−17	−9	−12	−7	−8	−5	−1	−6	−3	−3

Source: OECD PSE/CSE database, 2005.

Figure 2.8. **PSE by country, EU[1] and OECD, 2000-03 average**

As per cent of gross farm receipts

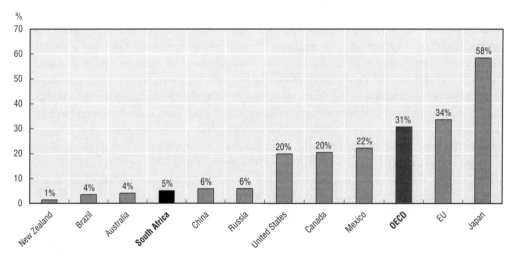

1. 2000-03: EU15.

Source: OECD PSE/CSE database, 2005.

A comparison of producer support in South Africa and the principal world agricultural players shows that support in South Africa is at the same level as in China and Russia, and somewhat above that in Brazil, New Zealand and Australia – the latter three being the countries with the lowest measured policy interventions (Figure 2.8). The percentage PSE in South Africa is nevertheless far below the OECD average (31%).[11]

The moderate average level of support in South Africa, however, disguises marked year to year variations – especially in the initial and the most recent years of the analysed period – with the percentage PSE fluctuating between 2% and 16% (Figure 2.9).

The strong variations in the support level are the result of diverse – at times complementing, at times opposing – policy impacts. One major force was the progressive overall trade deregulation, with the reduction in border protection and elimination of export subsidies. This overall pressure towards lesser protection, and therefore, lesser

Figure 2.9. **Composition of Producer Support Estimate, 1994-2003**

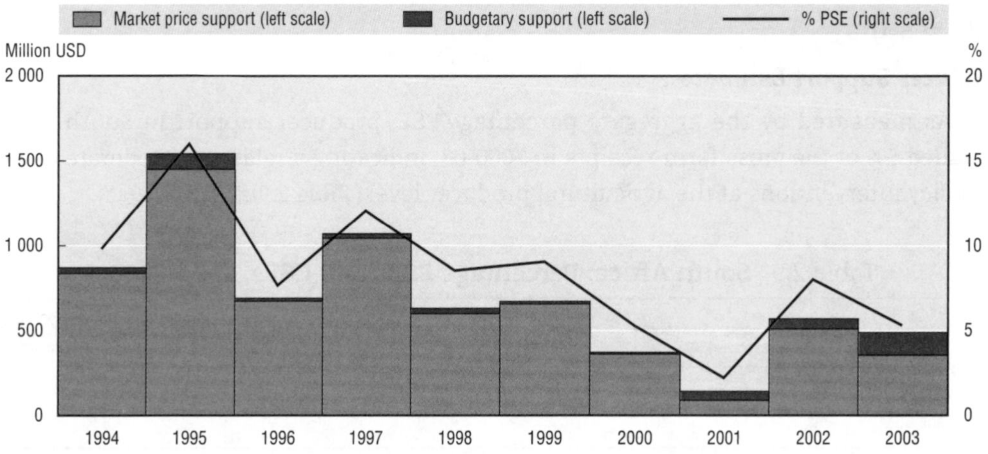

| ■ Market price support (left scale) | ■ Budgetary support (left scale) | —— % PSE (right scale) |

Source: OECD PSE/CSE database, 2005.

Box 2.3. **Fluctuations in exchange rates and world prices:
Implications for interpretation of producer support**

The discussion of annual PSE changes in South Africa shows that exchange rate and world price fluctuations have an important impact on the measured producer support. The origin of these impacts is in the Market Price Support (MPS) component of the PSE, which is estimated on the basis of price gaps between domestic and world prices.

Before the domestic market price can be compared with world price, it has to be converted into domestic currency, and the exchange rate is introduced into the calculations. Therefore, movements in world prices and exchange rates, which are not accompanied by an equivalent change in domestic prices, affect the measured MPS and the PSE. This may lead to a conclusion that the PSE, which is a measure of agricultural policies, captures non-agricultural policy impacts and may give rise to the following question: "Is it possible that agricultural policies do not change, but the MPS and the PSE change?" In this respect it is useful to consider the interplay between exchange rate and world price variations, agricultural policies and the functioning of markets.

In the model of an ideally functioning market economy, where the law of one price holds (i.e. arbitrage eliminates price differences between locations except for transaction costs), and in the absence of agricultural policies that alter the prices farmers receive for their output, the domestic market price is identical with the world market price (except for transaction costs). Hence, all changes in the world market price, expressed in domestic currency, are directly reflected in the domestic price, regardless of whether it is the world market price in foreign currency or the exchange rate that has changed. In this case, the gap between domestic and world price is zero and not affected by exchange rate variations. With an agricultural policy that insulates the domestic price against changes in the world market price, a non-zero price gap is measured. This is the explicit policy component of MPS that results directly from policy parameters set by governments. Even if these parameters are not changing, the price gap would change with variations in both the world market price in foreign currency and the exchange rate. In this situation it would not be correct to interpret the PSE change that is related to a movement in the exchange rate as being a result of currency developments. This is a result of an agricultural policy that has shielded the domestic market against influences originating in the world market and prevented domestic prices to adjust in line with the world prices. This is the implicit working of policy due to the fact that domestic policy settings do not adjust to current market developments. In fact, a situation where, for example, domestic support price (and hence the domestic market price) remains constant, while the border price (expressed in domestic currency) fluctuates, can be described as one in which the explicit policy component is unchanged, while implicit policy component varies over time. The total policy effect being the sum of the explicit and the implicit policy components then also varies over time.

In the real world, the law of one price does not hold perfectly, and hence there may be price gaps between domestic and world markets even in the absence of specific agricultural policies that create price wedges. This has to be considered when interpreting the price-related component of the PSE. The issue is particularly relevant for countries with imperfectly functioning markets and experiencing macroeconomic instability. Lags in market response due to adjustment processes may involve time for domestic prices to respond to a change in the world market price (resulting from either a price change in foreign currency or a variation in the exchange rate). In many non-OECD countries, with South Africa being no exception, such lags in market response have been rather pronounced, particularly in the years of sharp exchange rate adjustments.[*] In such periods,

Box 2.3. **Fluctuations in exchange rates and world prices:**
Implications for interpretation of producer support (cont.)

a variation in the exchange rate may result in a change in the price gap, which emerges independently of applied agricultural measures. Ideally this effect should be filtered out before the price-related component of the PSE is measured. However, this highly complicated task goes far beyond the realistically feasible MPS measurement effort. Thus, the results may be affected to a greater or lesser degree by exchange rate variations over and above the pure effects of agricultural measures applied. The interpretation of the PSE results for countries undergoing considerable economic adjustment, such as South Africa, should therefore carefully keep this in mind.

* A lag in market response may also be seen as partly due to government policies, or more precisely, a lack of appropriate policies for development of systems, which facilitate the pass-through of international price signals, such as transport infrastructure, communications, and market information.

Source: The text draws strongly on Tangermann, S. (2003), "Agricultural Policies in OECD Countries Ten Years After the Uruguay Round: How Much Progress?". Paper presented at the International Conference on Agricultural Policy Reform and the WTO: Where Are We Heading? Capri, 23-26 June 2003; Tangermann, S. (2005), "Is the Concept of the Producer Support Estimate in Need of Revision?" Working Paper, OECD, Paris.

producer support, was partly counter-balanced by the system of variable import tariffs, which were maintained for some principal commodities, such as maize, wheat and sugar. Over and above these specific policies, substantial exchange rate fluctuations produced shifts in relative levels of domestic and external prices, thus strongly contributing to annual changes in the measured support.[12] Thus, an appreciation of the *rand* in 1995, without an immediate equivalent transmission to domestic agricultural product prices, led to a temporary strengthening of domestic prices against external prices, and the consequent increase in the Market Price Support (MPS). In the following year the percentage PSE more than halved, as domestic prices adjusted to currency appreciation. The continued phasing-out of export support programmes added to the fall in support. The support stayed at around this level until 1999, except when it peaked in 1997, due mainly to weakening of external prices, which was not fully transmitted to South Africa's domestic markets.

The accelerated depreciation of the *rand* in 2000 and, particularly, in 2001, strongly dampened domestic prices relative to world levels, MPS declined and drove the percentage PSE down. Although the currency depreciation continued into 2002, its dampening effect on the relative level of domestic prices was offset by the weakening of the dollar world prices for many important commodities. An additional factor contributing to the pick-up of the PSE in 2002 was an almost doubling of the domestic price for white maize – a commodity with an important production weight in South Africa. The outcome was a marked rise in the overall level of support in 2002. In 2003 the percentage PSE was approximately at its level in the late 1990s, reflecting the appreciation of the *rand* and an increase in budgetary allocations.

Composition of the PSE

As is seen from Figure 2.9, the overwhelming share of producer support in South Africa is delivered in the form of Market Price Support (MPS). This suggests that overall price distortions continue to be a feature of agricultural markets in South Africa. Budgetary transfers, although showing a tendency to increase in the current decade (mainly due to the introduction of the fuel tax rebate and spending on land reform), have marginal importance as a source of producer support.

Consumer Support Estimate

The Consumer Support Estimate (CSE) is an indicator which measures the cost of producer support to consumers of agricultural products. In the OECD PSE methodology the consumer is understood as the first stage buyer of these products. In South Africa the CSE represents a mirror image of the Market Price Support provided to farmers, as there are no budgetary transfers to consumers. The South African percentage CSE fluctuated between – 1% and –17% in 1994-2003, averaging –3% for the 2000-03 period (Table 2.9), indicating a burden placed on food consumers.

Total Support Estimate

The Total Support Estimate (TSE) is the broadest indicator of support, representing the sum of transfers to agricultural producers (as measured by the PSE), expenditure for general services to the sector as a whole (as measured by the GSSE), and direct budgetary transfers to consumers.

The General Services Support Estimate (GSSE) encompasses all types of public provision of common and shared support to the agricultural sector. This sector-wide provision of support (as opposed to individual provision of support to farms) is what distinguishes the general services support from that measured by the PSE. The GSSE includes public expenditures on agricultural research, education, infrastructural development, crop and veterinary inspection, marketing and promotion, etc. Direct budgetary transfers to consumers represent the subsidy destined to reduce the effect of agricultural price support on prices paid by consumers. No such payments are made in South Africa.

The aggregate TSE in South Africa reached ZAR 6.3 billion (USD 748 million) per year in 2000-03 (Table 2.10). Expressed in per cent of GDP, the TSE indicates the relative cost of support to the overall economy. The South African percentage TSE fluctuated over the analysed period, reaching on average 0.6%, which is slightly above one half of the OECD level, and about the same percentage TSE level as Russia and Brazil. The cost of total support to the economy in South Africa is however, far less than in China or Turkey – countries with significant weights of the agricultural sectors in their economies (Figure 2.10).

Table 2.10. **Total support to South African agriculture, 1994-2003**

	1994	1995	1996	1997	1998	1999	2000	2001	2002	2003	2000-03 average
Total support estimate (TSE), million ZAR	5 116	7 464	5 207	6 758	5 490	6 130	4 701	3 575	8 907	7 985	6 292
of which:											
Producer support estimate (PSE)	3 091	5 033	2 961	4 926	3 503	4 107	2 586	1 210	5 997	3 689	3 371
General services (GSSE)	2 025	2 430	2 246	1 833	1 986	2 023	2 116	2 365	2 911	4 296	2 922
Transfers to consumers from taxpayers	0	0	0	0	0	0	0	0	0	0	0
Total support estimate (TSE)											
Million USD	1 441	2 283	1 211	1 466	989	1 002	676	415	846	1 055	748
Million EUR	1 215	1 746	954	1 294	884	940	734	463	898	941	759
TSE as share of GDP, %	1.2	1.5	0.9	1.1	0.8	0.8	0.6	0.4	0.8	0.7	0.6

Source: OECD PSE/CSE database, 2005.

Figure 2.10. **Total Support Estimate in South Africa and selected countries, 2000-03 average**

As % GDP

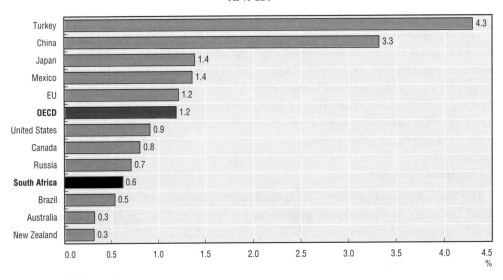

Source: OECD PSE/CSE database, 2005.

Figure 2.11 illustrates the relative importance of each component – the PSE and the GSSE – in South Africa's TSE. Around 55% of total support to agriculture in 1994-2003 was delivered in the form of the transfers to producers (the PSE). The remaining assistance was provided through the general services to the sector. The budgetary spending on general services finances mainly the research, development and training, the investments in infrastructure, inspection and control services, and administration of land reform. Most of the general services (*e.g.* training and infrastructure) are increasingly targeted to the emerging small farmers benefiting from the land reform.

Figure 2.11. **Composition of the Total Support Estimate in South Africa, 1994-2003**

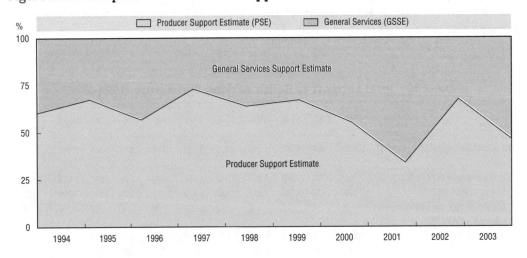

Source: OECD PSE/CSE database, 2005.

Commodity profile of producer support

Level of producer support by commodities

There are marked differences in the levels of support across individual commodities – with the average percentage PSE ranging from 23% for sugar to around zero for a range of other commodities (Figure 2.12). A wide cross-commodity spread in the level of support indicates considerable distortions in the allocation of resources in the sector.

Sugar is the most supported commodity receiving support far above the average level. This is notable given that sugar is one of South Africa's key exports (around one-half of sugar production is exported). The situation is explained by the pricing system under which South African sugar producers are effectively compensated for export losses by higher prices for domestic sales compared to that destined for exports.

Sheepmeat, milk and maize are the other commodities receiving the above-average support, which is however far below that for sugar and closer to the average level. Support for these commodities is based predominantly on border protection. It should be also noted that a relatively high average PSE for maize in 2000-03 is largely explained by an abnormal price spike for white maize in 2002. The latter also explains a relatively high feed cost and the resulting negative average PSEs for poultry and eggs in 2000-03.

Distribution of producer support across commodities

The distribution of total producer support across commodities reflects not only the relation between domestic and international price levels and the scale of budgetary assistance to specific commodities, but also the relative importance of these commodities to overall agricultural production. The cross-commodity distribution of total producer support is strongly skewed in South Africa (Figure 2.13). One half of the aggregate transfers to producers in 2000-03 were directed to just two products, maize and sugar cane, and another 16% to sheepmeat and milk. These are the four commodities which also receive the highest relative support (as measured by the percentage PSEs). Aggregate policy transfers to (from) other products are low or marginal.

Figure 2.12. **South African PSEs by commodity, 2000-03 average**

As per cent of gross farm receipts

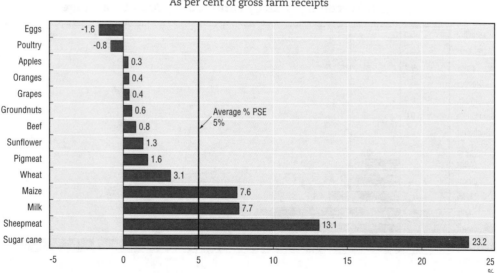

Source: OECD PSE/CSE database, 2005.

Figure 2.13. **Distribution of total producer support by commodity, 2000-03 average**

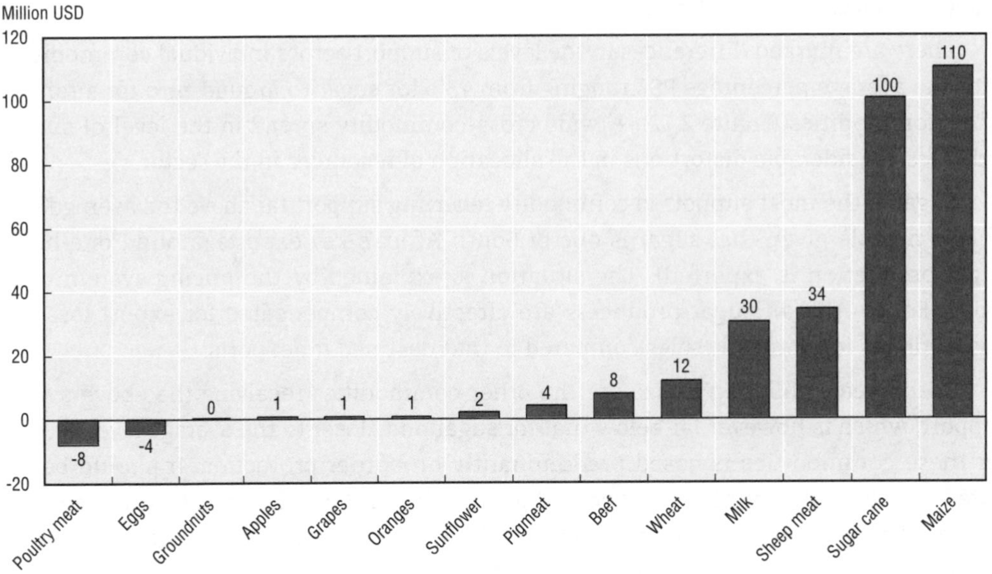

Million USD

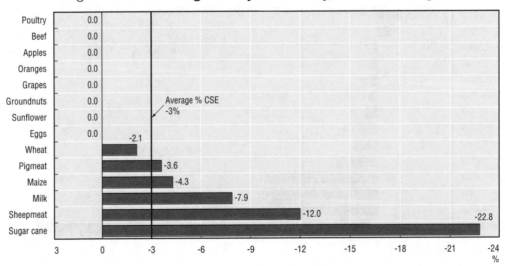

Source: OECD PSE/CSE database, 2005.

The Producer Nominal Protection Coefficient (NPCp) corresponds to an effective tariff, protecting agricultural commodities from competing imports. The aggregate producer NPC (a weighted average of commodity-specific NPCs) shows that policies in South Africa created an overall level of domestic market protection equivalent to an effective average tariff of 5% (a NACp of 1.05 in 2000-03). Among individual commodities, sugar and sheepmeat are under the highest protection, while other commodities receive either relatively moderate or no effective tariff protection.

The percentage CSEs by commodity (Figure 2.14) indicate that policies tax consumers mostly on sugar cane, sheepmeat and milk. For other products policy distortions affecting consumers are marginal.

Figure 2.14. **Percentage CSE by commodity, 2000-03 average**

Source: OECD PSE/CSE database, 2005.

OECD REVIEW OF AGRICULTURAL POLICIES – ISBN 92-64-03679-2 – © OECD 2006

Conclusions

The analysis of agricultural support in South Africa leads to the following general conclusions.

- The average percentage PSE in South Africa indicates rather moderate policy distortions at the agricultural producer level, with producer support far below the OECD average and close to that in other non-OECD countries monitored.

- The moderate average level of producer support, however, disguises marked annual changes. The latter were largely driven by the exchange rate and world price fluctuations, resulting in strong shifts in relative levels of domestic and world market prices and consequently, the measured support.

- Assistance to producers is almost entirely provided in the form of Market Price Support – through border protection and the regulated pricing system in the sugar sector. Budgetary transfers to producers are low relative to the Market Price Support, but tend to rise in recent years.

- The cross-commodity spread of support levels is important. Sugar receives the highest support, which is far above the average; this sector is the major source of overall price distortions in the agricultural sector.

- Within the total transfers to the agricultural sector (the TSE), producer support (the PSE) is the most important component, accounting for 55% of the TSE. The remaining support is provided through general services, which become increasingly focused on emerging small farmers who are the beneficiaries of the land reform.

- The cost of agricultural support to the South African economy (%TSE) is roughly one-half of the OECD average. Compared with other non-OECD countries, %TSE in South Africa is close to that in Brazil or Russia, but much less than in China.

Notes

1. The permanent closure of some control boards have not been achieved up to date due to outstanding legal issues.

2. Thus, wherever in the text below we refer to the Land Redistribution for Agricultural Development sub-programme, or "LRAD", we exclude the municipal and tribal commonage aspect.

3. Before 1994, the commercial farmers were divided into three categories according to their financial situation: Category I – farmers serviced by commercial banks; Category II – farmers serviced by Land bank; Category III – farmers serviced by the Agricultural Credit Board (ten-year mortgage loans and short-term production loans).

4. Between April 1994 and April 1996 the ACB handled 5 458 successful applications; 4 709 of these applications were for production loans and half of these were handled via 21 ACB agents (applications were mainly for land purchase, tractors and implements, with small amounts for irrigation and dairy equipment and livestock). In the same period the ACB handled 217 applications for debt consolidation, at an average of ZAR 10 955 and totalling ZAR 2.4 million.

5. While the ACB and the Land Bank have historically served mostly white commercial farmers, black emerging farmers have been served by Provincial Development Finance Corporations (PDFCs), such as the KwaZulu Finance Corporation, Agriwane, the Agricultural Development Banks of Ciskei and Transkei, and the Agribank of the North West Province. Evaluations of the PDFCs show that their outreach has been poor and their costs extremely high.

6. Given recent increases in the Land Bank interest rates, this observation may no longer be true.

7. The SADC is not a customs union contrary to SACU.

8. Under the sugar agreement, a price pooling system is applied and the producers are given quotas of production to be sold on domestic markets. The South African Sugar Association (SASA) is the only exporter of sugar.

9. Wheat, maize, sunflower, groundnuts, sugar cane, apples, oranges, table grapes, milk, beef, pigmeat, sheep, poultry, and eggs.

10. For more detailed results see Annex Table 2.A1.5 to 2.A1.8, and Annex Figures 2.A1.1 to 2.A1.11.

11. For additional country-comparative data see Annex Table 2.A1.7.

12. See Box 2.3 for discussion of the impact of exchange rate and world price fluctuations on the measured support and its interpretation.

ANNEX 2.A1

Supporting Tables and Figures

Table 2.A1.1. **The roles of Departments serving agriculture**

	Land Affairs	Agriculture	Water Affairs and Forestry	Environmental Affairs	Trade and Industry
National	Policy formulation	Policy formulation	Policy formulation	Policy formulation	Policy formulation
	Regulatory framework	Regulatory framework	Regulatory framework	Regulatory framework	Regulatory framework
	Strategies allocation	Budgeting	Strategies allocation	Strategies allocation	Strategies allocation
	Budget	Design institutional framework	Budget	Budget	Budget
Provincial	Adapt strategy	Design provincial strategy	Adapt strategy	Adapt sStrategy	Adapt strategy
	Setting of operational targets	Manage implementation	Setting of operational targets	Setting of operational targets	Settting of operational targets
	Implementation	Budgeting	Implementation	Implementation	Implementation
		Support services			
		Extension, research, training, finance			
Local	Management, Design and implementation of integrated development plans				

Source: Meyer, N. (2004).

Table 2.A1.2. **Import duties applied on maize and wheat, 1998-2005**

Date published	Duty ZAR/ton	Ad valorem equivalent	
Maize			
6 May 1998	25.50	3.92	
1 January 1999	84.00	15.16	
5 November 1999	153.00	28.36	
24 December 1999	151.03	27.59	
24 December2000	107.00	18.34	
30 June 2000	67.00	10.61	
18 May 2001	137.40	19.91	
4 October2002	43.60	3.63	
24 November2002	0.00	0.00	
30 July 2003	16.50	2.14	
11 February 2004	0.00	0.00	
8 October2004	31.68	5.02	
13 January 2005	84.24	13.40	
23 September 2005	11.92	3.29	
	Duty ZAR/ton	USA Ad valorem equivalent	Argentina Ad valorem equivalent
Wheat			
8 April 1998	105.00	13.13	17.07
21 August 1998	0.00	0.00	0.00
14 April 1999	181.00	19.86	25.17
11 June 1999	269.00	30.55	34.71
12 January 2001	196.00	16.64	25.04
16 September 2002	43.60	3.23	3.45
23 September 2002	0.00	0.00	0.00
4 July 2003	32.80	2.65	3.32
30 July 2003	105.20	8.49	10.65
22 August 2003	217.92	17.85	21.34
3 October 2003	22.00	1.61	2.01
16 January 2004	0.00	0.00	0.00
13 August 2004	18.67	1.82	2.32
27 July 2005	*	2.00	2.00

* Change to *ad valorem* duty.

Source: Grain, South Africa.

Table 2.A1.3. **Import duties applied for sugar, 1994-2005**

Date of trigger and application to ITAC	Duty adjustment level ZAR/Ton	*Ad valorem* gazetted duty %	Date of official introduction
04 March 1994	613		
05 April 1994	737		
11 November 1994	589		
04 January 1995	425		
22 March 1996	765		
07 November 1997	756		
01 February 1998	883		
30 April 1998	1 082		
30 June 1998	786		
30 December 1999	1 014		
29 May 2000	934		
08 December 2000	666	34.7%	23 March 2001
23 July 2001	501		Not implemented
06 September 2001	784	34.5%	16 November 2001
02 April 2002	1 312	67.3%	16 August 2002
14 August 2002	1 582		Not implemented
28 November 2002	1 105	54.2%	31 January 2003
05 March 2003	742	48.0%	06 June 2003
13 May 2003	862	58.2%	22 August 2003
13 October 2003	1 018	84.6%	02 December 2003
07 April 2004	718	52.1%	02 July 2004
19 August 2004	550	35.3%	08 October 2004
01 August 2005	233	12.4%	23 September 2005

Source: South African Sugar Association.

Table 2.A1.4. **Settled restitution claims: cumulative statistics, 1995 to 30 June 2005**

Province	Claims	HH's	Beneficiaries	Area	Land cost	Financial compensation	RDG	SPG	Total
		Numbers		Hectares		Million ZAR			
Eastern Cape	16 012	42 146	157 375	56 686	210.5	581.7	66.5	31.9	890.6
Free State	1 714	3 562	18 742	45 750	17.5	31.7	5.9	2.4	57.5
Gauteng	13 132	12 948	58 221	3 555	62.5	619.3	5.2	1.1	688.1
KwaZulu/Natal	10 596	29 240	177 155	260 828	711.6	517.7	54.1	22.2	1 312.0
Mpumalanga	1 604	28 955	145 391	92 103	342.3	83.6	73.3	37.7	536.9
North West	2 686	14 728	80 361	77 485	113.1	122.1	35.3	16.9	287.5
Northern Cape	2 302	6 160	36 162	237 398	74.5	74.1	14.3	5.6	168.5
Limpopo	1 361	25 424	133 710	139 564	353.7	49.7	61.3	27.4	492.1
Western Cape	12 720	15 620	87 049	3 101	8.1	456.1	11.0	2.6	477.7
Total	62 127	178 783	894 166	916 470	1 893.8	2 535.94	327.0	147.80	4 910.9

RDG – Restitution Discretionary Grant.
SPG – Settlement Planning Grant.
Note: These statistics have been compiled based on information reflected in the database of Settled Restitution Claims. In order to improve the accuracy of statistics the database of the Settled Restitution Claims is subject to internal auditing on an ongoing basis. Please note that the number of hectares restored is currently under review, both with regard to existing data, as well as outstanding data on state land. The total restitution award also includes the cost of solatium that was paid out, *i.e.* KwaZulu-Natal [ZAR 6 367 000] and Western Cape [ZAR 47 000].
Source: Commission on Restitution of Land Rights.

Table 2.A1.5. **Total Estimate of Support to South African Agriculture**

	Units	1994	1995	1996	1997	1998	1999	2000	2001	2002	2003
I. Total value of production (at farm gate)	mn ZAR	31 585	31 305	39 008	40 988	41 280	45 683	49 421	55 450	75 030	69 603
1. Share of standard PSE commodities (%)	%	77	72	74	74	71	72	74	75	78	73
II. Total value of consumption (at farm gate)	mn ZAR	28 996	33 685	34 572	37 446	39 555	42 066	44 183	48 905	65 350	64 815
1. Standard PSE commodities	mn ZAR	22 413	24 096	25 684	27 764	28 077	30 281	32 696	36 460	51 106	47 016
III.1 Producer Support Estimate (PSE)	mn ZAR	3 091	5 033	2 961	4 926	3 503	4 107	2 586	1 210	5 997	3 689
A. Market price support	mn ZAR	2 973	4 743	2 896	4 805	3 326	4 016	2 512	756	5 374	2 685
1. Standard PSE commodities	mn ZAR	2 298	3 393	2 151	3 563	2 361	2 891	1 859	564	4 203	1 947
B. Payments based on output	mn ZAR	0	0	0	0	0	0	0	0	0	0
1. Based on unlimited output	mn ZAR	0	0	0	0	0	0	0	0	0	0
2. Based on limited output	mn ZAR	0	0	0	0	0	0	0	0	0	0
C. Payments based on area planted/animal numbers	mn ZAR	25	14	8	10	5	0	0	0	0	0
1. Based on unlimited area or animal numbers	mn ZAR	0	0	0	0	0	0	0	0	0	0
2. Based on limited area or animal numbers	mn ZAR	25	14	8	10	5	0	0	0	0	0
D. Payments based on historical entitlements	mn ZAR	0	0	0	0	0	0	0	0	0	0
1. Based on historical plantings/animal numbers or production	mn ZAR	0	0	0	0	0	0	0	0	0	0
2. Based on historical support programmes	mn ZAR	0	0	0	0	0	0	0	0	0	0
E. Payments based on input use	mn ZAR	69	67	56	53	151	92	73	448	527	670
1. Based on use of variable inputs	mn ZAR	65	66	22	3	21	8	8	333	398	373
2. Based on use of on-farm services	mn ZAR	0	0	2	3	7	4	3	6	6	13
3. Based on use of fixed inputs	mn ZAR	3	1	32	48	124	80	63	110	122	284
F. Payments based on input constraints	mn ZAR	22	9	0	0	0	0	0	0	0	4
1. Based on constraints on variable inputs	mn ZAR	0	0	0	0	0	0	0	0	0	0
2. Based on constraints on fixed inputs	mn ZAR	22	9	0	0	0	0	0	0	0	4
3. Based on constraints on a set of inputs	mn ZAR	0	0	0	0	0	0	0	0	0	0
G. Payments based on overall farming income	mn ZAR	1	201	2	57	21	0	0	6	96	331
1. Based on farm income level	mn ZAR	1	201	2	57	21	0	0	6	96	331
2. Based on established minimum income	mn ZAR	0	0	0	0	0	0	0	0	0	0
H. Miscellaneous payments	mn ZAR	0	0	0	0	0	0	0	0	0	0
1. National payments	mn ZAR	0	0	0	0	0	0	0	0	0	0
2. Sub-national payments	mn ZAR	0	0	0	0	0	0	0	0	0	0
III.2 Percentage PSE	%	10	16	8	12	8	9	5	2	8	5
III.3 Producer NAC		1.11	1.19	1.08	1.14	1.09	1.10	1.06	1.02	1.09	1.06
IV. General Services Support Estimate (GSSE)	mn ZAR	2 025	2 430	2 246	1 833	1 986	2 023	2 116	2 365	2 911	4 296
I. Research and development	mn ZAR	1 741	2 162	2 083	1 147	1 200	1 180	1 242	1 117	1 372	2 442
J. Agricultural schools	mn ZAR	0	0	0	0	0	0	0	0	0	0
K. Inspection services	mn ZAR	74	79	55	305	236	292	317	292	401	574
L. Infrastructure	mn ZAR	167	131	73	219	383	388	409	576	628	1 112
M. Marketing and promotion	mn ZAR	6	10	0	0	0	0	2	3	0	0
N. Public stockholding	mn ZAR	0	0	0	0	0	0	0	0	0	0
O. Miscellaneous	mn ZAR	37	49	35	162	168	163	144	377	510	168
V.1 Consumer Support Estimate (CSE)	mn ZAR	–3 263	–5 805	–3 002	–4 633	–2 757	–3 208	–2 055	–289	–3 843	–1 818
P. Transfers to producers from consumers (–)	mn ZAR	–2 899	–5 263	–2 712	–4 316	–2 732	–3 059	–2 052	–319	–4 958	–1 778
1. Standard PSE commodities	mn ZAR	–2 241	–3 765	–2 015	–3 200	–1 939	–2 202	–1 518	–238	–3 877	–1 290
Q. Other transfers from consumers (–)	mn ZAR	–364	–940	–292	–340	–24	–170	–7	30	52	–40
1. Standard PSE commodities	mn ZAR	–281	–672	–217	–252	–17	–122	–5	22	41	–29
R. Transfers to consumers from taxpayers	mn ZAR	0	0	0	0	0	0	0	0	0	0
S. Excess feed cost	mn ZAR	0	398	2	23	0	21	4	0	1 063	0
V.2 Percentage CSE	%	–11	–17	–9	–12	–7	–8	–5	–1	–6	–3
V.3 Consumer NAC		1.13	1.21	1.10	1.14	1.07	1.08	1.05	1.01	1.06	1.03
VI. Total Support Estimate (TSE)	mn ZAR	5 116	7 464	5 207	6 758	5 490	6 130	4 701	3 575	8 907	7 985
T. Transfers from consumers	mn ZAR	3 264	6 203	3 004	4 656	2 757	3 229	2 059	289	4 906	1 818
U. Transfers from taxpayers	mn ZAR	2 217	2 201	2 495	2 442	2 757	3 071	2 650	3 256	3 950	6 207
V. Budget revenues (–)	mn ZAR	–364	–940	–292	–340	–24	–170	–7	30	52	–40

Source: OECD PSE/CSE database, 2005.

OECD REVIEW OF AGRICULTURAL POLICIES – ISBN 92-64-03679-2 – © OECD 2006

Table 2.A1.6. **Producer Support Estimate by commodity**

	1994	1995	1996	1997	1998	1999	2000	2001	2002	2003
Wheat										
PSE (mn ZAR)	203	11	231	88	4	310	241	33	45	37
Percentage PSE	14	1	9	4	0	19	9	1	1	2
Producer NPC	1.17	1.00	1.10	1.04	1.00	1.23	1.09	1.00	1.00	1.00
Producer NAC	1.17	1.01	1.10	1.05	1.00	1.23	1.09	1.01	1.01	1.02
Maize										
PSE (mn ZAR)	1	579	2	466	10	203	5	116	4 248	177
Percentage PSE	0	20	0	8	0	4	0	2	27	2
Producer NPC	1.00	1.24	1.00	1.08	1.00	1.04	1.00	1.00	1.35	1.00
Producer NAC	1.00	1.25	1.00	1.08	1.00	1.04	1.00	1.02	1.36	1.02
Sunflower										
PSE (mn ZAR)	0	3	0	1	2	66	0	18	29	31
Percentage PSE	0	1	0	0	0	4	0	2	1	2
Producer NPC	1.00	1.00	1.00	1.00	1.00	1.04	1.00	1.00	1.00	1.00
Producer NAC	1.00	1.01	1.00	1.00	1.00	1.05	1.00	1.02	1.01	1.02
Groundnuts										
PSE (mn ZAR)	0	2	0	1	1	1	0	7	6	4
Percentage PSE	0	1	0	0	0	0	0	1	1	1
Producer NPC	1.00	1.00	1.00	1.00	1.00	1.00	1.00	1.00	1.00	1.00
Producer NAC	1.00	1.01	1.00	1.00	1.00	1.00	1.00	1.01	1.01	1.01
Sugar cane										
PSE (mn ZAR)	342	576	486	556	879	1 151	425	617	1 080	1 259
Percentage PSE	29	35	27	22	31	41	15	16	29	32
Producer NPC	1.41	1.52	1.36	1.28	1.45	1.71	1.18	1.19	1.41	1.46
Producer NAC	1.41	1.53	1.36	1.29	1.46	1.71	1.18	1.19	1.42	1.47
Grapes										
PSE (mn ZAR)	0	4	0	1	3	1	1	5	6	10
Percentage PSE	0	1	0	0	0	0	0	0	0	1
Producer NPC	1.00	1.00	1.00	1.00	1.00	1.00	1.00	1.00	1.00	1.00
Producer NAC	1.00	1.01	1.00	1.00	1.00	1.00	1.00	1.00	1.00	1.01
Oranges										
PSE (mn ZAR)	1	5	1	3	3	2	1	5	7	12
Percentage PSE	0	1	0	0	0	0	0	0	0	1
Producer NPC	1.00	1.00	1.00	1.00	1.00	1.00	1.00	1.00	1.00	1.00
Producer NAC	1.00	1.01	1.00	1.00	1.00	1.00	1.00	1.00	1.00	1.01
Apples										
PSE (mn ZAR)	1	8	1	3	4	1	1	4	6	11
Percentage PSE	0	1	0	0	0	0	0	0	0	1
Producer NPC	1.00	1.00	1.00	1.00	1.00	1.00	1.00	1.00	1.00	1.00
Producer NAC	1.00	1.01	1.00	1.00	1.00	1.00	1.00	1.00	1.00	1.01
Milk										
PSE (mn ZAR)	598	543	46	614	981	756	375	−223	281	504
Percentage PSE	39	31	2	30	39	29	16	−12	10	16
Producer NPC	1.65	1.52	1.02	1.43	1.65	1.40	1.20	0.88	1.15	1.18
Producer NAC	1.65	1.45	1.02	1.43	1.65	1.40	1.20	0.89	1.11	1.20
Beef										
PSE (mn ZAR)	80	1 004	729	370	13	4	4	58	−78	240
Percentage PSE	2	26	18	9	0	0	0	1	−1	3
Producer NPC	1.00	1.35	1.21	1.09	1.00	1.00	1.00	1.00	1.00	1.00
Producer NAC	1.02	1.35	1.22	1.10	1.00	1.00	1.00	1.01	0.99	1.03
Pigmeat										
PSE (mn ZAR)	82	−50	0	2	2	0	0	2	−95	196
Percentage PSE	6	−7	0	0	0	0	0	0	−9	15
Producer NPC	1.07	1.00	1.00	1.00	1.00	1.00	1.00	1.00	1.00	1.17
Producer NAC	1.07	0.93	1.00	1.00	1.00	1.00	1.00	1.00	0.92	1.17

Table 2.A1.6. **Producer Support Estimate by commodity** (*cont.*)

	1994	1995	1996	1997	1998	1999	2000	2001	2002	2003
Sheep meat										
PSE (mn ZAR)	823	638	311	497	517	423	828	218	−255	128
Percentage PSE	61	51	27	42	44	29	46	13	−13	6
Producer NPC	2.53	1.99	1.36	1.71	1.78	1.41	1.85	1.15	0.88	1.03
Producer NAC	2.57	2.03	1.37	1.71	1.79	1.41	1.85	1.16	0.89	1.06
Poultry meat										
PSE (mn ZAR)	276	396	383	1 028	13	4	4	15	−428	54
Percentage PSE	7	9	8	18	0	0	0	0	−4	0
Producer NPC	1.08	1.16	1.09	1.21	1.00	1.00	1.00	1.00	1.00	1.00
Producer NAC	1.08	1.10	1.09	1.21	1.00	1.00	1.00	1.00	0.96	1.00
Eggs										
PSE (mn ZAR)	0	−97	0	3	4	1	1	4	−208	16
Percentage PSE	0	−8	0	0	0	0	0	0	−7	0
Producer NPC	1.00	1.00	1.00	1.00	1.00	1.00	1.00	1.00	1.00	1.00
Producer NAC	1.00	0.93	1.00	1.00	1.00	1.00	1.00	1.00	0.93	1.00

Source: OECD PSE/CSE database, 2005.

Table 2.A1.7. **Estimates of support to agriculture in selected non-OECD and OECD countries**

	Units	1994	1995	1996	1997	1998	1999	2000	2001	2002	2003	2004
Australia												
PSE	mn AUD	2 312	1 636	1 740	1 811	1 828	1 982	1 317	1 578	1 948	1 639	1 479
	mn USD	1689	1212	1362	1343	1148	1279	763	815	1058	1063	1085
GSSE	mn USD	586	579	591	564	490	1100	457	442	469	582	668
TSE	mn USD	2275	1791	1953	1907	1637	2379	1098	1148	1412	1505	1595
	% GDP	0.68	0.50	0.48	0.47	0.45	0.61	0.29	0.32	0.35	0.30	0.26
Percentage PSE	%	9	6	6	6	6	6	4	3	5	4	4
Producer NPC		1.07	1.03	1.03	1.03	1.03	1.03	1.00	1.00	1.00	1.00	1.00
Producer NAC		1.10	1.06	1.06	1.07	1.06	1.07	1.04	1.04	1.06	1.04	1.04
Brazil												
PSE	mn BRL	n.c.	−615	630	401	4 157	1 106	3 665	2 748	4 285	7 013	5 952
	mn USD	n.c.	−670	626	372	3 580	609	2 003	1 168	1 462	2 283	2 034
GSSE	mn USD	n.c.	2 691	3 010	3 384	3 014	1 567	1 224	1 374	894	703	867
TSE	mn USD	n.c.	2 021	3 641	3 795	6 654	2 180	3 259	2 597	2 364	2 986	2 913
	% GDP	n.c.	0.29	0.47	0.47	0.85	0.41	0.54	0.51	0.51	0.59	0.48
Percentage PSE	%	n.c.	−1	1	1	6	1	4	3	3	4	3
Producer NPC		n.c.	0.97	0.97	0.97	1.03	0.97	1.03	1.00	1.00	1.01	1.01
Producer NAC		n.c.	0.99	1.01	1.01	1.07	1.01	1.04	1.03	1.03	1.04	1.03
Canada												
PSE	mn CAD	5 320	5 702	4 808	4 410	5 092	5 540	6 618	5 668	7 533	8 488	7 428
	mn USD	3 895	4 155	3 525	3 184	3 433	3 729	4 456	3 660	4 798	6 051	5 714
GSSE	mn USD	1 459	1 355	1 511	1 312	1 327	1 297	1 329	1 416	1 462	1 617	1 776
TSE	mn USD	5 354	5 510	5 050	4 497	4 759	5 026	5 785	5 076	6 261	7 729	7 490
	% GDP	0.95	0.93	0.82	0.71	0.77	0.76	0.80	0.71	0.85	0.89	0.75
Percentage PSE	%	20	20	16	15	17	18	20	16	21	25	21
Producer NPC		1.19	1.12	1.11	1.12	1.14	1.14	1.13	1.11	1.12	1.16	1.13
Producer NAC		1.26	1.24	1.18	1.17	1.20	1.22	1.25	1.19	1.26	1.34	1.27
China												
PSE	mn CNY	8 122	109 426	27 535	30 490	15 880	−60 928	65 411	121 142	168 965	208 392	n.c.
	mn USD	942	13 103	3 312	3 678	1 918	−7 360	7 901	14 636	20 414	25 177	n.c.
GSSE	mn USD	8 468	10 467	11 160	12 917	17 098	17 741	21 112	24 237	25 341	26 469	n.c.
TSE	mn USD	9 705	23 860	14 713	16 821	19 229	10 703	29 296	38 956	45 828	51 718	n.c.
	% GDP	1.8	3.4	1.8	1.9	2.0	1.1	2.7	3.3	3.6	3.7	n.c.
Percentage PSE	%	1	6	1	1	1	−3	3	5	7	8	n.c.
Producer NPC		1.00	1.07	0.97	0.99	0.98	0.95	1.02	1.04	1.06	1.08	n.c.
Producer NAC		1.01	1.06	1.01	1.01	1.01	0.97	1.03	1.06	1.08	1.09	n.c.
Japan												
PSE	bn JPY	7 465	6 891	6 288	5 659	6 050	5 978	5 799	5 430	5 532	5 553	5 283
	mn USD	73 022	73 253	57 786	46 768	46 223	52 490	53 772	44 699	44 162	47 874	48 737
GSSE	mn USD		24 605	18 561	15 175	16 337	12 945	13 463	11 801	11 280	12 393	12 074
TSE	mn USD	92 049	98 135	76 582	62 151	62 663	65 515	67 293	56 551	55 489	60 304	60 850
	% GDP	1.91	1.85	1.63	1.44	1.59	1.46	1.42	1.36	1.39	1.40	1.30
Percentage PSE	%	62	61	57	53	57	59	60	57	58	59	56
Producer NPC		2.54	2.48	2.23	2.06	2.26	2.36	2.38	2.24	2.29	2.33	2.20
Producer NAC		2.62	2.57	2.32	2.15	2.35	2.46	2.48	2.34	2.39	2.43	2.28
Mexico												
PSE	mn MXN	24 079	−7 212	10 259	34 652	47 795	52 780	71 360	64 780	86 564	71 868	61 638
	mn USD	7 106	−1 123	1 350	4 373	5 222	5 525	7 549	6 933	8 961	6 661	5 452
GSSE	mn USD	1 167	551	356	370	417	508	628	649	629	878	799
TSE	mn USD	10 247	290	3 107	6 116	6 725	6 720	8 848	7 730	9 685	7 573	6 287
	% GDP	2.44	0.10	0.93	1.52	1.60	1.40	1.52	1.24	1.49	1.21	0.95
Percentage PSE	%	23	−5	5	15	18	18	24	19	26	19	17
Producer NPC		1.17	0.89	0.97	1.11	1.16	1.17	1.25	1.16	1.27	1.14	1.09
Producer NAC		1.29	0.95	1.05	1.17	1.22	1.22	1.31	1.24	1.35	1.24	1.20

Table 2.A1.7. **Estimates of support to agriculture in selected non-OECD and OECD countries**
(cont.)

	Units	1994	1995	1996	1997	1998	1999	2000	2001	2002	2003	2004
New Zealand												
PSE	mn NZD	208	240	191	214	158	172	133	95	223	342	390
	mn USD	123	158	132	142	84	91	61	40	103	198	257
GSSE	mn USD	86	98	112	114	91	90	87	69	91	122	141
TSE	mn USD	209	256	244	256	175	181	148	108	194	320	398
	% GDP	0.41	0.43	0.37	0.39	0.32	0.32	0.29	0.21	0.33	0.41	0.42
Percentage PSE	%	2	3	2	2	2	2	1	1	2	2	3
Producer NPC		1.02	1.02	1.01	1.02	1.01	1.01	1.01	1.00	1.01	1.02	1.02
Producer NAC		1.02	1.03	1.02	1.02	1.02	1.02	1.01	1.01	1.02	1.03	1.03
Russia												
PSE	mn RUR	−11 550	23 038	58 775	89 670	62 861	46 303	35 542	74 280	89 573	8 460	n.c.
	mn USD	−5 241	5 059	11 470	15 501	6 475	1 881	1 264	2 546	2 857	276	n.c.
GSSE	mn USD	1 003	788	762	3 987	471	444	498	438	611	694	n.c.
TSE	mn USD	−4 039	5 847	12 232	19 488	6 946	2 325	1 762	2 984	3 468	970	n.c.
	% GDP	−1.5	1.7	2.8	4.4	2.5	1.2	0.7	1.0	1.0	0.2	n.c.
Percentage PSE	%	−20	13	24	34	23	8	5	9	9	1	n.c.
Producer NPC		0.66	0.96	1.16	1.42	1.21	1.01	0.97	1.00	0.96	0.90	n.c.
Producer NAC		0.83	1.15	1.31	1.53	1.31	1.09	1.05	1.10	1.10	1.01	n.c.
South Africa												
PSE	mn ZAR	3 091	5 033	2 961	4 926	3 503	4 107	2 586	1 210	5 997	3 689	n.c.
	mn USD	871	1 539	689	1 068	631	671	372	140	569	487	n.c.
GSSE	mn USD	570	743	522	398	358	331	304	274	276	567	n.c.
TSE	mn USD	1 441	2 283	1 211	1 466	989	1 002	676	415	846	1 055	n.c.
	% GDP	1.2	1.5	0.9	1.1	0.8	0.8	0.6	0.4	0.8	0.7	n.c.
Percentage PSE	%	10	16	8	12	8	9	5	2	8	5	n.c.
Producer NPC		1.10	1.21	1.08	1.13	1.09	1.10	1.05	1.01	1.10	1.04	n.c.
Producer NAC		1.11	1.19	1.08	1.14	1.09	1.10	1.06	1.02	1.09	1.06	n.c.
United States												
PSE	mn USD	29 008	20 180	28 963	29 768	46 144	55 942	53 670	51 838	39 105	35 618	46 504
	mn USD	29 008	20 180	28 963	29 768	46 144	55 942	53 670	51 838	39 105	35 618	46 504
GSSE	mn USD	27 135	26 459	25 757	24 739	22 840	23 328	22 902	25 126	26 953	30 803	34 149
TSE	mn USD	76 552	67 792	76 358	76 178	89 824	100 328	97 513	98 610	90 020	92 199	108 696
	% GDP	1.09	0.92	0.98	0.92	1.02	1.08	0.99	0.97	0.86	0.84	0.93
Percentage PSE	%	14	10	13	13	21	26	24	22	18	15	18
Producer NPC		1.09	1.05	1.08	1.08	1.15	1.20	1.17	1.16	1.10	1.07	1.11
Producer NAC		1.17	1.11	1.15	1.16	1.27	1.35	1.31	1.29	1.22	1.18	1.22
European Union (15)												
PSE	mn EUR	90 180	96 779	93 199	95 318	100 917	107 173	93 338	93 061	96 989	104 474	107 686
	mn USD	106 966	126 517	118 305	108 023	112 867	114 192	86 018	83 343	91 407	118 028	133 386
GSSE	mn USD	9 091	8 797	11 207	13 125	10 036	10 222	7 879	8 206	8 801	9 997	12 748
TSE	mn USD	121 721	140 769	133 943	125 910	127 322	128 650	97 508	94 841	103 643	132 431	150 568
	% GDP	1.76	1.65	1.55	1.52	1.49	1.50	1.23	1.19	1.20	1.26	1.25
Percentage PSE	%	36	36	33	34	37	39	33	32	34	36	33
Producer NPC		1.43	1.38	1.30	1.32	1.41	1.48	1.32	1.27	1.31	1.34	1.29
Producer NAC		1.57	1.56	1.49	1.51	1.58	1.65	1.49	1.46	1.52	1.56	1.49
OECD												
PSE	mn USD	273 570	267 257	254 561	234 373	253 583	272 853	242 971	219 500	226 451	256 752	279 527
GSSE	mn USD	62 583	68 564	64 774	63 114	59 332	57 519	54 280	54 471	55 946	62 028	65 834
TSE	mn USD	365 673	364 908	348 223	326 524	340 404	357 020	322 712	299 306	310 130	349 421	377 938
	% GDP	1.68	1.53	1.45	1.37	1.42	1.42	1.26	1.18	1.17	1.18	1.16
Percentage PSE	%	34	31	29	29	33	35	32	29	31	30	30
Producer NPC		1.42	1.34	1.29	1.29	1.36	1.42	1.35	1.28	1.30	1.29	1.28
Producer NAC		1.52	1.45	1.41	1.40	1.48	1.55	1.48	1.42	1.44	1.44	1.43

n.c.: not calculated.

Source: OECD PSE/CSE database, 2005.

Table 2.A1.8. **Consumer Support Estimate by commodity**

	1994	1995	1996	1997	1998	1999	2000	2001	2002	2003
Wheat										
CSE (mn ZAR)	−248	0	−203	−91	0	−426	−238	0	0	0
Percentage CSE	−14	0	−9	−4	0	−18	−8	0	0	0
Consumer NPC	1.17	1.00	1.10	1.04	1.00	1.23	1.09	1.00	1.00	1.00
Consumer NAC	1.17	1.00	1.10	1.04	1.00	1.22	1.09	1.00	1.00	1.00
Maize										
CSE (mn ZAR)	0	−422	0	−311	0	−162	0	0	−2 188	0
Percentage CSE	0	−10	0	−8	0	−3	0	0	−17	0
Consumer NPC	1.00	1.23	1.00	1.09	1.00	1.03	1.00	1.00	1.34	1.00
Consumer NAC	1.00	1.11	1.00	1.08	1.00	1.03	1.00	1.00	1.21	1.00
Sunflower										
CSE (mn ZAR)	0	0	0	0	0	−41	0	0	0	0
Percentage CSE	0	0	0	0	0	−4	0	0	0	0
Consumer NPC	1.00	1.00	1.00	1.00	1.00	1.04	1.00	1.00	1.00	1.00
Consumer NAC	1.00	1.00	1.00	1.00	1.00	1.04	1.00	1.00	1.00	1.00
Groundnuts										
CSE (mn ZAR)	0	0	0	0	0	0	0	0	0	0
Percentage CSE	0	0	0	0	0	0	0	0	0	0
Consumer NPC	1.00	1.00	1.00	1.00	1.00	1.00	1.00	1.00	1.00	1.00
Consumer NAC	1.00	1.00	1.00	1.00	1.00	1.00	1.00	1.00	1.00	1.00
Sugar cane										
CSE (mn ZAR)	−342	−448	−375	−309	−477	−561	−199	−272	−543	−575
Percentage CSE	−29	−34	−27	−22	−31	−41	−15	−16	−29	−31
Consumer NPC	1.41	1.52	1.36	1.28	1.45	1.71	1.18	1.19	1.41	1.46
Consumer NAC	1.41	1.52	1.36	1.28	1.45	1.71	1.18	1.19	1.41	1.46
Grapes										
CSE (mn ZAR)	0	0	0	0	0	0	0	0	0	0
Percentage CSE	0	0	0	0	0	0	0	0	0	0
Consumer NPC	1.00	1.00	1.00	1.00	1.00	1.00	1.00	1.00	1.00	1.00
Consumer NAC	1.00	1.00	1.00	1.00	1.00	1.00	1.00	1.00	1.00	1.00
Oranges										
CSE (mn ZAR)	0	0	0	0	0	0	0	0	0	0
Percentage CSE	0	0	0	0	0	0	0	0	0	0
Consumer NPC	1.00	1.00	1.00	1.00	1.00	1.00	1.00	1.00	1.00	1.00
Consumer NAC	1.00	1.00	1.00	1.00	1.00	1.00	1.00	1.00	1.00	1.00
Apples										
CSE (mn ZAR)	0	0	0	0	0	0	0	0	0	0
Percentage CSE	0	0	0	0	0	0	0	0	0	0
Consumer NPC	1.00	1.00	1.00	1.00	1.00	1.00	1.00	1.00	1.00	1.00
Consumer NAC	1.00	1.00	1.00	1.00	1.00	1.00	1.00	1.00	1.00	1.00
Milk										
CSE (mn ZAR)	−571	−564	−42	−610	−949	−703	−377	268	−354	−489
Percentage CSE	−39	−34	−2	−30	−39	−29	−16	13	−13	−15
Consumer NPC	1.65	1.52	1.02	1.43	1.65	1.40	1.20	0.88	1.15	1.18
Consumer NAC	1.65	1.52	1.02	1.43	1.65	1.40	1.20	0.88	1.15	1.18
Beef										
CSE (mn ZAR)	0	−1 183	−861	−416	0	0	0	0	0	0
Percentage CSE	0	−26	−18	−9	0	0	0	0	0	0
Consumer NPC	1.00	1.35	1.21	1.09	1.00	1.00	1.00	1.00	1.00	1.00
Consumer NAC	1.00	1.35	1.21	1.09	1.00	1.00	1.00	1.00	1.00	1.00
Pigmeat										
CSE (mn ZAR)	−51	0	0	0	0	0	0	0	0	−183
Percentage CSE	−6	0	0	0	0	0	0	0	0	−14
Consumer NPC	1.07	1.00	1.00	1.00	1.00	1.00	1.00	1.00	1.00	1.17
Consumer NAC	1.07	1.00	1.00	1.00	1.00	1.00	1.00	1.00	1.00	1.17

Table 2.A1.8. **Consumer Support Estimate by commodity** *(cont.)*

	1994	1995	1996	1997	1998	1999	2000	2001	2002	2003
Sheep meat										
CSE (mn ZAR)	−1 001	−755	−327	−498	−530	−410	−707	−211	311	−72
Percentage CSE	−60	−50	−27	−41	−44	−29	−46	−13	14	−3
Consumer NPC	2.53	1.99	1.36	1.71	1.78	1.41	1.85	1.15	0.88	1.03
Consumer NAC	2.53	1.99	1.36	1.71	1.78	1.41	1.85	1.15	0.88	1.03
Poultry meat										
CSE (mn ZAR)	−309	−668	−421	−1 193	0	0	0	0	0	0
Percentage CSE	−7	−14	−8	−17	0	0	0	0	0	0
Consumer NPC	1.08	1.16	1.09	1.21	1.00	1.00	1.00	1.00	1.00	1.00
Consumer NAC	1.08	1.16	1.09	1.21	1.00	1.00	1.00	1.00	1.00	1.00
Eggs										
CSE (mn ZAR)	0	0	0	0	0	0	0	0	0	0
Percentage CSE	0	0	0	0	0	0	0	0	0	0
Consumer NPC	1.00	1.00	1.00	1.00	1.00	1.00	1.00	1.00	1.00	1.00
Consumer NAC	1.00	1.00	1.00	1.00	1.00	1.00	1.00	1.00	1.00	1.00

Source: OECD PSE/CSE database, 2005.

Figure 2.A1.1. **WHEAT: Percentage PSEs, producer and reference prices**

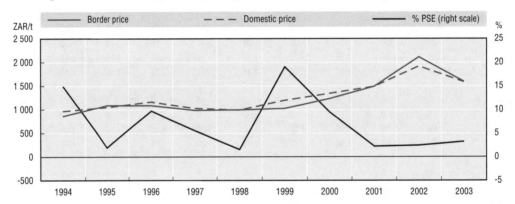

Source: OECD PSE/CSE database, 2005.

Figure 2.A1.2a. **WHITE MAIZE: Percentage PSEs, producer and reference prices**

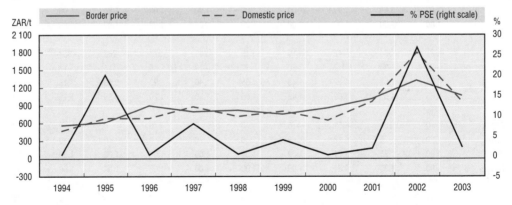

Source: OECD PSE/CSE database, 2005.

Figure 2.A1.2b. **YELLOW MAIZE: Percentage PSEs, producer and reference prices**

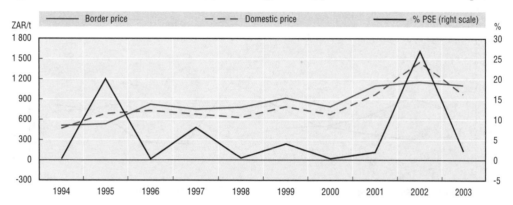

Source: OECD PSE/CSE database, 2005.

Figure 2.A1.3. **SUNFLOWER: Percentage PSEs, producer and reference prices**

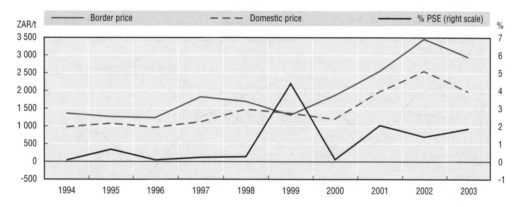

Source: OECD PSE/CSE database, 2005.

Figure 2.A1.4. **GROUNDNUTS: Percentage PSEs, producer and reference prices**

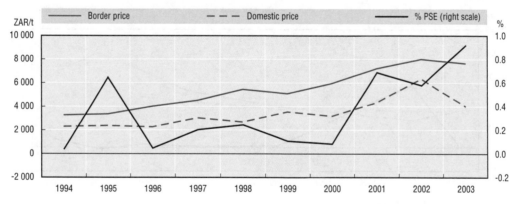

Source: OECD PSE/CSE database, 2005.

Figure 2.A1.5. **SUGAR CANE: Percentage PSEs, producer and reference prices**

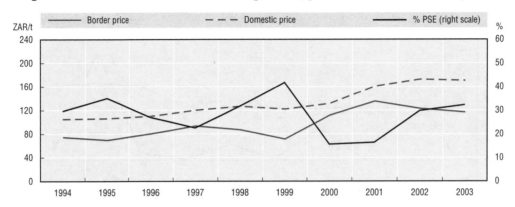

Source: OECD PSE/CSE database, 2005.

Figure 2.A1.6. **MILK: Percentage PSEs, producer and reference prices**

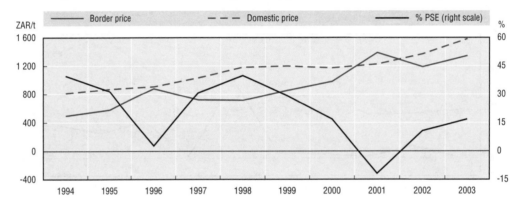

Source: OECD PSE/CSE database, 2005.

Figure 2.A1.7. **BEEF: Percentage PSEs, producer and reference prices**

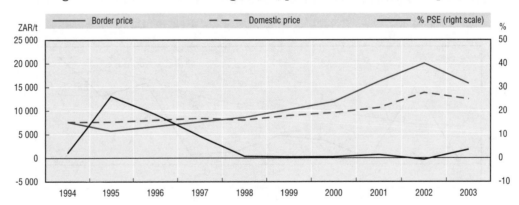

Source: OECD PSE/CSE database, 2005.

Figure 2.A1.8. **PIGMEAT: Percentage PSEs, producer and reference prices**

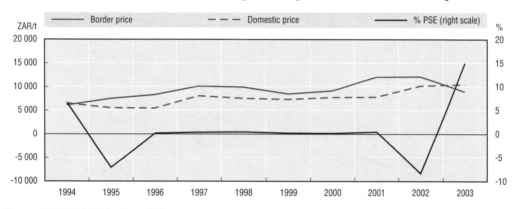

Source: OECD PSE/CSE database, 2005.

Figure 2.A1.9. **SHEEP MEAT: Percentage PSEs, producer and reference prices**

Source: OECD PSE/CSE database, 2005.

Figure 2.A1.10. **POULTRY MEAT: Percentage PSEs, producer and reference prices**

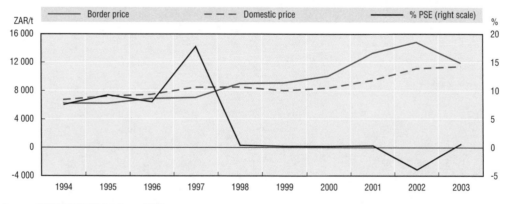

Source: OECD PSE/CSE database, 2005.

Figure 2.A1.11. **EGGS: Percentage PSEs, producer and reference prices**

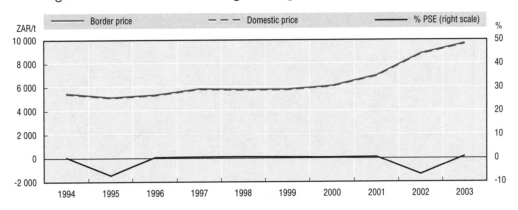

Source: OECD PSE/CSE database, 2005.

ISBN 92-64-03679-2
OECD Review of Agricultural Policies
South Africa
© OECD 2006

Chapter 3

Policy Effects

This Chapter examines various effects of existing policies and potential policy reforms. Section 3.1 looks at the tariffs faced by South Africa in its key export markets. Section 3.2 provides estimates of sectoral and economy wide welfare gains of own and multilateral trade liberalisation for South Africa. Section 3.3 explores how those gains are likely to be distributed among different types of households and the Provinces. Section 3.4 analyses the impact of OECD, South Africa and multilateral liberalisation on South African agricultural commodity markets. Finally, Section 3.5 examines how recent and ongoing sectoral and economy-wide policies contribute to food security and poverty reduction.

South Africa is one of the world's largest exporters of wine, fresh fruits and, to a lesser extent, sugar, which together account for almost one-third of total agro-food exports. Market access is widely regarded as the most important and most difficult element in the current round of international trade negotiations. This Chapter examines the market access barriers confronted by South Africa in its major agricultural export markets.

Another special feature of this review is an analysis of the potential effects of own and multilateral trade liberalisation (in the areas of market access, export subsidies, and domestic support). Estimates of sectoral and economy wide impacts for South Africa are provided along with an analysis of the distributional effects across different types of households and Provinces. The impact of OECD, South Africa and multilateral liberalisation on South African agricultural commodity markets is also examined.

Finally, this Chapter looks at the links to food security and poverty reduction: the impact of recent and ongoing sectoral and economy-wide policies; how the withdrawal of most of the support services to commercial farmers and the liberalisation of international trade has influenced food availability and labour markets; whether the deregulation and planned elimination of the control boards may affect food price instability for vulnerable households; and how land act revisions, government programmes and jurisdictional restructuring have affected land reform beneficiaries, farm workers, and the poor non-farm rural and urban households.

3.1. Market access barriers to South African agricultural exports

The 1994 Uruguay Round Agreement on Agriculture codified and disciplined border measures and all trade distorting domestic measures. In the URAA, nearly all non-tariff barriers were converted into tariffs and all agricultural tariffs were bound. Current and minimum access provisions created Tariff Rate Quotas (TRQs) in order to ensure minimum market access. The tariffs that resulted from this process were very high in many instances (often so high as to prevent trade from occurring). Tariff peaks (tariffs in excess of 100%) were common and tariff escalation (tariffs that rise as the commodity is further processed) was also prevalent. Many countries maintained very high levels of protection for sensitive products that had traditionally been heavily supported and protected. These commitments are now the basis for the round of current negotiations. This Section reviews the current situation faced by South Africa for its most important agricultural exports – wine, fresh fruits and sugar.

The discussion of market access that follows is supported by Figures showing *ad valorem* equivalent (AVE) tariffs faced by South Africa in its principal export markets.[1] In all cases, both the weighted average and the maximum tariff applied to imports from South Africa are reported. The weighted average tariff accounts for seasonal variations in tariffs, as well as tariff concessions granted to South Africa, with the weights being the import values. The maximum tariff indicates the highest tariff rate faced by South African exporters at any time in a particular market. A more detailed commodity information is presented in Annex 3.A1.

Generally low tariffs on wine

South Africa ranks among the world's top ten exporters of grape wines. The country's wine exports have been rapidly growing since the mid-1990s, becoming the country's leading agro-food export item with USD 0.53 billion per year from wine exports in 2002-04. Wine is a strongly differentiated product as is the protection from imports, in particular wine market segments. The focus below is on South Africa's dominant export group consisting of non-fortified natural wines.[2]

Geographic concentration of South Africa's trade in this group of wines is striking. About 86% of all exports are absorbed by the European Union (Table 3.A1.1). Under bilateral agreement between the European Union and South Africa, the latter receives a Tariff Rate Quota (TRQ) allocation for duty free exports to the Union. However, actual supplies far exceed the TRQ, most probably due to the fact that the over-quota tariff is a modest 6%.[3] Taking into account the in-quota and over-quota supplies, the average tariff faced by South Africa is estimated at 5% (Figure 3.1). Tariff protection in other segments of the EU wine market, *e.g.* sparkling or fortified wines, is higher but these segments have less significance for South Africa as outlets for its tradable wines.

The next most important but far less sizeable markets are the United States, Canada and Japan. The United States grants South Africa duty free entry, as foreseen by its commitments under the Generalised System of Preferences (GSP) and the African Growth and Opportunity Act (AGOA). This is a relatively modest concession given that the general US tariff is low, with an AVE equalling 1.5%. Canada applies a similarly low tariff at 2% (AVE). The most protected of the OECD markets is the Japanese market where the duty rate is set at 15% *ad valorem* and is subject to a minimum specific tariff.

Figure 3.1. **Tariff protection of the wine sector in South African export markets, 2005**

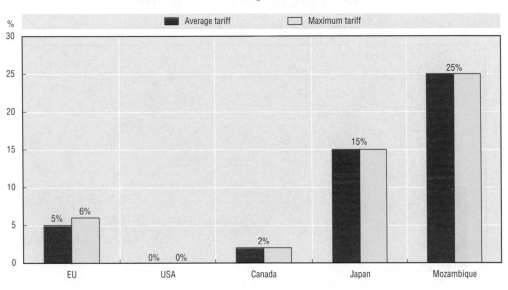

Source: MAD-ATD; TARIC; USITC, WITS.

Seasonal elevation of tariffs on fresh fruits

South Africa is also one of the world's largest exporters of fresh fruit. In 2002-04, exports of table grapes, oranges and apples were valued at USD 0.54 billion a year – a revenue comparable with that from total wine exports. As in the case of wine, fresh fruit exports are also strongly oriented towards the EU market, which absorbs over 80% of all South Africa's exports of table grapes, almost one-half of oranges and 60% of apples (Table 3.A1.2). The European Union operates a complex seasonal tariff regime for fresh fruits. The EU regime also incorporates the tariff setting system based on "entry prices" and seasonal TRQs under which in-quota and over-quota tariffs are also defined according to the entry price.[4] The maximum tariff South Africa faces under this regime is 14% for table grapes, 16% for oranges, and 9% for apples (Figures 3.2 to 3.4). If seasonal variations in tariffs and trade volumes, as well as tariff concessions (in the case of grapes), are taken into account, the average tariff level comes down to 6% for table grapes, 3% for oranges, and 2% for apples. This can be considered a quite low level of protection; however, the differential between the average and maximum tariff indicates seasonal variability of the EU protection system, which may effectively limit South Africa's supplies to this market. An additional impediment is embedded in the entry price system. This regime means that exporting countries cannot ship large quantities without potential risk of undercutting the selling price below the minimum entry price, which effectively puts exporters in a position of exercising some kind of voluntary export restraints.

Exports to important non-EU markets, such as Hong Kong (China), Russia, Saudi Arabia, and Malaysia, are typically duty free or incurring relatively low tariffs. The only exception is high and seasonally differentiated tariff imposed by Russia on apple imports.

High over-quota tariffs and tariff escalation for sugar

South Africa is an important exporter on the world sugar market, selling 0.7 million tonnes of raw and 0.3 million tonnes of refined sugar per year (Table 3.A1.3). As shown by

Figure 3.2. **Tariff protection of the fresh grapes sector in South African export markets, 2005**

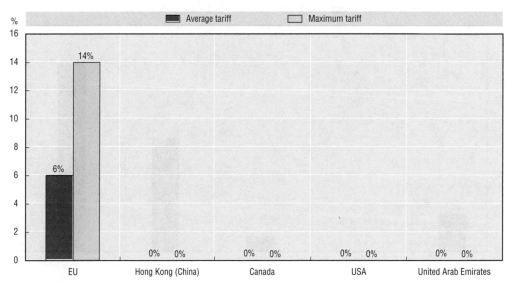

Sources: MAD-ATD; TARIC; USITC.

Figure 3.3. **Tariff protection of the fresh oranges sector in South African export markets, 2005**

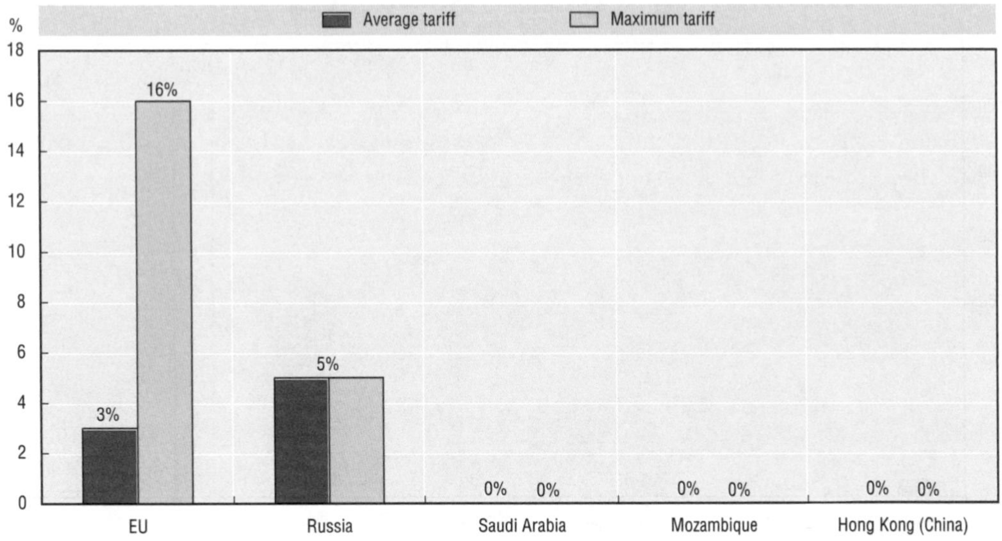

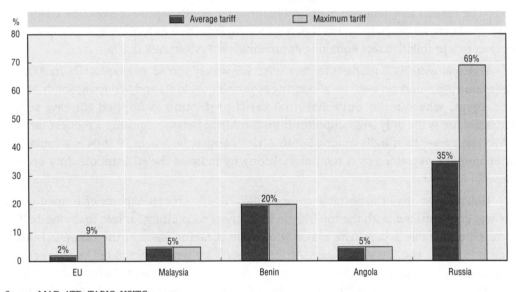

Source: MAD-ATD; TARIC; USITC.

Figure 3.4. **Tariff protection of the fresh apples sector in South African export markets, 2005**

Source: MAD-ATD; TARIC; USITC.

the estimated Nominal Protection Co-efficient (see Chapter 3), domestic sugar prices in South Africa are 1.3 times the world levels (on average in 2001-03). This suggests that South Africa has little comparative advantage in exporting sugar, but exports are actually made possible due to price discrimination between production destined for exports and for domestic consumption.

Around 40% of South Africa's raw sugar exports are destined for three OECD countries: South Korea, Japan, and the United States. To support the domestic refining sector, South

Figure 3.5. **Tariff protection of the raw sugar sector in South African export markets, 2005**

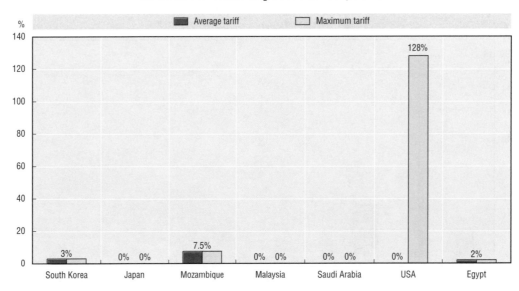

Source: MAD-ATD; USITC.

Korea applies low protection for raw sugar for refining, with *ad valorem* tariff set at 3% (Figure 3.5). Import into the Japanese market is duty free, but through a single State Trading Enterprise (STE).[5] All South African exports to the United States are under the general WTO TRQ. The regular in-quota rate is 6% (AVE); however, South Africa receives GSP treatment from the United Sates, which sets the in-quota sugar at zero duty. Over-quota imports are subject to a prohibitive rate equalling approximately 128% in AVE tariffs.

Principal non-OECD markets for raw sugar are widely spread geographically. In 2002-04, the main sugar markets were neighbouring Mozambique, India and Malaysia, Saudi Arabia and Egypt, where no or only marginal tariff protection is applied for raw sugar. Mozambique is the only large importer from the Africa region, imposing a modest tariff of 7.5%. The presence of India among South Africa's largest buyers in 2002-04 is a transitory phenomenon, explained by a temporary lifting by India of the 60% import duty on raw sugar.[6]

Unlike other major exportable commodities, South African exports of refined sugar are less concentrated, with the top five trade partners accounting for less than one-half of total exports (Table 3.A1.3). The majority of trade is taking place in the non-OECD area, mainly in Africa and the Middle East. African exports are largely facilitated by the regional free trade agreements, notably the Southern African Development Community (SADC), with the result that South Africa faces relatively low tariff barriers for refined sugar from its major buyers in the region. Trade links with the Middle East are rather sporadic, as indicated by the fact that the composition of particular destinations varies from year to year. In 2002-04, the two main Middle East sugar markets were Syria and Jordan, both applying relatively low tariff protection at 7% and 5% respectively (Figure 3.6). OECD countries absorb only 3% of South Africa's refined sugar exports, which are almost entirely directed to the European Union. A TRQ of around 1.3 million tonnes allows preferential imports of raw sugar for refining into the European Union at zero duty. The bulk of the quota (1.29 million tonnes) is allocated to ACP countries, with the balance (10 000 tonnes)

Figure 3.6. **Tariff protection of the refined sugar sector in South African export markets, 2005**

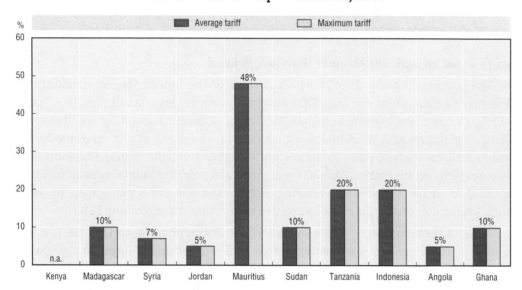

Source: MAD-ATD.

going to India. South Africa has no quota for duty free entry and therefore faces the over-quota tariff for refined sugar of around 93% (AVE), plus special safeguard measures which are essentially prohibitive.

Summary

A major share of South Africa's key exports is directed to just a few destinations, among which the OECD markets – in particular the European Union – are the most important. In general, wine and fresh fruit exports face relatively low levels of border protection, in part due to bilateral and general tariff concessions to South Africa. However, these preferences do not exclude South Africa from the seasonal elevation of tariff barriers, built, in particular, into the EU regime for fresh fruits, which limits exports during the peak seasons. The seasonal elevation of tariffs affects the possibility of exporting fruit production from South Africa's provinces with harvesting seasons similar to those in Europe, as these provinces have a potential to increase their production. OECD sugar markets are effectively restricted to raw sugar exports. Although reduction in protection of the sugar sector in the large OECD economies could provide important gains for the low-cost sugar producers, South Africa with domestic prices higher than world levels, is unlikely to have the comparative advantage to reap those gains.

3.2. Welfare impacts of trade and agricultural policy reforms

The effects of multilateral trade and domestic policy reforms on the South African economy are evaluated based on GTAPEM, a modified version of the standard GTAP model, developed by the OECD Secretariat. GTAP is a global general equilibrium trade model that is widely used in applied agricultural and trade policy analysis. Its key strengths are its global scope, its coverage of all sectors of the economy, and its depiction of the way in which resources are allocated across different sectors. In GTAPEM, the standard GTAP model is modified to provide a more realistic representation of the structure of the agricultural sector (notably in the allocation of land between alternative uses), and to accommodate a representation of policy interventions that is accurate and consistent with the way in which domestic support is classified and measured for the PSE, WTO export subsidy notifications, and import tariffs.[7] In addition, the data used in this analysis take account of the trade preference schemes operated by a number of countries.

Tariffs levied on agriculture lower than tariffs faced

The relative importance of various sectors of the South African economy is a necessary vantage point for understanding the potential impacts of simulated policy reform. The agro-food sector accounts for 11% of domestic output, of which 4% is in primary agriculture and 7% in processed agriculture. The share of processed products in total agriculture output (65%) is significantly higher than the average for non-OECD countries (47%). By comparison, the share of processed products in total agriculture output for OECD countries is 76%. Manufacturing, textiles and wearing apparel make up 38% of South African domestic output, while services account for the remaining 51%.

Table 3.1 summarises the tariffs South Africa levies on imports, and the tariffs it faces on exports. These are compared with the average tariffs levied and faced on aggregate by OECD and by non-OECD countries.[8] South Africa imposes a relatively low level of protection on agriculture. The average tariff levied on agricultural imports (9%) is lower than the average for non-OECD countries (14%), and slightly over half the average tariff levied by OECD countries (17%).

As is the case for most countries, tariffs levied increase with the level of processing (8% for primary agriculture compared to 9% for processed). This well known phenomenon of "tariff escalation" is particularly apparent in the tariffs facing South Africa on its agricultural exports (14% for primary compared to 17% for processed). The average tariffs faced by South Africa for primary and processed agriculture are similar to those faced by both OECD and non-OECD countries.

Generally, the tariffs levied by South Africa on agricultural imports are lower than those it faces for its agricultural exports. Therefore, if all tariffs are reduced in equal proportion, South Africa would gain a competitive advantage in agriculture vis-à-vis its trading partners, as the cut in absolute value for tariffs levied would be smaller than the cuts on tariffs faced. This is true on average for agriculture; however there is significant variation amongst commodities. Tariffs levied by South Africa on wheat, dairy products, and processed sugar from certain countries, for example, are higher and in some cases exceed 50%.

Table 3.1. **Tariffs[1] levied and faced**

%

	Tariffs levied on imports into			Tariffs faced on exports by		
	South Africa	OECD	non-OECD	South Africa	OECD	Non-OECD
Agriculture	9	17	14	15	17	16
Primary agriculture	8	15	9	14	14	14
Processed	9	17	17	17	18	17
Manufactures	5	1	8	4	4	3
Textiles and wearing apparel	22	7	14	7	9	10

1. Trade weighted average of applied rates. Includes ad valorem, specific and TRQs (in ad valorem equivalents) as applied in 2001.

Source: OECD calculations based on GTAP version 6 database (final release).

The levels of protection in the non-agriculture sectors in South Africa are generally higher than in OECD countries, and South Africa generally levies higher non-agriculture tariffs than it faces. The most protected South African sector is textiles and wearing apparel. Given the large economic weight of the non-agriculture sectors, reductions in protection in these sectors contribute significantly to the total welfare changes in South Africa arising from global liberalisation.

South Africa benefits from OECD agricultural reforms

GTAPEM is used to simulate the effects of a 50% reduction in tariffs for all countries and all sectors, a 50% cut in agricultural export subsidies for all countries, and a 50% reduction in domestic farm support in OECD countries and South Africa. The results are comparative static (i.e. they show the one-off gains from a change in policies) and are based on data for 2001. Accordingly, the most recent policy changes, including the current US Farm Act (2002) and the introduction of the single farm payment in the European Union (2003), are not considered. Policy changes as a result of China's WTO accession are also excluded, with the exception of tariff reductions made on grains and oilseeds. The results should be interpreted to be the medium-term impact of the policy change after all necessary adjustments on consumption and production have taken place (about five years).

The outcome of the scenario is summarised in Table 3.2. For each country/region, the total welfare gain, as measured by the equivalent variation (shown in the first column), is decomposed into the impact of agricultural reform (within and outside OECD) and the impact of reform in non-agricultural sectors (also within and outside OECD). The global welfare gains from all reforms in all countries are about USD 46 billion. Of this total, three-quarters accrue to OECD countries, resulting mostly from the reform of their own agricultural policies and the reform in non-agricultural sectors outside OECD. Non-OECD countries capture about one-quarter of global welfare gains, which come mainly from the reform in OECD countries, in particular in their non-agriculture sectors, but also in agriculture.

For South Africa, around 65% of the welfare gains are due to liberalisation of non-agriculture sectors, and mostly outside OECD area, i.e. within the "south-south trade" (Figure 3.7). The net welfare effect of multilateral agricultural liberalisation for South Africa is positive, contributing 35% to overall South Africa's welfare gains. Much of this contribution is due to liberalisation of OECD agriculture (25%), with the reform of non-OECD agriculture

Table 3.2. **Welfare effects of multilateral policy reform**

Equivalent variation of income, million USD

		Policy liberalised			
	All policies	OECD agriculture	Non-OECD agriculture	OECD non-agriculture	Non-OECD non-agriculture
World	45 642	22 905	3 919	6 752	12 066
OECD	33 758	20 974	2 068	99	10 617
Non-OECD	11 884	1 931	1 851	6 653	1 449
Brazil	1 575	1 093	49	368	66
China	4 126	61	31	3 313	721
India	1 767	64	562	381	760
South Africa	**251**	**63**	**25**	**23**	**141**

Source: OECD Secretariat, GTAPPEM.

Figure 3.7. **Welfare gains (losses) in South Africa by source of liberalisation**

Million USD

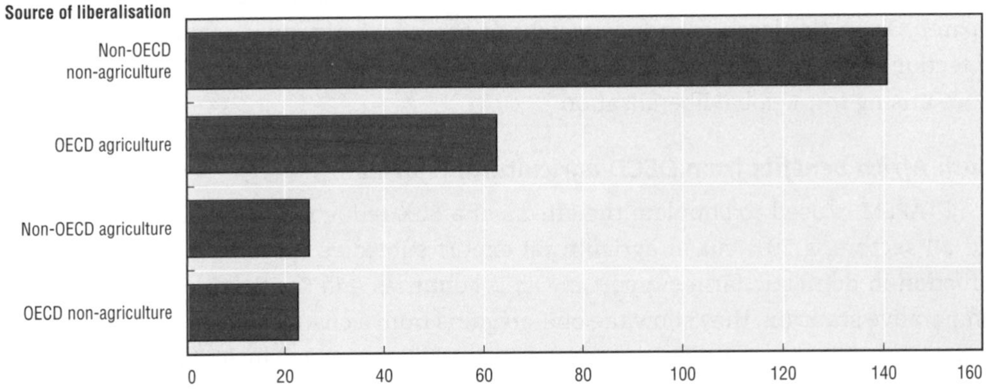

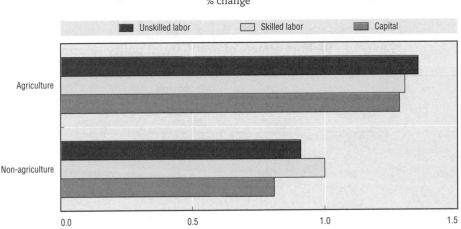

Source: OECD Secretariat, GTAPEM.

responsible for the remaining 10%. In other words, agricultural policy reform in the OECD area would clearly bring benefits to South Africa. In terms of commodities, the most important contributions are from liberalisation in the wheat, fruit and vegetable, dairy products, processed sugar, and other processed food sectors.

Liberalisation favours returns to agriculture

The simulated policy reforms of global liberalisation increase returns to both agriculture and non-agriculture factors of production (labour and capital). The results (per unit returns) for South Africa are shown on Figure 3.8. Real returns to labour and capital increase more for agriculture than for non-agriculture. That is, the economic incentives associated with global liberalisation would retain more factors in agriculture than would otherwise be the case, and/or marginal resources would shift from the non-agricultural sectors into agriculture. As there is little difference in the post-liberalisation returns to

Figure 3.8. **Real factor per unit returns to agriculture and non-agriculture**

% change

Source: OECD Secretariat, GTAPEM.

capital and labour within agriculture, the distributional effects of reform would depend more on the shift of resources between sectors.

The simulation results discussed so far have included the standard assumption of full employment in the economy. While this assumption may be reasonable for developed economies, it is less so for countries where education and other factors critical for human capital are not equally accessible to all. Indeed, a key characteristic of the labour market in South Africa is the relatively high rate of unemployment, particularly for unskilled labour.

Hence, an alternative scenario assuming a fixed real wage rate for unskilled labour (thereby assuming an infinite supply) was analysed. The results show that the assumption of fixed real prices for unskilled labour has important consequences for other factor prices. An unlimited pool of unskilled labour permits labour intensive industries to expand more aggressively. However, because factors of production are not perfectly substitutable, prices for skilled labour, land, capital and natural resources are all bid up. At the economy-wide level, the change in welfare is significant. The welfare benefits accruing to the manufacturing industries, which are more capital and skilled labour intensive, are amplified. At the household level (more fully explored in Section 3.3 and Annex 3.A2), this may result in a more unequal distribution of income even though poverty is reduced as new jobs are created for unskilled workers.[9]

Summary

Around two-thirds of the welfare gains to South Africa that may arise from multilateral trade liberalisation are due to liberalisation of non-agriculture sectors, and mostly by countries outside OECD area. Nevertheless, the gains from agricultural reform are also important, accounting for one-third of total welfare gains, with the most significant contribution from liberalisation of OECD agricultural policies. Under the standard assumption of full employment, agriculture factor returns increase slightly more than non-agricultural returns. However, an alternative assumption of no constraints on the unskilled labour supply shows that factor income inequality could be increased, though the poor would benefit from new jobs for unskilled workers.

3.3. Household impact of trade and agricultural policy reforms

South Africa has a heterogeneous agriculture with a commercial export-oriented sector co-existing with subsistence and semi-subsistence households. Non-agricultural income plays an important role in most rural households, including large commercial farms. South Africa is also a highly urbanised country, with large numbers of poor consumers, whose real incomes are dependent on the price of food. Given this structural diversity, it is important to understand how agricultural policy reforms, and trade liberalisation, will affect the incomes of different constituencies.

This section uses an economy-wide framework to address such questions by assessing the distributional impacts of global trade liberalisation on the economy of South Africa using a single country computable general equilibrium (CGE) model.[10] The data inputs to the study were vectors of (percentage) price changes for imports and exports that were derived from results of the global liberalisation scenario analysed through the GTAPEM model, and a social accounting matrix (SAM) for South Africa that was provided by the PROVIDE project.

Large income disparities by region and race

It is important to identify the existing income disparities in various households (representative households by region and race) when trying to estimate the impact of policy reform at the household level. Summary statistics for the distribution of incomes and expenditures by province support the observation that income distribution is highly skewed. Western Cape, Northern Cape and Gauteng all demonstrate per capita (adult equivalent) incomes greater than 140% of average national per capita incomes, while Limpopo and Eastern Cape have incomes per capita less than 60% of the national average (Figure 3.9).

The summary statistics for household incomes and expenditures by race demonstrate an even more skewed distribution of income. African households account for about 80% of the adult equivalent population, while total income is less than 50% of national household incomes resulting in per capita incomes and expenditures of just over 50% of the national average. Asian and coloured households receive 13% of total income while accounting for 11% of the adult equivalent population, and consequently their incomes and expenditures are some 120% of the national household averages. Interestingly, even higher education African households do only marginally better in terms of incomes per capita than the average for Asian and coloured households. Conversely, white households represent only 9% of the population but account for 42% of income and have per capita incomes and expenditures 4.7 times higher than the national average (Figure 3.10).

Higher incomes and redistribution of welfare

Annex 3.A2 provides a detailed analysis of the changes in the macroeconomic aggregates, as well as subsequent changes in production activities and factor incomes associated with the trade liberalisation simulation applied to South Africa. The results in terms of welfare gains from liberalisation[11] at the household level, disaggregated by region

Figure 3.9. **Household incomes and consumption expenditures by region**

Per capita income as % of the national average

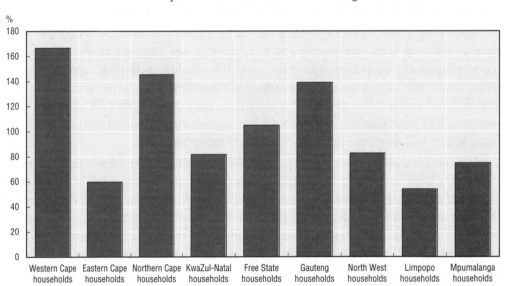

Source: Social Accounting Matrix – PROVIDE project.

Figure 3.10. **Household incomes and consumption expenditures by race**

Per capita income as % of the national average

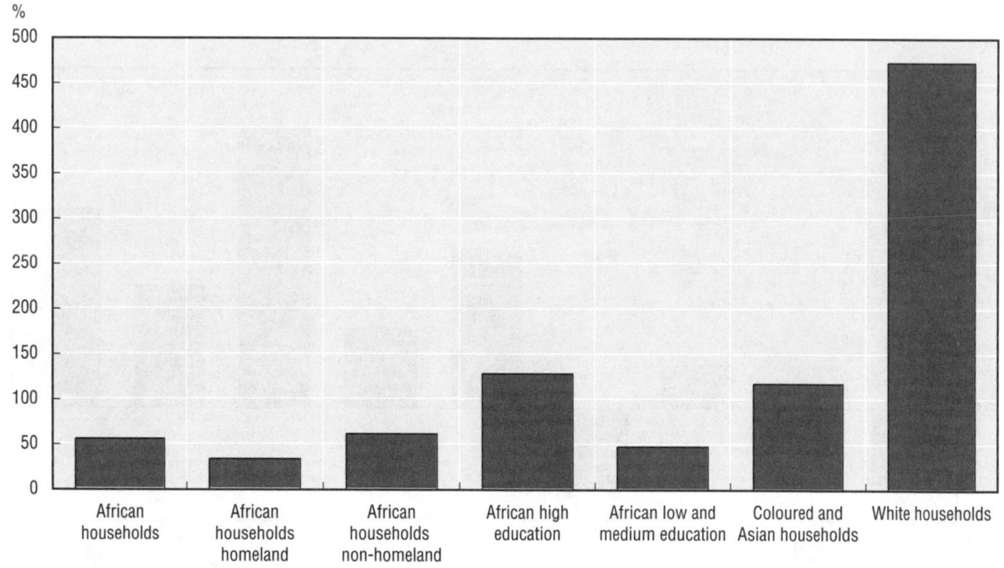

Source: Social Accounting Matrix – PROVIDE project.

and race, are summarised below. The welfare implications differ with respect to racial group, residential area and level of education. This suggests that the reasons are not simply related to changes in the prices of consumption commodities but also come about as a result of appreciable changes in factor prices and/or production structure. There is also some evidence that the welfare gains are inversely related to income.

The coastal provinces, Western and Eastern Cape and KwaZulu-Natal, show losses in welfare (over 0.5%), while the inland provinces show welfare gains (over 2%), with strongest gains for the North West and Mpumlanga (Figure 3.11). Non-white households gain while white households lose (about 0.6%). Africans living in the former homelands realise smaller welfare gains than Africans living elsewhere in South Africa. Coloured and Asian households are only affected marginally (Figure 3.12).

These welfare changes are primarily driven by income gains. The primary sources of household incomes are the returns from factor services, realised either as direct payments for labour, capital and land services or indirectly through the ownership of incorporated business enterprises. In both cases the starting point is factor incomes. As indicated by Figure 3.13, there is, with the exception of land, a generalised increase in the incomes to different (aggregate) factor types, although the range of increase in factor incomes by labour type is substantial. Consequently, a large part of the reason for the increase in household incomes is the generalised increase in factor incomes. As fiscal neutrality implies increased taxes to recapture lost government revenue after liberalisation, this cost is disproportionately borne by the rich which significantly reduces white household income gains.

Figure 3.11. **Equivalent variation in household welfare by province –
Based on consumption**

% change

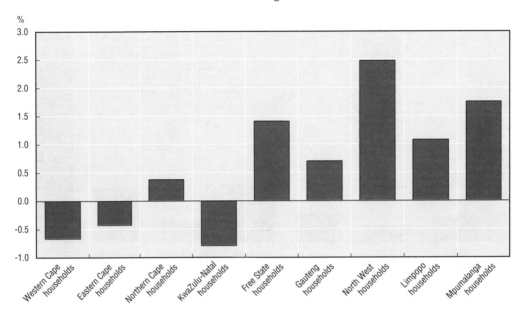

Source: Simulation results.

Figure 3.12. **Equivalent variation in household welfare by race –
Based on consumption**

% change

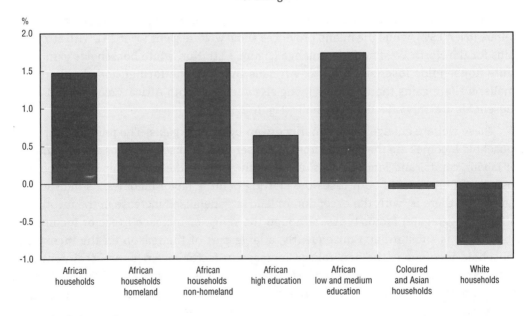

Source: Simulation results.

OECD REVIEW OF AGRICULTURAL POLICIES – ISBN 92-64-03679-2 – © OECD 2006

Figure 3.13. **Summary changes in factor incomes – 50% cut in South Africa's trade barriers with full employment and fiscal neutrality**

%

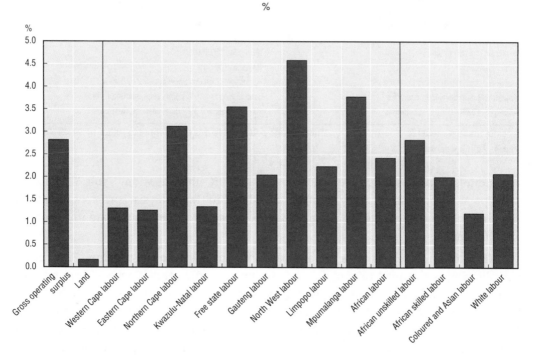

Source: Simulation results.

Summary

Multilateral liberalisation results in a generalised expansion of economic activity with income increases across all household groups in South Africa. There is evidence of redistribution in welfare terms both between racial groups and provinces, with the coastal provinces and white households being subjected to some small declines in welfare while the inland provinces and non-white households experience some increase in welfare. Liberalisation produces a small shift in the allocation of resources towards minerals, manufacturing and service activities. A modest expansion in food and agricultural activities is primarily a consequence of a generalised expansion of the South African economy.

It is important, however, to recognise that the results presented here are produced in the setting of a comparative static model. The presumption that the relative productivities of economies are unchanged by the policy of liberalisation is embedded within both the GTAPEM and the single country CGE models. Ultimately, the ability of the South African economy to respond to the increased market opportunities associated with liberalisation, by increasing its relative efficiency, may be more important than the short-term effects of liberalisation.

3.4. The impact of liberalisation on South African agricultural commodity markets

This section explores, with the use of a partial equilibrium model (Aglink-Cosimo), the potential implications that a significant cut in trade and domestic policies could have on South Africa's production, consumption and net trade of major agricultural commodities over a ten year future period. For all market related policies, including trade

Table 3.3. **Principal assumptions of the liberalisation scenarios**[1]

Policy	Scenario assumptions, relative to 2004 policy levels
Tariffs (in quota, out-of quota and non quota)	Reduction by 50%
Tariff rate quotas	Increase by 50%
Limits on subsidised exports	*Reduction by 50%*
Direct payments	*Reduction by 50%*
Support prices, target prices, loan rates	*Reduction of total support benefits by 50%*
Adjustment path developed countries	5 equal steps of 10% points each, starting from 2005
Adjustment path developing countries	10 equal steps of 5% points each, starting from 2005

1. Note that the model for South Africa does not include policy measures represented in italics in this table.
Source: Aglink-Cosimo.

and domestic policies, the scenarios assume a 50% liberalisation. Table 3.3 lists the principal assumptions on policy changes considered in this analysis, corresponding to the relevant policies represented in Aglink-Cosimo. These reform measures are implemented simultaneously.

Three alternative scenarios are analysed in comparison to the baseline. First, partial liberalisation is assumed to apply to OECD countries only, while South Africa and other non-OECD countries' policies are held at baseline levels. As described in Table 3.3, the liberalisation in most OECD countries would take place in five equal increments of 10 percentage points starting from 2005 (*i.e.* the full 50% cut in support would be reached as of 2009), while the developing countries' scheme is assumed to apply to South Korea[12] where liberalisation would take place over a longer period. This scenario shows the effects of OECD member policies on South Africa.

Second, South Africa is assumed to unilaterally liberalise. A 50% liberalisation of South African trade policies is assumed, keeping OECD and other non-OECD countries' policies unchanged (Box 3.1). Note that the developing countries' scheme implies that the full 50% cut in protection and support would be reached only by the year 2014 (*i.e.* only after the end of the simulation period which currently is 2013). This scenario shows the effects of South Africa's policies on its own and world markets. Finally, a third scenario assumes a multilateral liberalisation including policy changes in the countries represented in the model used for this analysis, *i.e.* China, India, South Africa, and OECD countries.

It should be noted (Box 3.1) that reductions in the border measures examined in this section start from the bound levels agreed to in the URAA. In contrast, reductions in

Box 3.1. **Implementation of assumed South Africa policy changes**

Policies explicitly considered for South Africa in this analysis include border measures, tariff rate quotas and non-quota tariffs. For tariffs a gradual reduction in annual 5% increments is assumed starting from 2005 (in other words, tariffs are assumed to be 95% of their baseline levels in 2005, 90% of their baseline levels in 2006, etc.) to reach a 45% reduction by 2013 when the simulations end (a 50% reduction would be reached by 2014 which however is not covered by the simulation period). Only MFN bound tariffs are reduced. Applied tariffs are held constant at their last known level, usually 2003. The tariff rate quotas are assumed to gradually increase by annual 5% increments, again starting from 2005. Changes in tariffs and tariff rate quotas are calculated from the final levels committed within WTO, which were reached in 2004.

domestic supports start from actual levels. Thus, the scenarios examined here are somewhat different from the scenarios discussed in Sections 3.2 and 3.3 dealing with multisectoral liberalisation where actual protection levels are reduced. Here, reductions up to 50% of tariffs and export subsidies and increases in TRQs may lead to much less or even no effective liberalisation, depending on the commodity and country. This is because in many cases there is considerable latitude to reduce bound levels without significantly altering effective protection. Furthermore, all instruments, although reduced, remain in place. In some cases, even though an instrument may not have been binding in the baseline, it can become binding in the scenario, thus counter-acting the liberalisation effects of other instruments and leading to lower effects on world and domestic markets than may have occurred otherwise.

Impacts on world and South African crop markets

Liberalising OECD markets

A partial liberalisation of OECD policies by 50% confirms the expectation that the biggest changes take place in the OECD countries where reforms occur and for products with relatively high levels of protection. For example, dairy is among the most protected sectors in many OECD countries. Partial OECD liberalisation leads to declining domestic prices in countries that reform their dairy policies. On average, the US domestic butter price is 5% below the baseline (as much as 11% below in 2009); in Canada, the domestic cheese price is 20% below its baseline level; the EU butter price is 15% below and coarse grains 6% below their baseline levels; and in Japan the rice price is some 9% lower. In each of these cases, of course, larger price changes are evident in certain years. In contrast, for products with relatively low or no effective protection, the changes are more modest. For example, on average, oilseed prices in the European Union and the United States respectively are about 0.6% and 0.7% below their baseline levels.

The effects of OECD liberalisation on world markets are muted by producer and consumer response in other countries. For example, OECD liberalisation has relatively small impacts on world cereal prices. It triggers slightly higher world prices for coarse grains (0.8%) and rice (0.8%) on average for the 2005-13 period (Figure 3.14). In the case of coarse grains, the changes in the European Union dominate. Production in the European Union falls 2.7% on average, leading to lower exports (down 25% on average). Other countries, notably the United States, respond by expanding production and exports, thus mitigating the rise in the world price. In the rice market, increased imports by Japan dominate the results. OECD rice policies represented in the model are Korea's and Japan's. For Korea, the rice quota is assumed to remain unchanged. Japan's rice TRQ is liberalised through expanding the quota and lowering the tariffs. These policy changes are sufficient to generate larger rice imports in Japan leading to a higher world price. Nevertheless, OECD countries comprise a small share of the world rice market, hence relative modest changes.

At the same time, support reduction leads to land reallocation in the European Union. EU production and exports of wheat would grow (exports increase about 15% on average), mostly offsetting falling exports from other exporting countries leading to slightly declining world wheat prices of about 0.7% on average.

Figure 3.14. **Impact of 50% liberalisation on world crop markets, 2005-13 average**

World market price impacts

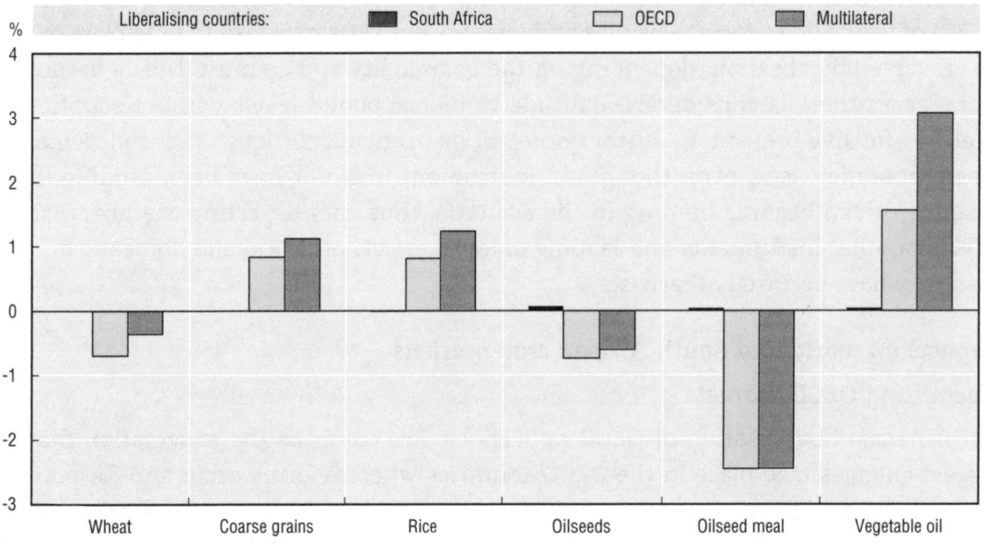

Source: OECD, Aglink-Cosimo simulation results.

Assuming no change in South African policies, the price changes for coarse grains and wheat would be largely transmitted to the domestic markets in South Africa (Figure 3.15). This will lead to some reduction in domestic use (mostly of coarse grains for feed); at the same time production of coarse grains will increase, albeit modestly. By contrast, the lower wheat price leads to a slight expansion in wheat use (mostly for food) and an equally small drop in production. The contrasting movements in world prices imply a small drop in coarse grains imports (0.5% on average) and a small increase in wheat imports (0.7% on average over the projection period).

Oilseeds are relatively less protected than other crops in OECD markets. OECD liberalisation leads to oilseed area and production expansion in the European Union, resulting in a lower world price. Reduced oilseed meal imports by the European Union and Japan also moderately lowers world prices, and both of these price developments are passed on to South Africa's domestic markets. As a result of lower oilseed and oil meal prices, production declines very modestly. The prices of vegetable oils in international markets on the other hand are higher following OECD liberalisation. Most of this is transmitted to South Africa's market. But even with slightly higher domestic prices, lower oilseed production leads to lower production of vegetable oils as well. It is important to note that the discussed changes are very slight. It appears that for the crop sectors, OECD liberalisation has minor effects on the international markets and therefore, on South Africa's markets as well.

Liberalising South African markets

Compared to a partial liberalisation in all OECD countries, liberalising South African trade policies by 50% would have an even smaller effect on world prices. This is not surprising given that South Africa is a relatively small country in world markets as far as analysed products are concerned (although South Africa is a relatively large exporter of fruits, wine and sugar not covered in AGLINK and hence not included in this part of the

Figure 3.15. **Impact of 50% liberalisation on South African crop markets, 2005-13 average**

Producer price impacts

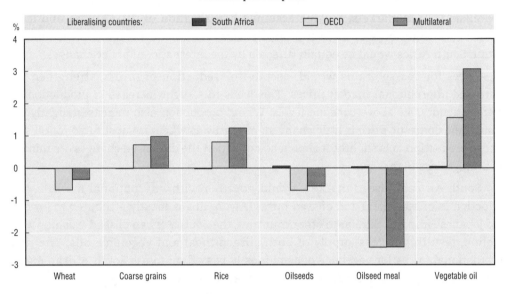

Crop production impacts

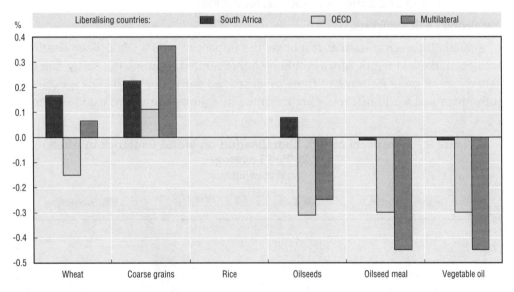

Source: OECD, Aglink-Cosimo simulation results.

analysis). Even in the domestic markets, the effects of South Africa's own liberalisation of border measures have relatively few effects. This is mostly attributable to the binding overhang existing in the South African crop markets whereby the applied rates are below the MFN bound rates and remain below even as the bound rates fall 45% by the end of the period. Furthermore, even though South Africa has scheduled many TRQs including for wheat, coarse grains, oilseeds and oil meals, they are not enforced. The administration method for most commodities is applied tariffs and, as mentioned, these are below bound rates. Consequently, there is little effective liberalisation, and a relatively small impact on domestic markets.

Liberalising all markets

A multilateral liberalisation would result in market impacts that represent the total of the above-mentioned scenarios. World price changes would be dominated by the effects of liberalising OECD markets, but the assumed liberalisation of the Chinese and Indian markets also contribute to the world price effects. The impact on the domestic markets within South Africa would be equally affected by the international policy changes.

Prices for coarse grains would, despite the reduction of tariffs, strengthen with increased international market prices. This leads to a slight increase in production – on average about 0.4% above baseline levels. Wheat production also increases slightly even though the domestic price is little changed, primarily as wheat is substituted for oil seeds whose production falls slightly. It should be noted that the discussed changes are minimal, on average, less than 0.3%.

South African oilseed markets would, together with international markets, see a reduction in oilseed meal and oilseed prices. Again, this is mostly attributed to lower EU and Japanese imports. Similar to other countries, the South African oilseed crushing would decline, resulting in less supply of both oilseed meal and vegetable oils. The rising international prices for vegetable oils are mostly passed on to the South African market, nonetheless vegetable oil production falls as a result of lower crushing.

Impacts on world and South African livestock markets

Liberalising OECD markets

Similar to the crop market response, the impact of a 50% OECD liberalisation on livestock markets in South Africa would be rather limited (Figure 3.16), partly due to the relatively small trade for some of these products and partly due to the linkages between South Africa and world markets as represented in Aglink-Cosimo. For example, the beef

Figure 3.16. **Impacts of 50% liberalisation on world livestock markets, 2005-13 average**

World price impacts

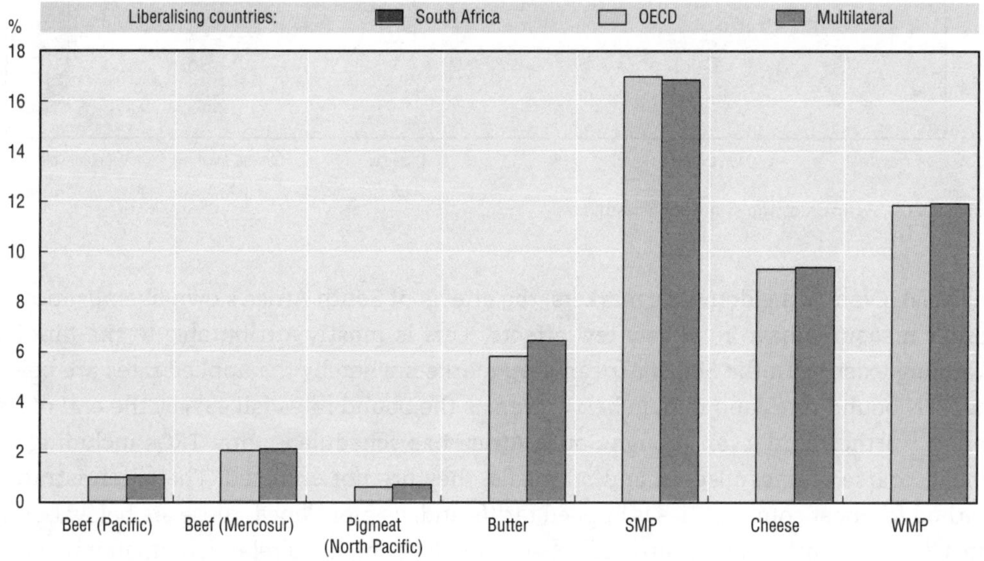

Source: OECD, Aglink-Cosimo simulation results.

and pigmeat markets are segmented between the foot and mouth disease free zone (the Pacific market) and other markets. South Africa is connected to the pigmeat markets of the regions where foot and mouth disease is endemic and which are disconnected from most OECD markets. OECD liberalisation therefore, has limited influence on this market, and because of binding overhang, South Africa's own liberalisation also has no impact as shown in Figure 3.17. South Africa's beef market is also delinked from the Pacific beef market and therefore from most OECD markets. For this market too, OECD liberalisation has relatively small direct effects on South Africa as shown in Figure 3.17. South Africa, however, is linked to the Mercosur beef market and thus is somewhat affected by changes

Figure 3.17. **Impact of 50% liberalisation on South African livestock markets, 2005-13 average**

Producer price impacts

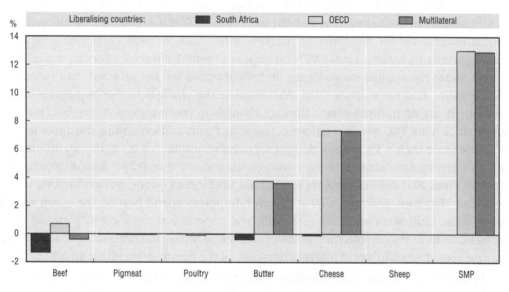

Livestock production impacts

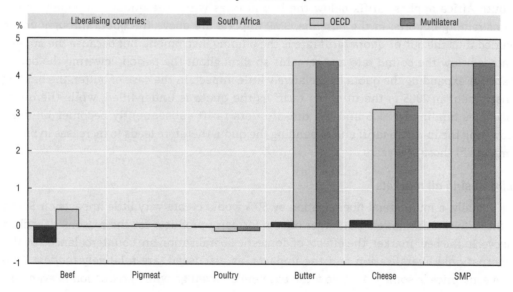

Source: Aglink-Cosimo simulation results.

in the EU's beef market. Changes in the EU's beef market lead to an increase in the Mercosur beef price (2% on average) which results in about a 4% drop in imports, most of them occurring in the last two years.

OECD liberalisation has nevertheless relatively large impacts on world dairy markets, especially skim milk powder (SMP), and South Africa is linked to these world markets. Higher world prices for these products are transmitted to the South African markets, leading to a drop in imports (some 21% for cheese, 28% for butter and 8% for SMP). As the higher prices are passed on to domestic markets, South Africa's butter and SMP production expands about 4% above baseline levels (3% for cheese) while cheese consumption drops to about 3%, SMP consumption falls some 2%, and butter consumption is about 1% below the baseline.

Liberalising South African markets

A 50% liberalisation of South Africa's livestock markets has no effect on world prices, mostly because of the linkages, or lack thereof between South African and world markets. Similar results hold for the domestic markets, other than for beef. Largely as a result of binding overhang, lower pigmeat MFN tariffs do not reflect effective liberalisation as they remain above the applied tariff. Hence, domestic prices are not affected, and therefore, neither production nor consumption. Also because the changes in the crop sector are so small, there are no indirect effects through changes in feeding costs. In the beef market, South Africa has a TRQ which is enforced. Lowering tariffs and expanding the quota results in a little more than a 1% drop in domestic prices, resulting in a 0.4% drop in production and 0.3% increase in consumption on average relative to the baseline. As a result imports increase. From 2007 to 2011, imports expand but the binding quota restricts imports to the expanded TRQ level. Starting in 2012 however, imports expand beyond the quota as the out-of-quota tariff becomes binding. Overall, beef imports average some 17% greater than the baseline from the combination of lower tariffs and higher import quota. None of these changes are reflected in world markets however, as the volumes are rather small.

In the dairy markets, South Africa's TRQs for cheese, SMP, and whole milk powder (WMP) are marginally impacted by the unilateral liberalisation. In these markets as well, South Africa applies tariffs below the bound rates while the quota component is not constraining imports. In the baseline, SMP imports are above the quota throughout the period thus the out-of-quota tariff rate is the binding instrument. But because the applied rate is below the bound rate and remains so throughout the period, lowering the bound tariff, or expanding the quota has relatively little impact. In the case of butter, the binding instrument in 2005 is the in-quota tariff as the quota is under-filled, while the quota becomes binding in 2006 and the out-of-quota tariff subsequently becomes binding. Lowering the in-quota tariff and expanding the quota therefore leads to increases in butter imports in those two years.

Liberalising all markets

Finally, a multilateral liberalisation by 50% would create very little impacts on South Africa's livestock markets but larger effects for dairy products for the reasons described above. In the beef market, the effects of domestic liberalisation are counterbalanced by the international liberalisation and the impacts, as discussed, are relatively modest. The domestic price is some 0.4% below the baseline on average while production is even less affected. The price impacts on dairy products would be more pronounced reflecting the more significant price changes on international markets.

Summary

Liberalising OECD and South African agricultural policies would, to some degree, have opposite and therefore partly offsetting effects on South African domestic markets for crops. For a number of commodities, the effects of a partial multilateral liberalisation would therefore be rather small. The effects of OECD and South African policies individually are generally more pronounced in dairy markets than in livestock. Partial liberalisation in OECD countries would result in higher world and domestic prices for most agricultural products and would therefore benefit South African producers, but at the same time negatively affect food consumers. However, given the size of price changes, the impacts remain small overall. Unilateral South African liberalisation on the other hand would have minor effects on world and domestic prices. The impact of unilateral liberalisation on South Africa's agricultural markets would also be relatively small, given that currently applied tariffs are well below bound rates.

3.5. The effects of policy reform on food security[13]

Food security and poverty reduction are dominant features of South Africa's national policy landscape, receiving consistent government policy attention, political will and budget resources. The government's policy agenda has been backed up with actions and resources. By the late 1990s, government agencies and departments had reoriented safety net and social programmes, making them more progressive and better targeted. The poor began to gain more than proportionately from social spending relative to their population size. Evaluations suggest that ongoing social assistance programmes make important contributions to rural poverty reduction (van der Berg, 2001).

Food security is a continuing problem

South Africa does not face a serious under nutrition problem in terms of chronically inadequate level of calorie intake. The country produces, exports and imports an increasingly wide range of foods. The Daily Energy Supply (DES) is more than 2 950 calories/per capita/day which is a relatively high quantity of calories available for consumption. In contrast, the average DES for Africa is 2 250 cal/cap/day. The average for developed countries is 3 300 cal/cap/day. According to the FAO methodology the proportion of undernourished population in South Africa is estimated at around 5% of total population.[14] This compares favourably to the sub-Saharan average of 33%. Food availability and access to food via targeted social programmes are contributing to the generally good calorie intake.

On the other hand, malnutrition remains a serious food security issue. The available quantity of total calories may be adequate, but the quantity of protein and nutrients, the diversity of foods, and the stability of access to food throughout the year are sources of concern. Estimates suggest that approximately 1.5 million South African children suffer from malnutrition, with 24% of the children stunted and 9% underweight. Among the poorest 20% of households, the stunting rate is 38%. Micro-nutrient related malnutrition is an unremitting public health problem. One-third of children show evidence of marginal vitamin A status, 20% are anaemic, and 10% are iron-deficient (May 2001). In addition, recent nutrition surveys indicate that a growing proportion of South Africa's population faces malnutrition from "excessive" calorie intake leading to health problems such as diabetes and heart diseases.

Like in much of Africa, poverty is predominately rural in South Africa. More than 70% of the poor live in rural areas, concentrated in communal lands. Unlike the large and small-scale commercial sector, agricultural activities in the former homelands (mainly on communal land) is constrained significantly by institutional rigidities, and is not nearly as responsive to market signals as commercial producers elsewhere in the country. However, rural poverty in South Africa appears to differ from other countries in three particular ways: a) among the rural poor, income generated directly from agricultural activities and food consumed from own farm production are minor components of household resources; b) migration patterns involve many household members continuously rotating between a rural and urban base; and c) rural society is linked tightly to the social and health problems of urban areas.

While South Africa is significantly wealthier than the other developing countries of Africa, it had a long history of discrimination and widespread inequality. South Africa's per capita GDP places it among the 50 wealthiest nations, while in overall human and social indicators it has a ranking of 120th out of 177 countries in the UNDP Human Development Indicators (UNDP, 2005). The country has life expectancies among the 50 worst in the world and projections of mortality suggest that these will deteriorate further as deaths from the Aids epidemic increase.

Reduced support has not affected food availability

Overall, existing research examining specifically how recent policy reforms and domestic liberalisation efforts have impacted on food security concludes that at the national level, the food availability dimension of food security has not been compromised by liberalisation and related organisation and jurisdictional reforms (National Agricultural Marketing Council, 2001). Several reasons help explain the commercial sectors ability to provide stable food supplies.

Within the last ten years, South Africa's commercial agricultural sector has adapted well to the policy reforms which liberalised markets and reduced support to commercial farming. In general, commercial producers tend to be highly competitive, market oriented, and profit focused, responding to local, regional and international market opportunities. More specifically, commercial farmers have adapted to the new policy environment in three ways. First, there are increased opportunities for small and medium-scale businesses to process and distribute maize and maize products. This increased activity in the rural areas has provided a stimulus to rural economies. Second, there has been a marked increase in agro-tourism throughout the country. Third, small-scale commercial farmers tend to have better access to markets, now that the co-operatives, which once acted as agents under the single channel schemes (and which were only taking delivery in bulk), have lost their monopolies.

One of the few conspicuous efficiency issues for the commercially oriented agriculture sector is water use and irrigation policies. Irrigated agriculture provides more than one-third the country crop value-added on less than 10% of the arable land. However, one-third of this irrigated land accounts for two-thirds of the output value. A great deal of water is used to produce lower value crops with relatively little value-added and job creating potential. Appropriate water sector reforms could yield numerous new jobs and higher value outputs.

Market deregulation has provided farms with opportunities to adapt a wide range of strategies (increased part-time farming, contract farming, strategic selling throughout the season, and price hedging) and led to the development of market institutions (*e.g.* agricultural futures market, grain trading firms, brokerage firms, auction places) that enable producers to participate in markets with greater certainty and lower transaction costs. In the livestock sector, deregulation resulted in a rapid increase in the number of smaller abattoirs in the rural areas, mostly on-farm facilities that are combined with retail outlets or which supply directly to retailers in the formal market. The proportion of red meat sold in the informal sector directly into poor urban and peri-urban communities has increased which may be considered a positive development for food security. Market deregulation also resulted in greater involvement of commercial banking in the financing of the commercial farming.

The commercial farming benefits from a well developed public and private research, extension and analytical infrastructures, and is also well integrated into communications, financial and marketing services. Where developed, these networks also facilitate the market integration of new small and medium commercial producers as they can more easily obtain information and market products at relatively low costs. South Africa is unique among most developing economies in that it has sophisticated and well developed input markets especially in the financial and banking sector. However, in part due to the legacy of apartheid, the financial system excludes the majority of South Africans. As a result, financial markets are not geared to serve the needs of the poor rural households, subsistence farmers and farm workers. Similar situations are found in almost all other factor markets, the result of market segmentation and access barriers.

In an economy and society where access to land has been denied to some groups of the population, jobs on commercial farms provided the best opportunity to gain income for this population. The living standards, as well as security, are generally considered significantly higher for all those involved in commercial agriculture than their equivalents in the traditional sector, in the densely populated rural settlements, and in the urban informal settlements where unemployment is particularly high (see Cross *et al.*, 1999, Bekker, 2003). Of primary importance, is the fact that typically at least one member of the on-farm worker household is employed full-time. Though commercial producers have continually shed on-farm labour and farm worker dependants over the past 30 years, on-farm employment offers farm workers (and their households) relative advantages, especially if these are compared to individuals and households without fixed employment and residing in dense rural informal settlements.

Poor households affected by higher food prices

Overall, the commercial farming sector continues to expand production and provide jobs on farms and in upstream and downstream industries. Productivity increases help to maintain lower real food prices, while farm employment, associated with increased production, contributes directly to food security via income generation. However, several important food security and poverty related qualifications (and implications) should be made:

- Domestic food prices are now more aligned with international prices with fluctuations transmitted more quickly – good news for low income net food consumers when world prices of basic foods fall and/or the ZAR strengthens, but bad news when world prices rise and/or the ZAR weakens.

- New jobs are predominately skill-intensive in marketing, retailing, processing, packaging and financial services – the poor and unskilled require access to basic education and specialised training in order to take advantage of these jobs.

- Much of the expansion into horticultural activities tends to provide only part-time, less skilled, low paid employment.

- The country's stable interest rates and low inflation favour investments in more capital intensive technologies which lead to further labour shedding and reduced farm employment.

The vast majority of the poor population, both rural and urban, are net food purchasers. So how are recent liberalisation efforts affecting the poor as food consumers? Despite increasing concentration in the food manufacturing and retailing sector since the early stages of deregulation, food price inflation was rather moderate since the drought of 1991/92. It was only ten years later in 2001/2002 when basic food prices increased sharply in the wake of a sharp depreciation of the local currency. Vink and Kirsten (2002) conclude that these sharp increases in the farm gate prices of basic food commodities was a result of four factors: a) an increasing world price for these commodities; b) a lack of competition in the supply chain beyond the farm gate, especially at the retail level; c) a fast and severe depreciation in the value of the currency; and d) a shortage of maize in the SADC region.

The poor in South Africa have been adversely affected by higher retail food prices. So far, there is little evidence that small farmers have benefited from the new trading environment in agriculture. Most small farmers in South Africa are still poor, are net food buyers, and are as adversely affected by higher consumer prices for food as are the landless rural and urban poor. A successful land reform together with a well targeted small farmer support programme can contribute to the creation of an efficient small-scale sector in agriculture and hence to alleviate poverty in rural areas.

South Africa has mechanisms in place to address poverty and food security problems. The 1996 Constitution of South Africa guarantees progressive social rights that are deemed to be universal – in particular, for both rural and urban residents. The national government's current social policies have been built upon this foundation and have been deeply influenced by the Reconstruction and Development Programme (RDP), a mid-1990s White Paper proposing a policy framework for socio-economic progress in which the eradication of poverty and diminishment of inequality figured as two primary goals.

Rural areas and agricultural regions in particular, have been identified by the national government as a primary objective for their delivery of social welfare policy. One important reason for this new focus on rural welfare derives from the rebalancing of state policies that were previously focused primarily on urban residents. Both the rural as well as the urban poor are now targeted by the national welfare safety net.

The 1996 Constitution also implemented the idea of government in which local, provincial and national governments are defined as spheres (rather than as the more traditional tiers), and between which co-ordination and co-operation are encouraged. The Constitution also defines the developmental role that local governments (and their municipalities) are required to play a role beyond simple service delivery. Each municipality is expected to give priority to the basic needs of, and promote the social and economic development of, its "community". Today, South Africa's local government has

Table 3.4. **Profile of the South African social security public policy framework, 2002**

Social security policy domains	Social security policies	Main regulations	Intended target communities
Social assistance and poverty alleviation	Social assistance (monthly state grants)	Social Assistance Act	Children in need and foster children, disabled, the aged
	Poverty relief	Public works programmes	The poor and residents in rural poverty pockets
Social infrastructure	Education	SA Schools Act	Youth learners and adult education
	Health	National Health Bill	Universal primary health care, HIV/Aids infected
Economic infrastructure	Housing	White Paper on Housing, Housing Act	Grants for households < ZAR 3 500/month
	Water supply and sanitation	Water Services Act	Universal + free basic water
	Energy	White Paper on Energy	Universal electrification
	Land rights	White Paper on SA Land Policy	Extension of land ownership and security of tenure for poor and landless
Employment and production	Labour	Unemployment Insurance Act, Basic conditions of employment Act, Labour Relations Act	Employed and recently unemployed
	Agricultural support	Provincial Depts of Agriculture	All farmers with a focus on black farmers
Fiscal allocation within cooperative govermnent	Fiscal and Finance Committee formula	The Division of Revenue Act	Allocations to provinces privilege those with high rural % of population

Source: Bekker (2003).

become a primary agent responsible for the implementation of social security policy, in both rural as well as urban areas.

Table 3.4 summarises the major safety net programmes. Funds and related resources to provincial departments of agriculture include extension, production and infrastructural support to small scale-farmers, beneficiaries from the land reform. These programmes provide the basic foundations for the future success of agriculture with large investments in people's health, education, rights and local infrastructure. For example, land rights are a basic policy goal to increase access to resources through the redistribution of land and tenure rights among the poor and the historically dispossessed.

Promoting enhanced food security

While production for home consumption increases the availability of vegetables and increases micronutrient intake, the income "savings" derived from home production seems to have more positive influences on the nutritional status of rural populations, as they are used for increased purchases of energy-dense foods such as fats, oils and meat. Various South African expenditure studies confirm that increased household incomes are likely to increase local demand for meat, poultry, vegetables and fruit. While increased micronutrients have undisputed benefits for nutrition, increased protein and energy from fats and meat would contribute more significantly to reducing South Africa's unacceptably high rate of stunting among children, while simultaneously benefiting micronutrient deficiencies. Increased incomes from agricultural sales are also likely to increase the nutritional adequacy of rural diets, hence improve health, and increase resistance to disease. These developments have a potential to increase productivity and improve human capacity of the poor rural population.

Household level incentives are needed to encourage more production of farm tradables. The prospects of additional income and reasonable return from improved agricultural production could be provided by appropriate agricultural services, accessible, affordable inputs and technology, and access to marketing structures (including transport and storage facilities), and access to market information.

The nutritional benefits of agriculture will only remain positive if the dietary changes that do occur comply with dietary guidelines. Trends such as urbanisation and consumer preference for convenience foods (such as rice over maize), threaten the beneficial characteristics of traditional rural diets (usually low in fat and animal protein), compromising the health of rural and migrating populations and exposing them unduly to health risks. Lastly then, consumer preferences for commercial goods require behavioural changes to ensure maximum realisation of the nutritional benefits of agriculture-led growth. Effective promotion of the value of agriculture and the savings of home production should be part of any food security and/or poverty alleviation strategy.

Summary

The extensive deregulation and liberalisation of agriculture in South Africa has resulted in a sector that is economically better off – more is being produced with fewer resources, and exports have increased substantially. Unfortunately, most of the direct benefits have accrued to a relatively small group; some larger-scale commercial farmers and some farm workers who have remained in permanent employment. The population at large has arguably benefited indirectly through commodity prices that are lower because of the additional supply, and through the greater availability of foreign exchange earnings. However, historically disadvantaged farmers, smaller-scale commercial farmers, and a large number of former farm workers have not benefited, and some are worse off.

Notes

1. For each commodity five leading destinations are shown based on the average export volume in 2002-04. If the aggregate share of the top five in total export volume is below 80%, the list of partners is expanded to reach 80% threshold, as is done for raw and refined sugar.

2. See Footnote 2 of Table 3.A1.1 for more detailed description of the wine export group under consideration.

3. The 6% over-quota rate represents the weighted average of the over-quota rates for TARIC codes 22042179, 22042183 and 22042184 with weights being import values from South Africa under these codes.

4. According to the entry price system, products imported at or over an established entry price are charged an *ad valorem* duty only. If the import comes in at price lower than the entry price, on top of the *ad valorem* duty a specific duty is charged, which increases as import price falls.

5. Through the STE, Japan applies a high resale price on imports to protect the domestic industry. The import is only duty free to the STE that extracts a rent from resale to domestic processors.

6. Due probably to consecutive droughts in India that cut domestic production substantially, India's trade position shifted from a periodic exporter (with subsidies) to a large importer in those years. In 2004, duty-free imports of raw sugar were allowed under the advanced import licence scheme.

7. Tariff information includes MFN applied tariffs, the *ad valorem* equivalent of specific tariffs, tariff rate quotas, and preferential arrangements.

8. Trade weighted average of applied rates. Includes *ad valorem*, specific and TRQs (in *ad valorem* equivalents) as applied in 2001. This static view may understate the actual level of protection. Other policies affecting trade, such as import licensing, state trading agencies, etc., are not fully accounted for in this analysis. These other policies may have a significant impact on South Africa's trade depending on the time period chosen, and are therefore analysed in detail using the AGLINK world agricultural commodity market model.

9. The impact of factor price changes for a particular household depends on changes in factor employment, factor returns, and asset ownership structure.

10. As far as possible the core simulation was compatible with the simulation used in the GTAPEM to generate the global price changes. However, rather than running a single simulation a series of simulations was implemented so as to assess the sensitivity of the results to changes in specification; the additional simulations considered a range of trade liberalisation scenarios by South Africa and variations in the closure rules.

11. Global reforms (i.e. 50% cuts to all tariffs in all countries and 50% cut in agricultural domestic support in OECD countries) with and without South Africa partaking. The results presented in this Section relate to the case where South Africa participates in the liberalisation and where the closure rules are full employment and fiscal neutrality.

12. Note that due to the NAFTA no policy changes are assumed for Mexico in these scenarios.

13. This Section was contributed by the FAO (Randy Stringer), based on a report by Johann Kirsten (University of Pretoria) and Nick Vink (University of Stellenbosch). Their report was based on work for the FAO Roles of Agriculture Project and includes contributions by Julian May, Sheryl Hendriks, Mike Lyne, Cecilia Punt and Simon Bekker.

14. Personal communication with Jorge Mernies, Chief, Socio Economic Statistics and Analysis Service, FAO.

ANNEX 3.A1

Supporting Tables for Chapter 3, Section 3.1

Table 3.A1.1. **Protection of the wine sector in South African export markets**

Product/ South African exports	Country	Share of exports (2002-04)	Applied tariff 2005	Tariff type	TRQ	Tariff preferences	Other measures
Grape wines[1]							
USD 345 million	EU[2]	86%	5% (6%)	Specific	Yes	BA	..
160 thousand tonnes	USA[3]	3%	0% (1.5%)	Specific	–	GSP, AGOA	–
(2002-04 average)	Canada[4]	3%	2%	Specific	–	–	–
	Japan[5]	1%	15%	Mixed	–	–	–
	Mozambique	1%	25%	*Ad valorem*	–	–	–

Acronyms: GSP: Generalised System of Preferences; BA: Bilateral Agreement; AGOA: African Growth and Opportunity Act.

1. The data presented in the table concerns wines covered by the HS-220421 code, which includes wines in containers holding 2 litres and less. Tariff rates within this 6-digit code are in some countries strongly differentiated at lower levels of classification. The tariffs reported in the table are for table grape wines of alcoholic strength not exceeding 15%, representing the most traded South Africa's wines.
2. The EU tariff rates are for TARIC codes 22042179, 22042183 and 22042184. South Africa's wine exports under these three codes accounted for around 99% of total export under the 6-digit code 220421. The bilateral trade agreement grants South Africa a TRQ of 32 million litres per year which applies to codes 22042179, 22042180, 22042183 and 22042184, and provides for a zero in-quota duty and the average over-quota duty estimated at 6% (AVE). The weighted average import tariff, accounting for both in-quota and over quota supplies, is 5% (AVE).
3. South Africa's exports to the Unites States are duty free under GSP and AGOA. General weighted average tariff for wines under the group HS- 220421 is 1.5% (AVE).
4. The specific tariff is 0.0935 CAD/litre, or AVE of 2%.
5. The *ad valorem* tariff is 15%, or 125 JPY/litre, whichever is less; subject to a minimum duty of 67 JPY/litre.

Sources: MAD-ATD; TARIC; USITC.

Table 3.A1.2. **Protection of the fresh fruit sector in South African export markets**

Product/ South African exports	Country	Share of exports (2002-04)	Applied tariff 2005	Tariff type	TRQ	Tariff preferences	Other measures
Table grapes							
USD 199 million	EU[1]	82%	6% (14%)	Ad valorem	Yes	GSP, BA	–
215 thousand tonnes	China, Hong Kong	4%	0%	–	–	–	–
(2002-04 average)	Canada	2%	0%	–	–	–	–
	USA[2]	2%	0%	–	–	GSP, AGOA	–
	United Arab Emirates	1%	0%	–	–	–	–
Oranges							
USD 205 million	EU[3]	45%	3% (16%)	Ad valorem	–	–	–
708 thousand tonnes	Russian Federation[4]	12%	5%	Mixed	–	–	–
(2002-04 average)	Saudi Arabia	9%	0%	–	–	–	–
	Mozambique[5]	7%	0%	Ad valorem	–	SADC	–
	China, Hong Kong	6%	0%	–	–	–	–
Apples							
USD 137 million	EU[6]	60%	2% (9%)	Ad valorem	Yes	–	–
297 thousand tonnes	Malaysia	6%	5%	Ad valorem	–	–	–
(2002-04 average)	Benin	2%	20%	Ad valorem	–	–	–
	Angola	2%	5%	Ad valorem	–	–	–
	Russian Federation[7]	2%	35% (69%)	Specific	–	–	–

Acronyms: GSP: Generalised System of Preferences; BA: Bilateral Agreement; AGOA: African Growth and Opportunity Act; SADC – Southern African Development Community.

1. The TRQ for fresh grapes is in effect between 21 July and 31 October equalling 1 500 tonnes. The in- and over-quota tariff rates are differentiated according to the level of import value. South Africa is liable for an in-quota tariff of 9.0% and over-quota rate of 14.1%. The MFN tariff rate during the months when TRQ is not effective is 11.1% ad valorem; however, South Africa can benefit from a reduced GSP rate of 8% and from the bilateral concession rate of 4.8%. The annual weighted average tariff faced by South Africa is 6% (AVE), and the highest tariff applicable to South African exports during the year is 14% (reported in brackets).
2. The US tariff for fresh grapes is seasonally differentiated, with the tariff falling to zero between 1 April and 30 June. Under AGOA and GSP, imports from South Africa are duty free irrespective of the season.
3. Import tariff for fresh oranges is set in ad valorem terms and is seasonally differentiated, with rates ranging from 16.0% to 3.2%. The weighted average rate paid by South Africa is 3%, and the highest rate applicable during the year is 16% (reported in brackets). The EU grants no GSP or bilateral concessions to South Africa on imports of fresh oranges.
4. The tariff is 5%, but not less than 20 €/tonne.
5. The ad valorem MFN tariff is 25%; however, under SADC imports from South Africa are granted duty free entry.
6. There are three TRQs for fresh apples, each of 600 tonnes, effective between 1 April and 31 July. The in- and over-quota tariff rates are differentiated according to the level of import value. South Africa is liable for a zero in-and over-quota rates. The ad valorem MFN tariff rate during the months when TRQ is not effective ranges from 4% to 9%. The annual weighted average tariff faced by South Africa is 2% (AVE), and the highest tariff applicable to South African exports in during the year is 9% (reported in brackets). The European Union grants no GSP or bilateral concessions to South Africa on imports of fresh apples.
7. The specific tariff is 100 €/tonne (35% AVE), with the rate rising to 200 €/tonne (69% AVE) between 1 August and 31 December.

Sources: MAD-ATD; TARIC; USITC.

Table 3.A1.3. **Protection of the sugar sector in South African export markets**

Product/ South African exports	Country	Share of exports (2002-04)	Applied tariff 2005	Tariff type	TRQ	Tariff preferences	Other measures
Raw sugar							
USD 177 million	Republic of Korea	18%	3%	–	–	–	–
935 thousand tonnes	Japan	18%	0%	–	–	–	STE
(2002-04 average)	Mozambique	17%	7.5%	Ad valorem	..	–	–
	India	8%	60%[1]	Ad valorem	..	..	..
	Malaysia	7%	0%	–	–	–	–
	Saudi Arabia	6%	0%	–	–	–	–
	USA[2]	4%	0% (128%)	–	Yes	GSP	SSG
	Egypt	4%	2%	Ad valorem	–	–	–
Refined sugar							
USD 97 million	Kenya	11%	..	Ad valorem	–	–	–
416 thousand tonnes	Madagascar	10%	10%	Ad valorem	–	–	–
(2002-04 average)	Syria	8%	7%	Ad valorem	–	–	–
	Iraq	8%	..	..	..	..	..
	Jordan	7%	5%	Ad valorem	–	–	–
	Mauritius[3]	7%	48%	Ad valorem	–	SADC	–
	Sudan	5%	10%	Ad valorem	–	–	–
	Tanzania[4]	4%	20%	Ad valorem	–	SADC	–
	Indonesia	3%	20%	Specific	–	–	–
	Angola	3%	5%	Ad valorem	–	–	–
	Ghana	3%	10%	Ad valorem	–	–	–
	Iran	3%	4%	Ad valorem	–	–	–
	Saudi Arabia	3%	20%	Ad valorem	–	–	–
	Nigeria	2%	15%	Ad valorem	–	–	–
	Mozambique	2%	7.5%	Ad valorem	–	–	–

.. not available.

Acronyms: GSP: Generalised System of Preferences; SADC – Southern African Development Community; STE – State Trading Enterprise; SSG – Special Safeguard Provision.

1. The *ad valorem* tariff is 60%, but in 2004 it was temporary lifted, which explains high South African exports to this market in 2004 and the emergence of India among the top importers.
2. All South African raw sugar exports to the United States are under the TRQ, set at 1 117 195 tonnes per year. Within this overall quota, South Africa supplied 58 657 tonnes in 2002, 23 646 tonnes in 2003 and 23 401 tonnes in 2004. Under the GSP treatment, the in-quota tariff for South Africa is zero (compared to regular in-quota rate of 14.606 USD/tonne or an AVE of 6%). The over-quota rate is 338.7 USD/tonne or an AVE of 128%. SSG is applied.
3. MFN tariff is 65%; however, under SADC imports from South Africa are levied an *ad valorem* tariff of 48%.
4. MFN tariff is 100%; however, under SADC imports from South Africa are levied an *ad valorem* tariff of 20%.

Sources: MAD-ATD; USITC.

ANNEX 3.A2

Supporting Analysis for Chapter 3, Section 3.3

Results from a single country computable general equilibrium model applied for South Africa

To be read as a complement to Chapter 3, Section 3.3, this Annex provides more detailed results of the liberalisation simulation. The distributional impacts of global trade liberalisation on the South African economy are assessed using a single country computable general equilibrium (CGE) model. The data inputs to the study were vectors of (percentage) price changes for imports and exports that were derived by the OECD, using the GTAPEM model, and a social accounting matrix (SAM) for South Africa that was provided by the PROVIDE project. The version of the PROVIDE SAM used for this study is an aggregation of the full SAM. The CGE model used is discussed in brief and technical descriptions together with the details of the SAM aggregation are available on the OECD public website, *www.oecd.org/agr/ete*.

As far as possible the core simulation was compatible with the simulation used in the GTAPEM to generate the global price changes. However, rather than running a single simulation a series of simulations was implemented so as to assess the sensitivity of the results to changes in specification; the additional simulations considered a range of trade liberalisation scenarios by South Africa and variations in the closure rules.

The results for the real macroeconomic variables indicate that if South Africa does not reduce its own trade barriers the impact of global reforms upon South Africa is minimal and although marginally negative. This conclusion is unaffected by the choice of closure rules. On the other hand, if South Africa simultaneously reduces all its trade barriers by 50% there are some noticeable changes in the macroeconomic aggregates, with the following patterns emerging from the results[*] (Figure 3.A2.1).

- Measured GDP is unaffected under the full employment closures, but increases marginally under the presumption of unemployed unskilled labour (about 0.13%).

- Real absorption increases by some 0.5% in all cases, with (real) private consumption increasing by about 0.4%.

- Government (real) consumption declines by about 0.7%.

- Investment (real) consumption increases by about 2.5%.

---

[*] The discussion here concentrates upon the key indicators of national and household well being – a full set of results is available for a more in depth analysis.

Figure 3.A2.1. **Major real macroeconomic variables**[1]

% change

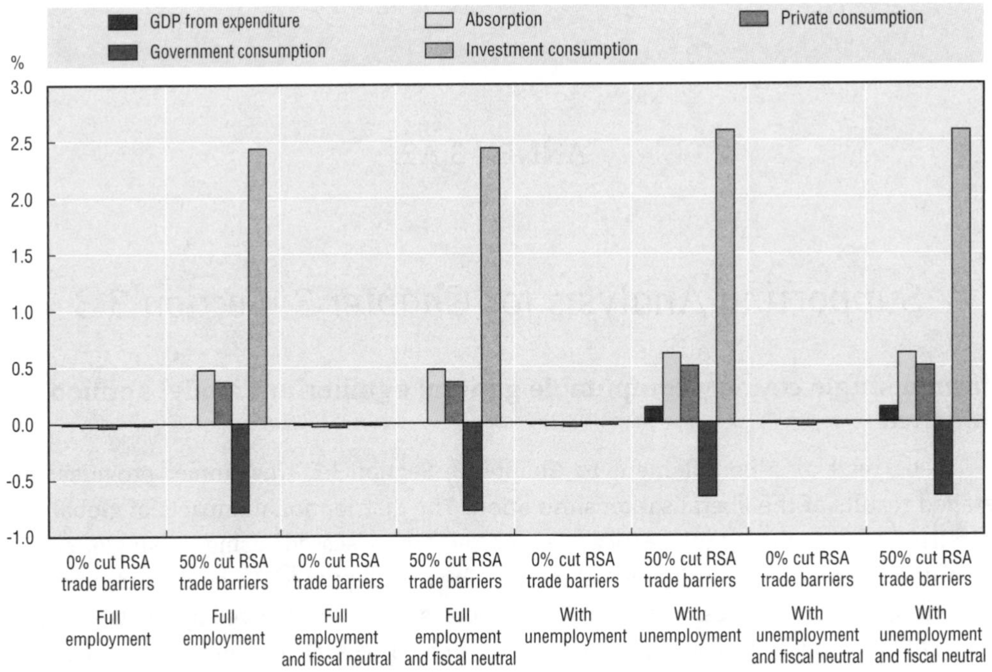

RSA: Republic of South Africa.
1. All real values are computed at base period prices.
Source: Simulation results.

Ultimately, these results are a consequence of changes in the prices of consumption commodities (Table 3.A2.1) and the consumption patterns of domestic institutions. In essence, the (weighted) average prices of household and investment consumption commodities decline, thereby allowing increases in real private and investment consumption, but the reverse is the case for government and hence, government real consumption declines. This indicates that if the government wishes to maintain its real consumption expenditure then the government must increase its share of domestic consumption expenditure, in which case the increase in consumption by households and/or investment would be smaller. The decline in the average price of investment commodities is important since it may facilitate increases in real investment which may have positive long-term implications.

The changes in commodity prices when South Africa liberalises unleash three major forces, all of which are consequences of the changes in relative commodity prices (Table 3.A2.2) associated with the different liberalisation scenarios. First is a substantial increase in exports of mineral products, for which the production activities are located in the inland provinces. Second is the generalised increase in domestic production, which is most heavily concentrated in the manufacturing activities (Table 3.A2.3). Third is the change in the structure of production.

The changes in production structure (Figure 3.A2.2) indicate that the main expansion takes place in minerals, manufacturing and service activities, with a particularly sharp expansion in minerals driven by an increased export demand. This is accompanied by a series of small increases in agriculture and food processing activities that appear to be primarily driven by the generalised expansion of the economy rather than the

Table 3.A2.1. **Imposed percentage changes in world prices of exports and imports**

Commodity	Change in world price of exports	Change in world price of imports
Summer cereals	0.259	1.508
Winter cereals	0.259	1.508
Oilseeds	1.66	0.534
Sugar cane	1.403	7.821
Other field crops	0.412	0.089
Potatoes and vegetables	0.746	0.775
Wine grapes	0.746	0.775
Citrus	0.746	0.775
Subtropical fruits	0.746	0.775
Deciduous fruits	0.746	0.775
Other horticulture	0.746	0.775
Livestock sales	0.249	−0.068
Milk and cream	0.121	−2.352
Animal fibres	0.083	0.244
Poultry	0.083	0.244
Game products	0.083	0.244
Other animals	0.083	0.244
Forestry	0.412	0.089
Wild flowers and other agric. products	0.412	0.089
Mineral products	0	0
Meat products	0.05	0.979
Processed fish products	−0.023	1.216
Fruit and vegetable products	0.023	−0.622
Oils and fats products	−0.205	0.762
Dairy products	−0.023	4.479
Grain mill products	0.167	3.386
Animal feeds	0.167	3.386
Bakery products	0.023	−0.622
Sugar products	0.243	−0.312
Other food products	0.023	−0.622
Beverages and tobacco	−0.327	−0.18
Textile products	−1.638	−0.707
Leather wood and paper products	−1.638	−0.707
Petroleum products	−0.327	−0.18
Fertilisers	−0.327	−0.18
Pesticides	−0.327	−0.18
Pharmaceutical products	−0.327	−0.18
All other chemical products	−0.327	−0.18
Non metallic products	−0.327	−0.18
Metal products	−0.327	−0.18
Machinery	−0.327	−0.18
Vehicles	−0.327	−0.18
Other manufacturing	−0.327	−0.18
Utilities	−0.327	−0.18
Construction and building	−0.327	−0.18
Trade and transport services	0.077	−0.061
Other services	0.077	−0.061

Source: Derived from GTAPEM results.

Table 3.A2.2. **Commodity price results**

% changes

Commodity	Export prices	Import prices	Domestic producer price	Domestic consumer price
Summer cereals	2.77	−0.56	4.87	5
Winter cereals	2.77	−6.91	−3.87	−5.31
Oilseeds	4.21	−2.37	1.47	0.08
Sugar cane	n.a.	n.a.	2.9	2.9
Other field crops	2.93	−2.03	0.81	−0.74
Potatoes and vegetables	3.27	1.46	−0.04	−0.03
Wine grapes	n.a.	n.a.	0.66	0.66
Citrus	3.27	−7.97	2.88	2.69
Subtropical fruits	3.27	−3.37	−0.26	−0.36
Deciduous fruits	3.27	−0.94	2.7	2.3
Other horticulture	3.27	−13.19	2.62	−10.86
Livestock sales	2.76	−4.9	1.33	1.19
Milk and cream	n.a.	n.a.	−2.04	−2.04
Animal fibres	2.59	−0.23	1.92	1.11
Poultry	2.59	−2.91	−0.84	−0.85
Game products	n.a.	n.a.	4.73	4.73
Other animals	2.59	−5.32	−2.94	−3.03
Forestry	2.93	−3.3	0.87	0.49
Wild flowers and other agric. products	n.a.	n.a.	0.57	0.57
Mineral products	2.51	1.16	1.57	0.14
Meat products	2.56	−6.11	0.61	0.34
Processed fish products	2.48	−1.35	0.91	0.27
Fruit and vegetable products	2.53	−8.03	0.28	−0.82
Oils and fats products	2.3	−2.76	−0.25	−1.28
Dairy products	2.48	−6.14	0.27	−0.03
Grain mill products	2.68	4.54	0.98	1.19
Animal feeds	2.68	−4.68	0.38	0.16
Bakery products	2.53	−13.6	0.83	0.67
Sugar products	2.76	−13.74	1.42	1.28
Other food products	2.53	−9.41	0.32	−0.84
Beverages and tobacco	2.17	−16.3	0.58	−0.8
Textile products	0.83	−12.2	−0.01	−2.25
Leather wood and paper products	0.83	−8.68	0.02	−1.24
Petroleum products	2.17	−1.63	0.76	0.38
Fertilisers	2.17	−4.61	0.78	−0.46
Pesticides	2.17	−5.02	−1.14	−2.99
Pharmaceutical products	2.17	−7.92	−0.25	−2.15
All other chemical products	2.17	−5.1	−0.12	−1.7
Non metallic products	2.17	−8.04	0.11	−1.7
Metal products	2.17	−4.36	0.51	−1.09
Machinery	2.17	−6.03	−0.68	−3.98
Vehicles	2.17	−5.37	−1.73	−3.59
Other manufacturing	2.17	−6.48	−0.19	−3.4
Utilities	2.17	−2.56	1.24	1.24
Construction and building	2.17	2.32	0.01	0.02
Trade and transport services	2.59	−2.16	1.16	0.79
Other services	2.59	−4.26	1.25	1.12

n.a.: not available.

Source: Simulation results.

Table 3.A2.3. **Commodity quantity results – Base volume (for imports and exports) and percentage changes**

Commodity	Exports		Imports		Domestic production	Domestic consumption
	Base	% change	Base	% change	% change	% change
Summer cereals	9.0	−3.4	1.9	13.2	0.6	1.6
Winter cereals	1.6	15.0	13.5	5.1	0.6	1.6
Oilseeds	2.4	6.0	2.5	5.5	0.5	0.4
Sugar cane	0.0	3.2	n.a.	n.a.	1.2	1.2
Other field crops	3.6	4.8	5.8	3.2	0.5	0.5
Potatoes and vegetables	0.8	7.3	2.1	−2.5	0.6	0.4
Wine grapes	n.a.	n.a.	n.a.	n.a.	1.1	1.1
Citrus	7.9	1.4	0.1	25.0	0.6	0.4
Subtropical fruits	0.5	7.9	0.1	6.8	0.6	0.5
Deciduous fruits	24.9	2.2	0.2	7.0	1.0	0.3
Other horticulture	10.8	1.9	3.1	7.8	0.6	2.3
Livestock sales	9.4	3.6	0.6	13.8	0.7	0.6
Milk and cream	n.a.	n.a.	n.a.	n.a.	1.0	1.0
Animal fibres	4.7	2.2	0.8	2.8	0.9	0.1
Poultry	0.2	7.8	0.0	5.0	0.7	0.7
Game products	n.a.	n.a.	n.a.	n.a.	0.3	0.3
Other animals	0.1	12.8	0.1	5.8	0.9	0.9
Forestry	0.9	4.8	8.2	9.4	0.6	1.3
Wild flowers and other agric. products	n.a.	n.a.	n.a.	n.a.	1.0	1.0
Mineral products	819.6	13.9	308.9	2.7	11.8	4.8
Meat products	6.0	4.2	12.3	15.0	0.2	0.7
Processed fish products	7.9	4.0	6.1	4.0	0.8	0.7
Fruit and vegetable products	18.8	5.7	3.5	17.0	1.1	0.6
Oils and fats products	2.4	4.5	28.0	4.0	−0.6	0.9
Dairy products	2.1	4.9	5.1	14.4	0.4	0.8
Grain mill products	3.7	4.6	11.8	−5.8	1.2	0.6
Animal feeds	0.4	7.0	2.5	13.3	2.3	2.7
Bakery products	0.4	3.7	0.9	36.5	0.3	0.5
Sugar products	4.2	3.3	0.3	38.7	0.7	0.7
Other food products	8.5	3.6	11.5	20.8	−0.8	0.8
Beverages and tobacco	33.0	2.6	16.6	42.4	−0.6	1.4
Textile products	33.2	−0.6	73.8	26.4	−2.2	2.0
Leather wood and paper products	72.2	2.0	101.1	19.9	0.3	2.6
Petroleum products	104.7	6.2	24.0	7.2	3.3	2.9
Fertilisers	11.2	5.4	10.5	13.1	2.6	3.8
Pesticides	8.4	13.7	7.9	9.9	6.5	5.4
Pharmaceutical products	10.5	4.1	39.5	15.5	−0.8	2.3
All other chemical products	109.0	6.3	191.6	10.5	1.5	3.0
Non metallic products	34.4	5.0	91.4	18.6	0.8	3.8
Metal products	384.5	9.1	132.2	12.3	5.6	4.9
Machinery	101.4	6.4	360.1	8.2	0.6	3.7
Vehicles	169.5	12.3	374.4	7.8	3.9	3.9
Other manufacturing	187.1	4.9	383.2	10.2	0.1	3.3
Utilities	0.0	5.6	0.1	12.0	3.7	3.7
Construction and building	1.3	7.7	2.3	−1.4	3.2	3.2
Trade and transport services	246.5	5.7	320.6	9.5	2.8	3.2
Other services	107.6	3.9	102.5	13.1	1.2	1.3

n.a.: not available.

Source: Simulation results.

Figure 3.A2.2. **Activity output**

% change

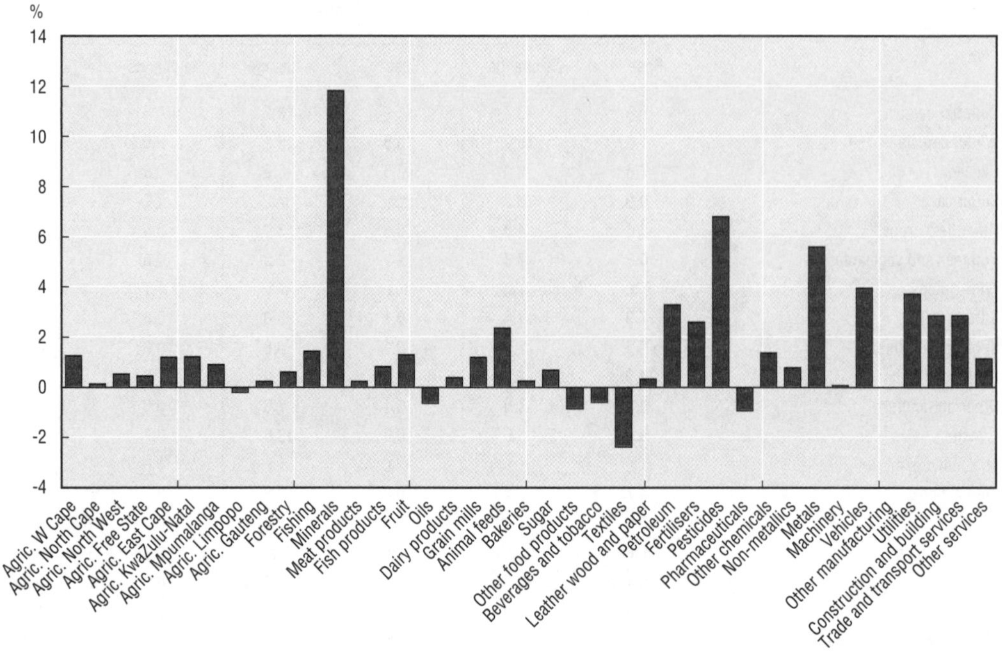

Source: Simulation results.

liberalisation. A number of activities show some decline in output, most notably textiles, but these are relatively small changes.

The changes in output are consistent with the changes in activity prices (see Annex Table 3.A2.4). Note here, however, that the allocation of primary inputs is driven by the price of value-added and not the output price, and it is the allocation of primary inputs, and the use of intermediate input that are the primary determinants of the scale of production. What is made most clear by the results for the activities is the extent to which the potential welfare gains for South Africa (see below) derive from non food and agriculture activities, and this is reflected in the small shift of resources (factors) towards the manufacturing and service activities.

The liberalisation by South Africa induces a generalised fall in import prices (Table 3.A2.1), which translates into a series of more selective changes in domestic consumer prices; in general, the prices of manufactured commodities decline with a resultant decline in the cost of living for most households. One notable consequence of this decline in consumer prices is that the prices of value-added increase far more than the activity prices (Table 3.A2.4). This produces a generalised increase in wage rates that in turn produces increases in factor prices of between 1.2% and 4.5%, except for land which only increases by 0.1% (see Chapter 3, Section 3.3, Figure 3.13 for a summary of the results). The reason why labour prices increase more in the inland provinces is because the changes in the structure of manufacturing result in a more rapid expansion of activities located in the inland provinces. This is especially the case for mining.

Table 3.A2.4. **Activity prices**

% change

	Output price	Aggregate intermediate price	Price of value added
Agric. W. Cape	0.73	−0.31	1.67
Agric. North Cape	1.5	−0.13	2.65
Agric. North West	1.55	−0.04	3.32
Agric. Free State	1.1	−0.11	2.72
Agric. East Cape	0.73	−0.19	1.49
Agric. KwaZulu-Natal	0.81	−0.17	1.67
Agric. Mpumalanga	1.15	−0.15	2.69
Agric. Limpopo	1.1	−0.22	2.28
Agric. Gauteng	0.73	−0.23	1.98
Forestry	0.88	−0.43	2.55
Fishing	1.14	−0.14	2.3
Minerals	1.45	−0.23	3.27
Meat products	0.65	0.59	2.28
Fish products	0.93	0.65	2.19
Fruit	0.29	−0.05	1.91
Oils	−0.07	−0.37	2.08
Dairy products	0.35	0.06	2.28
Grain mills	0.92	0.61	2.38
Animal feeds	0.38	0.07	2.37
Bakeries	0.85	0.55	2.12
Sugar	1.42	1.21	2.62
Other food products	0.43	−0.12	2.08
Beverages and tobacco	0.69	0.1	2.4
Textiles	0.1	−0.29	1.53
Leather wood and paper	0.07	−0.45	2.08
Petroleum	0.64	0.28	2.56
Fertilisers	0.45	0.09	2.6
Pesticides	−1.16	−1.54	2.38
Pharmaceuticals	−0.06	−0.36	2.27
Other chemicals	0	−0.42	2.32
Non metallics	0.13	−0.52	2.17
Metals	0.36	−0.25	2.43
Machinery	−0.42	−0.74	2.07
Vehicles	−1.59	−2.04	2.1
Other manufacturing	−0.1	−0.47	2.25
Utilities	1.21	−0.06	2.53
Construction and building	0.1	−0.78	2.19
Trade and transport services	1.14	0.1	2.28
Other services	1.27	0.04	2.11

Source: Simulation results.

These effects are primarily driven by the changes in the relative prices of imports, which change mainly as a consequence of South Africa's liberalisation rather than because of the global liberalisation. Indeed, in many cases the prices of imports to South Africa will rise as a consequence of global liberalisation and it is this generalised rise in import prices which is the key reason why global liberalisation without South Africa partaking does not produce any substantive gains for South Africa.

The relatively muted macroeconomic effects do not necessarily translate into similarly muted effects on household welfare. Indeed, the welfare results based on equivalent variations in welfare from consumption, are mixed (Figures 3.A2.4 and 3.A2.6). A fuller table of results is provided in Table 3.A2.5.

Some insight into the factors behind these welfare changes can be gained by examining the changes in household incomes under the different scenarios; these are reported in summary form in Figures 3.A2.3 and 3.A2.5. Again the impact of global liberalisation without liberalisation by South Africa is minimal across both provinces and racial groups. But when South Africa also liberalises there are generally positive consequences. These responses are somewhat larger under the assumption of unemployed unskilled labour and appreciably larger under the assumption of fiscal neutrality.

There remain differences across the provinces, with the inland provinces and the Northern Cape witnessing larger increases than the coastal provinces. Indeed, it is only the coastal provinces that experience negative changes in household incomes. In terms of the racial groups there are several distinctive patterns. The presumption of fiscal neutrality has a major impact upon the incomes of white households. Among the non-white households there is a stable pattern, with coloured and Asian households always gaining the least; followed by African households resident in the former homeland areas; then by African households with high education levels; and finally, African households with low and medium education levels having the highest gains.

Overall, it is noticeable that the percentage increases in household incomes are greater than the percentage increases in welfare, and that this is particularly so when the assumption of fiscal neutrality is imposed. It is therefore instructive to look more closely at the components of household incomes and consumption expenditures; this exploration will be reported for the scenario where there is global liberalisation and matching (50%) liberalisation by South Africa under the assumption of full employment and fiscal neutrality. The results for other closure options are broadly the same.

The primary sources of household incomes are the returns from factor services, realised either as direct payments for labour, capital and land services or indirectly through the ownership of incorporated business enterprises; in both cases the starting point is factor incomes. As indicated by Figure 3.13 there is, with the exception of land, a generalised increase in the incomes to different (aggregate) factor types, although the range of increase in factor incomes by labour type is substantial (1.2% to 4.5% in the aggregates and from –0.4% to 6.6% in the full set). Consequently, a large part of the reason for the increase in household incomes is the generalised increase in factor incomes.

However, it is of interest to decompose the linkages by which these changes in factor incomes are translated into changes in household incomes. In the model household incomes are made up of direct payments for factor services, indirect payments for factor services – via incorporated business enterprises, inter household transfers, transfers from the government and transfers from the rest of the world. The last three components do not change much in these simulations and therefore attention in instance focuses upon direct and indirect payments for factor services; these are reported in Table 3.A2.5.

The proportionate change in household incomes ranges from 0.9% to 5.7% across the 70 household groups. In the rank order of percentage increases in incomes, the lowest white household is ranked 32, whereas the top 5 households are non-white. Hence, white households do disproportionately well when households are ranked in terms of the proportionate increase in income; one reason for this can be identified from the shares of changes in income due to transfers from enterprises (HOENT). Typically, white households

Table 3.A2.5. **Components of household incomes – Base levels and changes**

	Base income	Change in income		Share of change due to	
		Absolute	%	YFDISP	HOENT
WC African high education	44.01	0.86	2	53.6	45.9
WC African low education	58.64	0.84	1.4	85	13.7
WC Coloured and Asian high education	188.17	3.21	1.7	55.9	44.4
WC Coloured and Asian mid education	123.85	1.97	1.6	50.2	49.6
WC Coloured and Asian low education	93.54	1	1.1	75.4	23.7
WC White high education	472.91	10.78	2.3	49.4	51.6
WC White low education	98.18	2.74	2.8	27.8	70.6
EC African farm	13.53	0.27	2	68.3	28.6
EC African homeland high education	90.25	1.6	1.8	74.5	25.6
EC African homeland low education	130.89	1.81	1.4	60.1	25.1
EC African high education	46.13	0.79	1.7	71.3	30.1
EC African low education	50.11	0.65	1.3	66.3	31.3
EC Coloured and Asian	62.01	0.72	1.2	66.8	34.7
EC White high education	168.9	3.96	2.3	44	57.3
EC White low education	25.13	0.54	2.2	55.2	44.9
NC African households	22.81	0.89	3.9	94	3.5
NC Coloured households	38.19	0.85	2.2	87.2	12.1
NC White households	96.29	3.23	3.4	58.9	41.1
FS African farm	3.69	0.21	5.7	92.5	0
FS African high education	63.43	1.69	2.7	85	14.1
FS African mid education	40.98	1.79	4.4	86.8	7.3
FS African low education	78.2	3.69	4.7	86.1	7.8
FS Coloured and Asian households	8.73	0.17	1.9	92.9	5.8
FS White high education	187.4	5.68	3	61.3	38.7
FS White low education	39.13	1.16	3	66.4	33.5
KZN African homeland farm households	10.24	0.18	1.8	77.5	18.9
KZN African farm households	12.49	0.23	1.8	85.8	10.8
KZN African homeland high education	73.36	1.29	1.8	84.4	15.7
KZN African homeland low education	58.35	0.9	1.5	52.5	34.1
KZN African high education	149.8	2.76	1.8	72.7	26.2
KZN African mid education	105.44	1.97	1.9	76.5	21
KZN African low education	141.38	1.78	1.3	82.8	13
KZN Asian high education	112.81	1.88	1.7	48.6	51.4
KZN Asian low education	84.52	1.08	1.3	36.4	63.7
KZN Coloured households	17.71	0.26	1.5	59.1	37.8
KZN White high education	367.83	9.68	2.6	44.3	58.6
KZN White low education	24.44	0.61	2.5	28.1	76.2
NW African farm	10.54	0.5	4.7	69.8	29.8
NW African high education	64.42	2.38	3.7	81.6	16.6
NW African mid education	91.1	3.65	4	79.8	13.9
NW African low education	77.4	3.26	4.2	88.2	4.9
NW African no education	32.32	1.12	3.5	85.3	9.8
NW Coloured and Asian households	8.18	0.19	2.4	87.8	11.1
NW White high education	85.71	3.06	3.6	70.8	29.2
NW White low education	27.87	1.05	3.8	65	33.3
GT African farm	13.15	0.26	1.9	99.6	0.2
GT African high education	115.34	2.14	1.9	91.7	7.7
GT African mid education	367.85	8.24	2.2	83.8	15.3
GT African low education	301.07	8.02	2.7	66.5	31.7
GT African primary education	222.83	5.3	2.4	83.4	15.3

Table 3.A2.5. **Components of household incomes – Base levels and changes** (cont.)

	Base income	Change in income		Share of change due to	
		Absolute	%	YFDISP	HOENT
GT African no education	75.04	1.62	2.2	89.6	8.8
GT Coloured household	92.93	1.73	1.9	90.1	9.6
GT Asian households	68.16	1.25	1.8	85.2	15.1
GT White high education	574.34	13.59	2.4	62.2	37.8
GT White mid education	457.92	11.18	2.4	57.4	42.4
GT White low education	115.35	3.35	2.9	40.2	59
MP African farm	8.35	0.29	3.5	93.7	4.5
MP African high education	63.64	1.72	2.7	79.9	18
MP African mid education	41.09	1.26	3.1	85.1	8.1
MP African low education	67.09	2.23	3.3	82	10.5
MP African no education	44.08	1.18	2.7	71.3	19.7
MP Coloured and Asian households	10.89	0.2	1.8	84.7	14.9
MP White households	81.59	3.43	4.2	89.4	10.2
LP African farm	8.35	0.2	2.4	96.7	2.1
LP African high education	120.62	2.49	2.1	80.3	17.5
LP African mid education	48.96	0.98	2	83	7.2
LP African primary education	78.49	1.71	2.2	69.8	20.7
LP African no education	68.2	1.48	2.2	42	47.5
LP Coloured and Asian households	4.83	0.04	0.9	100.4	0
LP White households	60.32	1.69	2.8	81.3	18.7

Notes: WC : Western Cape, EC: Eastern Cape, NC: Northern Cape, FS: Free State, KZN: KwaZulu-Natal, NW: North West, GT: Ganteng, MP: Mpumalanga, LP: Limpopo.
YFDISP: Changes in incomes from direct sales of factor services.
HOENT: Changes in incomes from indirect payments for factor services – via incorporated business entreprises.
Source: Simulation results

Figure 3.A2.3. **Household income by province**

% change

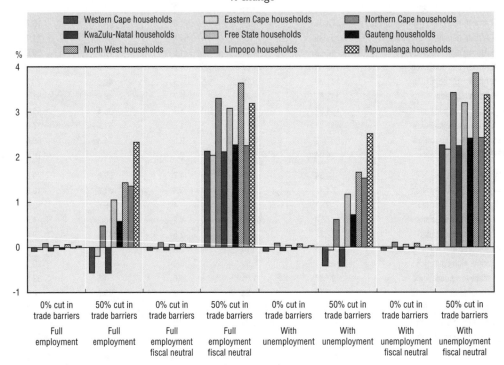

Source: Simulation results.

Figure 3.A2.4. **Equivalent variation in household welfare by province –
Based on consumption**

% change

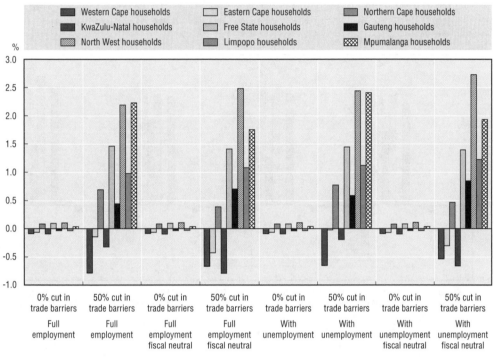

Source: Simulation results.

Figure 3.A2.5. **Household income by race**

% change

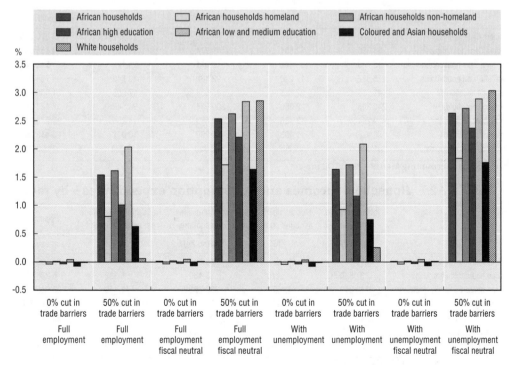

Source: Simulation results.

Figure 3.A2.6. **Equivalent variation in household welfare by race – Based on consumption**

% change

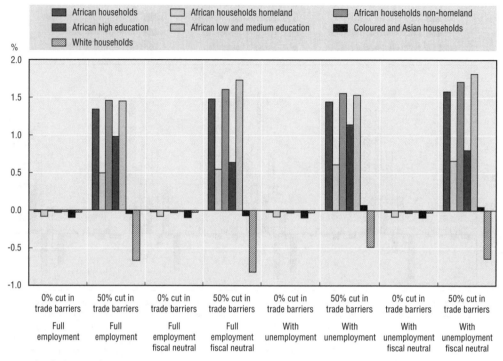

Source: Simulation results.

Table 3.A2.6. **Household incomes and consumption expenditures – by province**

	Total household income	Household income per adult equivalent	Total household expenditure	Household expenditure per adult equivalent	Population
	Million ZAR	ZAR	Million ZAR	ZAR	Adult equivalents
Western Cape households	107 930	35 156	88 715	28 897	3 070 066
Eastern Cape households	58 696	12 601	49 774	10 686	4 658 088
Northern Cape households	15 730	30 666	12 911	25 172	512 928
KwaZulu-Natal households	115 837	17 220	92 489	13 749	6 726 916
Free State households	42 158	22 125	33 636	17 653	1 905 426
Gauteng households	240 398	29 359	200 984	24 545	8 188 302
North West households	39 754	17 466	32 453	14 259	2 276 031
Limpopo households	38 977	11 403	34 290	10 031	3 418 250
Mpumalanga households	31 674	15 808	26 713	13 332	2 003 645

Source: Social Accounting Matrix – PROVIDE project.

Table 3.A2.7. **Household incomes and consumption expenditures – by race**

	Total household income	Household income per adult equivalent	Total household expenditure	Household expenditure per adult equivalent	Population
	Million ZAR	ZAR	Million ZAR	ZAR	Adult equivalents
African households	311 369	11 891	266 951	10 195	26 185 249
African households homeland	37 560	7 170	33 430	6 382	5 238 289
African households non-homeland	273 810	13 072	233 522	11 148	20 946 960
African high education	74 076	27 218	61 732	22 682	2 721 629
African low and medium education	237 293	10 113	205 220	8 746	23 463 620
Coloured and Asian households	91 453	24 784	79 806	21 627	3 690 027
White households	288 331	99 963	225 208	78 079	2 884 376

Source: Social Accounting Matrix – PROVIDE project.

receive a greater proportion of their income as payments from incorporated business enterprises. With three exceptions this is the case for all other province.

The exceptions are KwaZulu-Natal, where Asian households also receive substantial proportions of income from enterprises, and within Mpumalanga and Limpopo, where white households receive low payments from enterprises. These results reflect the historic patterns of asset ownership, whereby white households held disproportionately large shares of assets, and consequently, the shares of income coming from "direct" sales of factor services are typically lower for white than for non-white households. This simply emphasises the extent to which the comparative static income distribution effects will, to a greater or lesser extent, be driven by presumption that asset ownership patterns are unchanging.

There remains, however, the apparent anomaly of why white households appear to do so much worse under conditions of fiscal neutrality in welfare terms, while they do relatively well in terms of household income. This is a consequence (% change) of the larger shares of the cost of fiscal neutrality being borne by the richer households and white households are appreciably richer (on average) than non-white households. In essence this conclusion is a consequence of the presumption that fiscal neutrality is achieved by means of changes in income tax rates and that the changes in income tax rates are equiproportionate. Clearly, there are a range of alternative presumptions available – including allowing other tax rates to vary and/or reducing government absorption – but (non exhaustive) experiments indicate that the distributional effects of the alternatives would be generally less favourable in terms of their welfare effects.

Acronyms

ACB	Agricultural Credit Board
ACP	African, Caribbean and Pacific (group of countries)
AGOA	United States African Growth and Opportunity Act
AgriBEE	Black Economic Empowerment Framework for Agriculture
ARC	Agricultural Research Council
AVE	*Ad valorem* equivalent (tariff)
BATAT	Broadening Access to Agriculture Thrust
(BB)BEE	(Broad Based) Black Economic Empowerment
BLNS countries	Botswana, Lesotho, Namibia and Swaziland (other members of SACU)
CASP	Comprehensive Agriculture Support Programme
CGE	Computable General Equilibrium (model)
CPAs	Communal Property Associations
CPI	Consumer Price Index
CSE	Consumer Support Estimate
DBSA	Development Bank of Southern Africa
DES	Daily Energy Supply
DLA	Department of Land Affairs
DoA	Department of Agriculture
DTI	Department of Trade and Industry
DWAF	Department of Water Affairs and Forestry
EFTA	European Free Trade Association
EU	European Union
FACIA	Food and Agricultural Commodities Inspection Agency
FAO	Food and Agriculture Organisation of the United Nations
FTA	Free Trade Agreement
GAO	Gross Agricultural Outuput
GDP	Gross Domestic Product
GSP	Generalised System of Preferences
GATT	General Agreement on Tariffs and Trade
GEAR	Growth, Employment and Redistribution Strategy
GEIS	General Export Incentive Scheme
GSP	General System of Preferences
GSSE	General Services Support Estimate
GTAP	Global Trade Analysis Project
GTAPEM	Global Trade Analysis Project/Policy Evaluation Model
IDP	Integrated Development Plan
IFSS	Integrated Food Security Strategy
ISRDS	Integrated Sustainable Rural Development Strategy
ITAC	International Trade Administration Commission
LDO	Land Development Objective

LED	Local Economic Development
LRAD	Land Redistribution and Agricultural Development Programme
MAD-ATD	Market Access Database – Applied Tariff Database (of the European Commission)
MAFISA	Micro-Agricultural Finance Scheme for South Africa
Mercosur	Common Market of the South
MFN	Most Favoured Nation (status)
MLC	Metropolitan Councils
MPS	Market Price Support
MTEF	Medium Term Expenditure Framework
NACc	Consumer Nominal Assistance Coefficient
NACp	Producer Nominal Assistance Coefficient
NAFU	National African Farmers Union
NAMC	National Agricultural Marketing Council
NDA	National Department of Agriculture (of South Africa)
NFES	National Food Emergency Scheme
NPCc	Consumer Nominal Protection Coefficient
NPCp	Producer Nominal Protection Coefficient
NRWS	National Water Resource Strategy
OECD	Organisation for Economic Co-operation and Development
PAETA	Primary Agriculture Education and Training Authority
PPECB	Perishable Product Export Control Board
PPI	Producer Price Index
PSE	Producer Support Estimate
RDP	Reconstruction and Development Programme
SACU	South African Customs Union
SADC	Southern Africa Development Community
SAFEX	South African Futures Exchange
SAM	Social Accounting Matrix
SARB	South African Reserve Bank)
SASA	South African Sugar Association
SETAs	Sectoral Education and Training Authorities
SLAG	Settlement/Land Acquisition Grant
SMP	Skim Milk Powder
SPS	Sanitary and Phytosanitary measures
STE	State Trading Enterprise
TARIC	European Community Integrated Tariff
TAU	Transvaal Agricultural Union
TBT	Technical Barriers to Trade
TDCA	Trade, Development and Cooperation Agreement between South Africa and EU
TSE	Total Support Estimate
TRQ	Tariff Rate Quota
URAA	Uruguay Round Agreement of Agriculture
USD	United States Dollar
USITS	United States International Trade Commission
VAT	Value Added Tax
VPH	Veterinary Public Health policy
WITS	World Integrated Trade Solution
WTO	World Trade Organisation
ZAR	South African Rand (rand)

ISBN 92-64-03679-2
OECD Review of Agricultural Policies
South Africa
© OECD 2006

Bibliography

Abstracts (2004), *Abstracts of Agricultural Statistics*, Department of Agriculture, 2004.

Abstracts (2005), *Abstracts of Agricultural Statistics*, Department of Agriculture, 2005.

AfDB/OECD (2004), *African Economic Outlook 2003/2004*, Chapter on South Africa: 277-293, OECD, Paris 2004.

Aihoon, J.K., J.A. Groenewald and H.J. Sartorius von Bach (1997), "Agricultural Salinization in the Olifants River at Loskop Valley, Mpumulanga", *Agrekon* 36: 268-282.

Bbenkele, K.E. (2003), *Rural Finance Expansion: Experience in Commercialization: Selected South African Micro Finance Case Studies*, Johannesburg, Micro Enterprise Alliance.

Bekker, S. (2003), *The Social Role of Agriculture in South Africa, Roles of Agriculture Project*, FAO, Rome.

Beukes, D.J. (1995), *Benefits from Identifying and Correcting Soil Acidity in Agriculture*, Pretoria, ARC Brochure.

Bhorat, H. and J. Hodge (1999), "Decomposing Shifts in Labour Demand in South Africa", *South African Journal of Economics* 67: 348-380.

Bromberger, N. (1982), "Government Policies Affecting the Distribution of Income 1940-1980", in: Schrire, R. (ed.), *South Africa – Public Policy Perspectives*, Cape Town, Juta and Co.

Bruggemans, C. (2004), *The Labour Miracle Revisited*, First National Bank, Economic Division, Johannesburg.

Cassim, R., D. Onyango and D.E.N. Van Seventer (2002), *The state of trade policy in South Africa*. Unpublished document, Trade and Industrial Policy Strategies (TIPS).

Coetzee, G. (2003), "Agricultural Finance in South Africa", in: L. Nieuwoudt and J. Groenewald (eds.), *The Challenge of Change*, Pietermaritzburg, University of Natal Press.

Cross C., S. Bekker, N. Mlambo, K. Kleinbooi, L. Saayman, H. Pretorius, T. Mngadi and T. Mbela (1999), "An Unstable Balance: Migration, Small Farming, Infrastructure and Livelihoods on the Eastern Seaboard: Part Two – Eastern and Western Cape", *Final Report to Development Bank of Southern Africa* (DBSA), Halfway House, DBSA.

Doran, J.W. and T.B. Parkin (1994), "Defining and Assessing Soil Quality", *Soil Science Society of America Special Publication*, Nr. 35: 3-21.

Du Toit, M.E., C.C Du Preez, M. Hensley and A.T.M. Bennie (1994), "Die effek van bewerking op die organise materiaalinhoud van geselekteerde droelandgronde in Suid-Afrika"*South African Journal of Plants and Soil*, 11(2): 71-79.

Food Pricing Monitoring Committee (2003), Final Report of the Food Pricing Monitoring Committee, Pretoria, December 2003.

Goodland, R.J.A. (1995), *South Africa: Environmental Sustainability and the Empowerment of Women*, Washington, DC, The World Bank.

Hofmeyer, J.F. (1994), "The Rise in African Wages", *South African Journal of Economics*, 62: 198-215.

Humphris, R.B. (2001), "President's Report: The Fertilizer Society of South Africa", *FSSA Journal*, 2001: 3-5.

Humphris, R.B. (2004), "President's report: The Fertilizer Society of South Africa", *FSSA Journal*, 2004: 3-7.

Jooste, A. and P.R. Taljaart (2005), "Red Meat", in: J.A. Groenewald (ed.), *Medium Term Economic Review of the South African Agricultural Sector*, Pretoria: National Department of Agriculture (forthcoming).

Jordaan, A. and R. Mafaesa (2005), "Rural Finance and Capital Resources", in: Groenewald, J. (ed.), *Medium Term Economic Review of the South African Agricultural Sector*, Pretoria: National Department of Agriculture (forthcoming).

Kassier, W.E. and J.A. Groenewald (1992), "The Agricultural Economy of South Africa", in: C. Csaki, T. Dams, D. Metzger and J. Van Zyl (eds.), *Agricultural Restructuring in Southern Africa*, Windhoek: International Association of Agricultural Economists, in association with AGRECONA.

Kirsten, J.F. and N. Vink (2002a), "A note on a future agricultural marketing dispensation in South Africa", Pretoria, National Agricultural Marketing Council (NAMC), unpublished memorandum.

Kirsten, J. and N. Vink, (2002b), *Agricultural Policy Changes in South Africa 1996-2002*, Roles of Agriculture Project, FAO, Rome.

Lewis, J. (2001), Reform and opportunity: the changing role and patterns of trade in South Africa and SADC. *The World Bank, Africa Region Working Paper Series No. 14*; and Trade and Industrial Policy Strategies (TIPS) secretariat, Occasional paper.

Lombard, J.P., B.B. Halenwang, H.J.E. Uys and A.J. Van Der Merwe (1996), "The Physical-Biological Environment", in: Spies. P.H. (ed.), *Agrifutura 1995/96*, Stellenbosch, University of Stellenbosch.

Louw, A. and C.W. Mostert (1990), "Die doeltreffende aanwending van kapitaal in die landbou", *Agrekon* 29:216-229.

Louw, D. and M. Fourie (2005), "Fruit Sector Review" in: J.A. Groenewald (ed.), *Medium Term Economic Review of the South African Agricultural Sector*, Pretoria, National Department of Agriculture (forthcoming).

Makhura, M.T. (2001), "Overcoming Transactions Costs Barriers to Market Participation of Smallholder Farmers in the Northern Province of South Africa", PhD thesis, University of Pretoria.

Makhura, M. and M. Mokoena (2003), "Market Access for Small-Scale Farmers in South Africa", in: L. Nieuwoudt and J. Groenewald (eds.), *The Challenge of Change*, Pietermaritzburg, University of Natal Press.

Matungul, P.M., M.C. Lyne and G.F. Ortmann (2001), "Transaction Costs and Crop Marketing in the Communal Areas of Impendle and Swayimana", KwaZulu-Natal, *Development Southern Africa*, 18: 348-363.

Meyer, F.H. and M. Cutts (2005), "Poultry" in: J.A. Groenewald (ed.), *Medium Term Review of the South African Agricultural Secto*, Pretoria: National Department of Agriculture (forthcoming).

National Treasury (2004), *Trends in Intergovernmental Finances, 2000/01-2006/07*, Pretoria, August 2004, *www.treasury.gov.za*.

Poonyth, D, J. Van Zyl, N. Vink and J.F. Kirsten (2001), "Modelling the South African Production Structure and Flexibility of Input Substitution", University of Pretoria working paper.

Preston, G., T. Willems, B. Van Wilgen and C. Meiring (1996), *How Much Water do Alien Plant Invaders Use?* Pretoria, Department of Water Affairs and Forestry.

Skeen, J.B. (1996), "President's report: The Fertilizer Society of South Africa", *FSSA Journal* 1996: 3-9.

Spio, K. (2003), "The Impact and Accessibility of Agricultural Credit: A Case Study of Small-Scale Farmers in the Northern Province of South Africa", PhD thesis, University of Pretoria.

Taljaard, P.M. and M. Brussow (2005), "Wool and Mohair", in: J.A. Groenewald (ed.), *Medium Term Economic Review of the Agricultural Sector*, Pretoria, National Department of Agriculture (forthcoming).

Tyson, P.D. (1988), "Atmospheric Pollution and its Implications in the Eastern Transvaal Highveld", Pretoria, Council for Scientific and Industrial Research (CSIR), *National Scientific Programmes Report No. 150*.

Van den Brink, R., G. Thomas and H. Binswanger (2004), "Agricultural Land Redistribution in South Africa: Towards Accelerated Implementation", paper presented at the Harold Wolpe conference on land reform.

Van der Berg, S. (1998), "Incorporating the Poor into the Economic Mainstream: Global and South African Perspectives", paper to poverty seminar, Dept. of Health and Welfare, Provincial Administration of the Western Cape, Cape Town, 2 October 1998: 10 pp.

Van der Berg, S. (1997), "Fiscal Incidence in South Africa: An Overview of the Evidence", paper to the African Economic Research Consortium (AERC) training workshop, Kampala, 6-14 Augustus 1997, 25 pp.

Van der Merwe, A.J. (1995), "Wise Land Use: The Basis for Sustainable Growth and Development in South Africa", Pretoria, *Proceedings, ARC-ISCW Wise Land Use Symposium*.

Van der Merwe. A.J. and M.C. De Villiers (1998), "Soil Quality as Indicator of Sustainable Agriculture", University of Stellenbosch, *Proceedings of Conference on Farm and Farmer Organisation for Sustainable Agriculture in South Africa*.

Van Schalkwyk, H.D. and J.A. Groenewald (1992), "Regional Analysis of South African Resource Use and Productivity", *Agrekon* 31: 16-127.

Van Schalkwyk, H.D., J.A. Groenewald and A. Jooste (2003), "Agricultural Marketing in South Africa", in: L. Nieuwoudt and J. Groenewald (eds.), *The Challenge of Change*, Pietermaritzburg, University of Natal Press.

Van Zyl, J. and J.A. Groenewald (1988), "Flexibility in Input Substitution: A Case Study of South African Agriculture", *Development Southern Africa*, 5: 2-13.

Van Zyl, J. and C.J. Van Rooyen (1990), "Agricultural Production in South Africa: An Overview", *IDASA Rural Land Workshop*, March 1990.

Vink, N. (2003), "The Influence of Policy on the Roles of Agriculture in South Africa", Department of Agricultural Economics, University of Stellenbosch, *TIPS forum 2003 papers*.

Vink, N. (2005a), "The Use of Inputs in South African Commercial Agriculture", in: J.A. Groenewald (ed.), *Median Term Economic Review of the South African Agricultural Sector*, Pretoria, National Department of Agriculture (forthcoming).

Vink, N. (2005b), Background paper on agriculture prepared for the DBSA Development Report 2005.

Vink, N. and J. F. Kirsten (2003), *South African Case Study*, FAO.

Volkskas Bank (1991), "Kapitaaldoeltreffendheid in die landbou", *Ekonomiese soeklig*, February 1991.

Wilson, M. and M. Ramphele (1989), *Uprooting Poverty: The South African Challenge*, Cape Town and Johannesburg, David Philips.

World Bank (1994), South African Agriculture: Structure, Performance and Options for the Future, Washington, D.C, The World Bank.

OECD PUBLICATIONS, 2, rue André-Pascal, 75775 PARIS CEDEX 16
PRINTED IN FRANCE
(51 2006 01 1 P) ISBN 92-64-03679-2 – No. 54987 2006